Early Access to Hollywood -
cite the Neil   Ronald Colman, Laughton,
Sinyard article,   Conner
Rattlore, Book,
Niven/Simmons/Kerr/Ha[...]

British stars and stardom

Chaplin/Laurel   what makes [...]
                  Hollywood stardom?
                  what can Hollywood use?
{ David Niven
{ Hugh Grant   Deborah Kerr
                       Vivien Leigh
essences of
Englishness -   but not
Hollywood's   Wendy Hiller
idea of what   Roger Livesey
it is to be English

Hitchcock/Allen
on stardom

Genre stars
Horror
   Cushing, Lee,
   Pitt
Crime
   Baker
Roun'ter Comedy
   Hugh Grant

Peter Sellers

        Divas - quote from Selznick
             Hollywood wants out the local

    The character actor/stage star
             Ralph Richardson
Heightened Englishness: Alec Guinness
Deborah Kerr/   Charles Laughton
Julie Andrews

    Korda - the star-maker!
        Forging an international product -
        Robert Donat, Merle Oberon, Vivien Leigh

The Fan magazines   Gainsborough Melo
                       - a powerful
                        star-led cinema
                       Lockwood, Mason

    the limitations of
    a class-bound
    cinema - few
    British actors
    but through it

MANCHESTER
UNIVERSITY PRESS

Not the continuity   The great changes
in British cinema   late 50s/early 60s
the [...] to [...]   & British cinema discovers
the [...] it but at heart   the working class - a
                       great release for every
                       [...] at heart of stardom

intertextuality — you need a run of films + premieres to build a star persona: the difficulties of the industry made it difficult to provide these things.

It's no accident that it's the more successful periods of the industry that provided the stars.

Is O'Toole a British star?

Or Vivien Leigh?

No. They're international stars.

They're re-made — the earlier British associations are ~~REMADE~~ erased.

E.g. Vivien Leigh.

No one remembers St. Martin's Lane

extreme desirability, flightiness, vulnerability, and vulnerability

Scarlett, Cleopatra, Anna Karenina, Blanche, Lady Hamilton (statue scene) — it's an international qualities. British cover — with universal

MK treats the British film industry like a ~~potting shed of~~ a nursery — you could grow your stars to a certain size, but then you'd have to transplant them to a bigger pot: HOLLYWOOD.

VL or MO examples of this — MO — a kind of British Joan Crawford — show the tv "little neck" scene — a manufactured into universal, transnational rather than indigenous, commodities. The traces of an earlier indigenous persona easily enough erased.

1) The stage tradition supports most simple types.
The character actor who becomes a star

2) The drawing-room drama tradition holds

British stardom
Robert Parker G?y
Kind Hearts - Agatha
Kaji in Q?? Tent
Colonel Nicholson
The Arab Chieftain

BRITISH STARS and STARDOM

from Alma Taylor to Sean Connery

edited by Bruce Babington

3) relentlessly middle-class - Not good
for a mass medium because it's exclusive.
We've learned that an important ingredient
of the star persona is identification, well
it's v. difficult to identify with s.o. who
went to Eton or Rhodean and speaks
with plums in his or her mouth - unless you
went to Eton or Rhodean (extract from
Plumbing him). Quote from "Get out ?
Posh".
    In late 1950s. the old model
Onstage - the working class movie -
    Albert Finney H?????

The working class - the indigenous
returns

Manchester University Press

MANCHESTER AND NEW YORK
distributed exclusively in the USA by Palgrave

exportable:
Money from US pours into UK → Hollywood comes to Britain

Extract from ?????y of SNSM, TSL, IFb

4) who are the biggest stars ????? W + G → ????
with the idea of Englishness without going into the ????? ????

Published by Manchester University Press
Oxford Road, Manchester M13 9NR, UK
and Room 400, 175 Fifth Avenue, New York, NY 10010, USA
http://www.manchesteruniversitypress.co.uk

Distributed exclusively in the USA by
Palgrave, 175 Fifth Avenue, New York, NY 10010, USA

Distributed exclusively in Canada by
UBC Press, University of British Columbia, 2029 West Mall,
Vancouver, BC, Canada V6T 1Z2

British Library Cataloguing-in-Publication Data
A catalogue record for this book is available from the British Library

Library of Congress Cataloging-in-Publication Data applied for

ISBN 0 7190 5840 6 *hardback*
    0 7190 5841 4 *paperback*

First published 2001

10 09 08 07 06 05 04 03 02 01   10 9 8 7 6 5 4 3 2 1

Typeset in Scala with Meta display
by Northern Phototypesetting Co Ltd., Bolton
Printed in Great Britain
by Bookcraft (Bath) Ltd, Midsomer Norton

To my Mother, Father and Sue,
and those long-distant but well-remembered
five o'clock Queen Street cinema visits

Guinness - representative of a certain
kind of v. British tradition to which Larence
Olivier belongs - a different town, a
different role, a different disguise -
the tradition of the stage.

Other tradition - a new Hollywood
tradition - stardom as extension of
oneself. It's why the Method is
to appeal in Hollywood → it seems
to be about digging into one's existing
persona, rather than abandon it for a totally
new one - it allows for the melding of
self + role that is at the heart of the
construction of star personas.

Contents

Illustrations

Contributors

JUSTINE ASHBY is Lecturer in Television and Film Studies at the University of East Anglia. She is a contributor to *Dissolving Views: Key Writings on British Cinema*, and co-editor of *British Cinema, Past and Present*. She is currently writing a book about Betty Box and Muriel Box.

BRUCE BABINGTON is Reader in Film Studies at the University of Newcastle upon Tyne. He has co-authored *Blue Skies and Silver Linings: Aspects of the Hollywood Musical, Affairs to Remember: The Hollywood Comedy of the Sexes*, and *Biblical Epics*. His *Launder and Gilliat* is forthcoming.

CHARLES BARR is Professor of Film at the University of East Anglia. He is the author of *Laurel and Hardy, Ealing Studios, English Hitchcock*, and a forthcoming study of *Vertigo* He has edited the collection *All Our Yesterdays: 90 Years of British Cinema*, as well as writing many articles on British film and other subjects.

JONATHAN BURROWS is Lecturer in the Department of Film and Television Studies at the University of Warwick. His PhD thesis was on actors and acting in British cinema of the 1910s.

PAM COOK is Professor of European Film and Media at Southampton University. She has published several works on British cinema including *Fashioning the Nation: Costume and Identity in British Cinema* and *Gainsborough Pictures* (which she edited), and a study of Powell and Pressburger's *I Know Where I'm Going!*

CELESTINO DELEYTO teaches film and literature at the University of Zaragoza, Spain. He is the co-editor of a book on 1980s and 1990s romantic comedy, *Terms of Endearment*, and has recently completed a book-length study of *Smoke*.

PETER WILLIAM EVANS is Professor of Spanish at Queen Mary and Westfield College. He is the author of *The Films of Luis Buñuel* and *Women on the Verge of a Nervous Breakdown*, and co-author of *Blue Skies and Silver Linings: Aspects of the Hollywood Musical, Affairs to Remember: the Hollywood Comedy of the Sexes* and *Biblical Epics*.

ANDREW HIGSON is Professor of Film Studies at the University of East Anglia. His books include *Waving the Flag: Constructing a National Cinema in Britain, British Cinema, Past and Present* (co-editor), and '*Film Europe' and 'Film America': Cinema, Commerce and Cultural Exchange, 1920–1939*. He is currently working on a book on English Heritage cinema of the 1980s and 1990s.

MARCIA LANDY is Distinguished Professor of Literature and Film at the University of Pittsburgh. She is the author of *British Genres: Film and Society 1930-1960, Imitations of*

Life: A Reader on Film and Television Melodrama, Film, Politics and Gramsci, Cinematic Uses of the Past and *Italian Film.*

GEOFFREY MACNAB is a freelance writer who has written *J. Arthur Rank and the British Film Industry* and *Searching for Stars* as well as many articles and interviews on stars and other cinematic topics.

ANDREW MOOR studied at the University of Newcastle and now lectures in film at the University of Wales in Bangor. He has published on Derek Jarman, and both a book and an edited collection on Powell and Pressburger are forthcoming.

LAWRENCE NAPPER is researching a PhD in 'British Cinema and the Middlebrow Aesthetic' at the University of East Anglia.

JULIAN PETLEY teaches media and commication studies at Brunel University and he is Chair of the Campaign for Press and Broadcasting Freedom.

RICHARD W. SCHOCH is Lecturer in Drama at Queen Mary and Westfield College, University of London. He is the author of *Shakespeare's Victorian Stage* and is currently completing a book on Shakespearian burlesques and travesties.

NEIL SINYARD is Senior Lecturer in Film Studies at the University of Hull and author of a number of books on the cinema, including studies of Billy Wilder, Alfred Hitchcock. Richard Lester and Nicolas Roeg. His most recent book is on Jack Clayton. He is co-editor of the British Film Makers Series for Manchester University Press.

ANDREW SPICER teaches Film at the University of the West of England. He is the author of *Typical Men: The Representation of Masculinity in Popular British Cinema* and of essays on Stanley Baker, British male postwar stars and the New Zealander Bruno Lawrence.

MICHAEL WILLIAMS is researching a PhD in the ambiguous appeals of Ivor Novello at the University of East Anglia.

Acknowledgements

Thanks first of all to the contributors for their efforts towards this volume. Also to Matthew Frost at Manchester University Press for enthusiastically agreeing to the project, and getting it launched, and to various friends and colleagues whose discussions were valuable, in particular Peter Evans, Andrew Moor, Chris Perriam and Ron Guariento. To Charles Barr, Andrew Higson and Alan Kibble for help in finding films. To Helen Tuton for help with getting the manuscript into order and to her, Rowena Bryson and Hermann Moisl for their help in keeping it from getting lost in the electronic void. Finally to Khun Jiab for putting up with my excessive interest in 'Julie' and 'Margaret'.

BRUCE BABINGTON

Introduction: British stars and stardom

1

Holloway not Hollywood

> I wrote to her and obtained an autographed photograph, which I had
> framed and hung on the wall of my bedroom, where it still is.

In an early example of the 'ethnographic' approach to film, J. P. Mayer's
British Cinemas and their Audiences (1948), a twenty-one-year-old army
clerk confessed his attachment to the star Sally Gray. He relates how,
when watching films, he selected minor actresses as future stars.

> One of these was the British star Sally Gray, whom I first saw in *Mr Reeder
> in Room 13*. I was definitely impressed and decided to watch out for her
> next film. I made a point of seeing her in *Lambeth Walk*, *The Saint in
> London*, *A Widow in London* and *The Saint's Vacation*, all of which made me
> more certain that here was an actress who would be Britain's best.
>
> Up to late 1940 it had just been a case of seeing her name in the cast of
> a film and going along to see it. Then one day, on my way to work, I hap-
> pened to see a copy of *The Picturegoer* Xmas number, with a photograph of
> Miss Gray on the cover. I bought it, and that was the start. Since then, I've
> accumulated files of cuttings and data about this one actress. I started a
> collection of stills from her films and put them in albums. I wrote to her
> and obtained an autographed photograph, which I had framed and hung
> on the wall of my bedroom, where it still is.
>
> From my data I found her birthdate and sent her a birthday present
> which she acknowledged, later I sent other and more valuable gifts, and at
> the time I decided to join up I was saving to be able to send her a gift for
> Xmas. The reason for this heroine worship was brought about, I think, by
> a lack of interest in life which was caused by all my companions having left
> for the services, and it certainly did fill the void. A psychologist would be
> able to define it more clearly.[1]

Even if we ignore the temptations the last sentence offers, the account has
many points of interest. At a time when star theory has concentrated on
same-sex identification (the star as ego ideal or homosexual rather than

heterosexual object of desire), it reminds us that heterosexual desire has also been a factor in audience – star relations. It also reminds us that while fandom is most concentrated with adolescents and women, it is not confined to them.

The narrative also registers in its catalogue of mildly obsessive behaviour – the sense of power in discovering a potential star ('the Korda Syndrome'?), the accumulation of data, the establishing of a para-intimacy through gifts – the extra- filmic dimensions of fan behaviour which have lately been at the centre of theorists' interests. You certainly could not accuse Mayer's clerk of an abject imprisonment by the text! However, the account also returns to Sally Gray as film performer, since the respondent first saw her in a film that he clearly remembered, and then watched her in successive productions, all recalled by title. This underlines what the theorists John Ellis and Richard deCordova have argued, that film stars' screen appearances are privileged sites, the primary reason for their stardom.[2] This fan's accumulated cuttings perfectly illustrate the extra textual dimensions of stardom[2] but nevertheless they are ultimately dependent on the films.

We might also be interested in the narrative's self-conscious epilogue reviewing the writer's strange attachment, which he explains by his having inhabited a liminal space, ended by joining up. Though the episode is over, he admits that Sally Gray's photograph still hangs on his wall, as if, despite the exorcising of his passion by reason, he still clings to it, or yearns for the past when he was more possessed by it. In this we might think of him as not unlike the analyst of stars, detached by analytic method from the object of study, effecting a distance from erotic and narcissistic bonds by scanning the star for societal significances, yet with a favourite star's photo on the bedroom wall, not wholly free of the illusions he or she dissects.

Finally, Mayer's respondent was British (presumably English), and his star was also English, born in Holloway, and never went to Hollywood, but pursued a significant – if, like many others' – attenuated, career in the British cinema of the 1940s. Undoubtedly part of the fan's erotics here related particularly to the star's indigenousnesss, to the relative rarity of homegrown stars and to the tender triumph felt when one matched Hollywood's icons. Given that work by British critics has largely centred on those Hollywood stars, this is perhaps the most salutary reminder of all.

Gazing the other way: barely visible British stars

Three decades of analysis of the once neglected British cinema has seen the substantial charting of many areas – authors, genres, studios, producers, audiences etc. – but, with due respect to the minority who have written analytically on indigenous stars, there is still strangely little significant writing on what is the second subject of British popular discourse about film – Hollywood stars being the first – as witness the recent journalistic explosions based around Ewan McGregor, Kate Winslet and Catherine Zeta Jones. That there is a sea change is, however, clear. An acceleration of publications, of which this book is part, reflects the increasing, if belated, analysis of indigenous stars. Yet for a long time the new analytic focus on the British cinema neglected its stars, and it is worth briefly considering why.

The late 1970s saw 'star studies' instituted as a sub-discipline within academic film studies. Here the defining moment was the appearance of Richard Dyer's *Stars* (1979) with its formidable organisation of a disparate mass of previous material.[3] While it might have been expected that this new analytical sophistication would result in an immediate increase of significant work on British stars, for various reasons this failed to happen. Most obviously, dominant star theory, even when British in origin, was almost wholly Hollywood-oriented. This reflected Hollywood's unquestionable status as the paradigmatic site of stardom, and the great influence of Dyer's work was dependent on the clarity achieved by its strategic restriction of the subject. But Paul MacDonald's postscript chapter to the 1998 edition of *Stars* clarifies certain conservative emphases in star theory in the last twenty years with its resistance to almost any interests outside the new Hollywood megastars.[4] In retrospect it can be seen how later movements in star theory – psychoanalysis, audience reception, sexual subcultures' uses of stars, extra textuality over textuality – ignored Edgar Morin, who in *The Stars* (1962)[5] brought European (if not British) stars into his account, as well as Dyer's own brief hints on the extra-Hollywood deployment of star theory.[6] The combination of Hollywoodcentric film theorists acting on a film critical culture yet to pluralise into its present multiplicity, with an only slowly altering condescension towards the British cinema, is the primary explanation. And when eventually the British cinema lost its 'bad object' status, taxonomising of authors, genres and studios took precedence over the investigation of its stars.

That regression to a too-simple secondarisation is still possible can be seen in a recent highly acclaimed text, Jackie Stacey's *Star Gazing*, which studied British female film audiences of the 1940s and 1950s, but only as viewers of Hollywood female stars.[7] Given the hegemony of Hollywood throughout British film history, the book's subject is unexceptionable, but less so its exaggeration of part-truths into an unmitigated antithesis in which British stars (of huge appeal, this being the period of Lockwood, Roc, Calvert and others) are typed as the negative polarity to Hollywood's. Because of the book's timely conjunction of feminism, audience reception, psychoanalysis and 'ethnography', the oddity of a methodology which obscures its statistical evidence and, unlike its predecessors, Mayer and Mass Observation, dissolves the integrity of individual replies into mere selective corroboration of the author's argument, seems to have escaped observation. Most extraordinarily for research aiming to define attitudes to Hollywood and British stars, the answers to four questions allowing respondents to cite admiration for British stars simply disappear, allowing an exaggerated antithesis to stand unchallenged. Surely *someone* mentioned Margaret Lockwood![8]

Early on in *Stars* Dyer acknowledged the problematics of applying a theory based on Hollywood stars to other cinemas, writing that he believed that 'the theorizing and methodology' underpinning the book 'are broadly applicable' to stars of other cinemas, provided that 'the specificities of these other places where stars are to be found would always have to be respected'.[9] In other words, the institutions of film stardom exhibit major constants running across different film cultures, but each national cinema produces different inflections of them. The underlying questions in the rest of this introduction are: what exactly are the 'specificities' of the British cinema that have to be respected, and where and to what degree 'broadly applicable' needs redefining?

'British' (?) 'Stars' (?)

The title of this book, *British Stars and Stardom*, hides two complicated questions: the first concerning the terms 'English' and 'British', the second who, in the British context, can be called a star.

When, in response to political devolution and its attendant pressures, the British Broadcasting Corporation recently announced its intention of dropping, or at least severely limiting, its use of the word 'British', the prohibition did not extend to its own title which enshrined the word's previously acceptable meaning, the idea of a common but varied interest, based on geographical and historical contingency, shared by the English, Scots, and Welsh (the question of the Northern Irish always being more uneasy).[10] However, the proposed ban on further uses suggested, first, a pragmatic response to the widespread feeling (if the amount of journalism on the crisis of English identity can be believed) that the word 'British' is no longer used widely as a touchstone of an identity beyond 'English', 'Welsh', etc., and, second, a more politically pure reaction to a word suspected of being used to subsume others into an Englishness disguised as Britishness. The problem equally touches on questions of British cinema and its stars. Glancing at my bookcase, I can see eight books on this subject, from James Curran's and Vincent Porter's *British Cinema History* to Antonia Lant's *Blackout: Reinventing Women for Wartime British Cinema*, all of which use 'British' rather than 'English' (only one actually includes brief material on any non-English made films), though Alexander Walker's and Raymond Durgnat's titles (*Hollywood England: The British Film Industry in the Sixties* and *A Mirror For England: British Movies from Austerity to Affluence* respectively) gesture to the tension that other authors doubtless feel by managing to include both terms, and, by not quite conflating them, preserve some distance between them.[11]

In this book only one of seventeen chapters is on a star many of whose primary meanings derive from non-English Britain – the Scot, Sean Connery – though another is on the Austrian Anton Walbrook. The other fifteen are on English actors, who – even where there is a partial contrary claim (Novello's Welsh origins, Deborah Kerr's Scottish birth, Kenneth Branagh's Northern Irish beginnings) – are all highly anglicised in ethos.

Arguments in one case for 'English' over 'British' are made by Charles Barr in his recent *English* [i.e. not British] *Hitchcock* and convincing enough with that very English (and London-centred) director.[12] Indeed in this introduction 'English' (as, say, in the qualities embodied by Ronald Colman) is occasionally used as the more precise term. But overall, beyond the classificatory inconvenience Connery would pose to *English Stars and Stardom*, there are reasons for staying (warily) with traditional terminology. Its deployment recognises historical usages, the terms in which the cinema and surrounding culture(s) have dominantly addressed themselves, though that consensus looks to be declining. Though British cinema has been overwhelmingly English in its centres of production and ideological emphases (something underlined by recent films of the smaller nations' nascent industries), it has always drawn its personnel from all over Britain. Even if their non-Englishness is very much subsumed within an English cinema, it is hard to argue that this process is absolute. (Test this with such Welsh stars as Stanley Baker, Richard Burton and Anthony Hopkins.) Then, too, while England is the dominant centre of the indigenous cinema, its films frequently engage with other parts of Britain – and even if these representations of adjacent otherness are, to echo Durgnat's title, at best 'a mirror for England' (part of a long tradition whereby the Celtic Fringe, as in Gray's 'The Bard' and Collins's 'Ode on the Superstitions of the Highlands of Scotland', is used to define English preoccupations) – it is hard to argue that this process is always distortive, or all the preoccupations unshared.[13] Lastly, these English films were made for British audiences, for the cinemas of Edinburgh and Cardiff, as well as London and Manchester, and in some sense those audiences' expectations must have been taken into account. For all these reasons this book stays with 'British', leaving individual writers to provide their own cancellations and emphases, perhaps along the lines adopted by John Hill where, like other contributors to Robert Murphy's recent *British Cinema Book*, he stays with the established term but in his case complicates it with occasional inverted commas and terms such as 'English British'.[14]

Who is a star? Pragmatically, a performer who is called a star? (But how many times by how many people?) A performer whose name is displayed above the title of the film (which is what Edith Dodds at Rank told Dirk Bogarde)[15] – especially alone, as in 'REX HARRISON in THE RAKE'S PROGRESS', or, more pronouncedly, alone and before the title, as in 'CHARLES LAUGHTON in / Alfred Hitchcock's JAMAICA INN'? Should we talk of stars in a unitary way? Doubtless not, which means defining different kinds of stars – a spectrum running from Hollywood superstar to Hollywood star, to the star whose sphere is wholly or largely a national cinema, to significant performers (stars or not stars depending on one's definitions), to those who are just performers. To think only of Hollywood British as true British stars is transparently fallacious, leading to the untenable view that only those who found Hollywood pre-eminence are real stars. But more than a few of the indisputable stars of the British cinema (Gracie Fields, George Formby, Margaret Lockwood, Jessie Matthews, Ivor Novello) had either no Hollywood careers or very attenuated ones. And though James Mason had a larger audience from Hollywood, it is doubtful if any parts he played there had as much star charisma or created such excitement as his Gainsborough roles.

While it may be self-evident who is a Hollywood superstar and who a star of the first order within the national cinema, complications arise in defining the difference between a star and a major (household name) performer. This may be even more difficult within the British than within the Hollywood cinema, because of phenomena persisting through British film history, such as lesser specularisation (a test comparison for which might be King Vidor's more glamorising treatment of Robert Donat in *The Citadel* with his British roles), tendencies for films to be built less as star vehicles than as ensemble pieces, more restrained publicity, and more emphasis on the 'acting' and 'picture personality' discourses than on the 'star' one (to use Richard deCordova's terminology),[16] as well as persistent remnants of the suspicion of stardom documented circa 1910–12 by Jon Burrows.[17] All these lead not to an absence of stardom but certainly to a more muted version of it.

Usage provides a guide, but is so diverse that it is difficult to generalise from. David Shipman in *The Great Movie Stars: The International Years* includes not only Alastair Sim, Margaret Rutherford and Terry-Thomas but Kathleen Harrison and Glynis Johns.[18] Sue Harper and Vincent Porter note Basil Radford as a minor star whom audiences listed as a reason for attending a specific picture.[19] To call Radford – certainly a (middle-class) household name – or Harrison a star surely goes too far, giving rise to the critique that critics, in their search for new subjects, mis-define minor performers as stars.[20]

We might ask how candidates fulfil such central criteria of stardom as:

1 to constitute a – often the – major attraction of a film for substantial audiences
2 to bear the marks of special treatment, significant specularisation, within the films
3 to exhibit what is called 'personification' (i.e. an iconic transtextual sameness beneath variations),[21] and
4 to be the subject of 'star discourse' in intertextual media (newspaper, magazines, radio, television).

In the light of these Basil Radford and Kathleen Harrison are surely not stars in any mainstream sense, though Glynis Johns, particularly from the time of *Miranda* (1949), qualifies as some kind of minor star. With Alastair Sim, Margaret Rutherford and Terry-Thomas cases for minor stardom might be made. They fulfil the criteria: (1) albeit not on a Schwarzeneggerian scale; (2) though not in the primary (but not absolutely necessary) inflection of sexual glamour; (3) because as much as any actors we think of them primarily as themselves over the character acted in the diegesis; and (4) in a minor degree, sometimes posthumously (for example the revelations of Rutherford's fear of madness, her father's parricide, etc., the discovery of Terry-Thomas's MS and semi-destitu-tion).[22] All three are comic actors: the popularity of comedians in polls is often forgotten when thinking about stardom, and elderly comic eccentrics have an interestingly prominent role in the national cinema. The American sociologists Wolfenstein and Leites in their comparative study of the Hollywood, British and French cinemas made some inter-esting comparisons concerning the roles of parental (especially father) figures, suggesting that, while fathers in American films are insubstan-tial characters, those in British films are stronger and more idealised.[23]

Though their argument fails to register the possibility of ambivalence (there is something tyrannical about Will Fyffe and even vampiric about Sim), it does illuminate an interesting minor star type heightened in a pre 1960s societal context of greater authority and less mobility.

The point here is not to try to construct some infallible litmus test for stardom – as many will deny Terry-Thomas's claim as affirm it – but to suggest that the issue is less theoretically resolvable than is sometimes thought, especially within the British context, in which the various criteria of stardom are often underplayed.

It may be difficult also to recover the historical reality of star appeal, especially where performers' styles have gone out of fashion. How many readers know Jack Buchanan apart from his late Hollywood role in *The Band Wagon?* Yet Buchanan was a multimedia star (film, stage, recordings), and the amount of space Rachael Low gives him is testament to that.[24] Conrad Veidt's reputation as a British star is safer, but the citations in Mayer, projecting him as a star of demonic erotic force, might surprise: 'Only once have I fallen in love with a screen star. And that was Conrad Veidt. The magnetism, the compelling personality of him "got me". His voice, his mannerisms fascinated me. I hated him, I feared him, loved him.'[25] Apropos of other neglected performers, John Sedgwick's attempt to analyse star popularity through attendance statistics in the 1930s, has occluded figures such as the Hulberts, with Tom Walls and Elizabeth Bergner scoring surprisingly highly.[26]

The chapters in this book incorporate, first, major figures in the Hollywood cinema, such as Mason, Andrews, Connery, Kerr. Here a decision has been taken to limit the number of such stars dealt with to the few above. Either to wholly omit them or to deal only with their British films would neglect an ever-present reality of British film history. On the other hand, to include more would incline the book towards a history of Hollywood's representations of Britishness, which is not its primary purpose. Its main focus, then, is on the second category: major figures of the national cinema (sometimes featuring in the Hollywood cinema) such as Alma Taylor, Lockwood, Guinness, Fields, Dors, Novello, Finney, Trevor Howard, Branagh and Thompson, and from the German cinema Anton Walbrook. It also deliberately incorporates, third, figures whose claim to stardom is unsteady. Andrew Higson's chapter on Flora Robson deals with a star whose 'character acting' brought her international renown, and Charles Barr's with James Donald, an actor seen as nearly, but not quite, achieving stardom. Both chapters test concepts of stardom through ambivalent instances. Finally, fourth, the growing reality, with increasingly fragmented audiences, of cult stars is represented by Julian Petley's chapter on the sex film performer Mary Millington.

Stars, histories, repetitions

'I have been engaged to play in a big drama. I am allowed to choose my leading man – Henry Edwards. His actions, his eyes, his hair, and his clothes always held a fascination for me. And he is British. And so am I, so we make a good couple'.

Marjorie Harris (14), Birmingham

The statement comes from *Pictures and the Picturegoer* magazine (9–16 November 1918), which prints entries in a competition asking boys and girls 'to fancy yourselves as stars and then choose the player you would prefer to play opposite you and why'. In other letters Nancy Burn (10) of Bristol chooses 'Stewart Rome' 'because he is a true type of English gentleman, and because his kisses would be reel [*sic*] ones', and Herbert Burn (15) of Bristol (presumably Nancy's older sibling) opts for Alma Taylor 'because she is English and so simple, dainty and sweet'. Others imagine starring opposite Douglas Fairbanks, Mary Miles Minter and, of course, Mary Pickford, but 'Uncle Tim' surprisingly announces that 'Henry Edwards came out on top with six times more cards than any other player, male or female'. The competition hardly provides indisputable information. Popular though Henry Edwards was, no other evidence corroborates such precedence over American stars. Its significance lies in demonstrating how in Britain by 1918 the star system, since 1912 when Gladys Sylvani appeared on posters in the underground,[27] had become the major motivation for mass cinemagoing, and in its expression of a desire for British primacy. Another *Picturegoer* competition, 'Can you Film Phiz?', required the identification of stars from fragmented portraits, thus demonstrating contestants' intense specular knowledge of their favourites.[28] Here the preponderance of American 'phizzes' over British reflects more reliably the secondarisation (though not negligiblity) of indigenous stars. It is emblematic that when Chrissie White (1917) and Violet Hopson (1918) attained the cover of *Pictures and the Picturegoer*, in both cases the cover also advertised 'Mary Pickford's Life Story',[29] accidentally underlining Hollywood's dominance. This was also visible when British stars were referred to as reflections, as the 'The English Mary Pickford', 'the British Lillian Gish', etc. (appellations variously made of Alma Taylor, Joan Morgan, Chrissie White and Mabel Poulton, and historically continued in the desire for a 'British Monroe').[30]

In the 'starring opposite' fantasy the children's Great-War-heightened patriotism prefigures a constant future theme. Macnab's recent book on British stars is perceptively called *Searching for Stars*,[31] and that they were and still are sought for needs little theorising. Though Hollywood stars have almost always seemed more glamorous economically and libidinally (except perhaps for that brief 'swinging London' period in the early 1960s when to be British or, more particularly, English, was the ultimate glamour), British stars, like those of other indigenous cinemas, give things to home audiences that Hollywood luminaries cannot – reflections of the known and close at hand, typologies of the contingent, intimate dramatisations of local myths and realities – which, when they fit into Hollywood's categories, make the performers who embody them world stars, while others remain local stars – but no less meaningful for that.

Both *Picturegoer* competitions occur at the end of the concentrated process beginning circa 1911, which produced a recognisably modern film stardom. In Britain, however, this period constitutes an exception to the cartography that has taken place. Such neglect is due to historical distance, the non-survival, or non-circulation, of films, and the impossibility of viewing stars like Alma Taylor and Chrissie White outside of archives. Thus knowledge of British stardom's formative period has depended heavily on Rachael Low's pioneering *The History of the British Film* (published from 1948 on).[32] Extraordinary though Low's work is, it has unavoidable limitations here, being a massive production history, which recognises the centrality of stars in the commercial cinema but is necessarily constrained in dealing with them, both by space and by its predating sophisticated models of star analysis.

Low's treatment of incipient native stardom is dominated by two related factors which underlie all subsequent activity in the British film industry: first, the chronic economic weakness and unstable production base of the local industry,[33] and, second the dominance of American films and stars in British film culture.[34] Within this context three particular points are stressed: (1) the close connection between the West End theatre and the nearby film studios, with its economic and aesthetic consequences;[35] (2) the relative failure to generate the stars desired by both public and producers, because of both the poor quality of their films and insufficient investment in the basics of star-building;[36] and (3) that, when stars emerged, many abandoned the home industry for the greater rewards of Hollywood.[37]

As this primal period is reinspected, recent research by Jon Burrows (see his chapter on Alma Taylor) nuances Low's descriptions with evidence of a much more varied interest in, and range of popular debates about, local stars, as well as much greater activity in 'booming' them, than the dominant account maintains.[38] Rereading Low's account as modified by later research is to see not simply moments unique to that first phase but first versions of recurring constants.

Low's first point concerned cinema and theatre. From geographical proximity, economic necessity and the theatre's cultural primacy, cinema and theatre remained far more tightly coupled than in the United States. British cinema's initial reliance on theatrical actors never modulated as in the USA into a large class of cinema actors economically sustained by the cinema alone.

The unstable British production base underlaid this failure ever to arrive at the American pattern of economically powerful, stable studios able to contract performers for long periods to their own productions. The number of British organisations that significantly developed and exploited stars in the systematic Hollywood way is rather small. Walter West at Broadwest with Violet Hopson; Hepworth with his company; Michael Balcon with Jessie Matthews and Jack Buchanan at British Gaumont; Herbert Wilcox with Anna Neagle; Alexander Korda with Robert Donat, Charles Laughton, Laurence Olivier, Rex Harrison and Merle Oberon; Basil Dean with Gracie Fields and George Formby; the Ostrers and Edward Black at Gainsborough with Margaret Lockwood, James Mason, Stewart Granger, Phyllis Calvert and Jean Kent; and Rank in the 1950s, particularly with Dirk Bogarde, are most of the names that come to mind.[39] Elsewhere, the picture is much more haphazard. Peter Noble's *The British Film Yearbook 1949–50* accidentally dramatises the difference between the British scene and the Hollywood studio system, with its numerous photos of major freelance performers advertising themselves, but with only two of them, Patricia Roc (Rank) and Deborah Kerr (MGM), contracted. All the others, including such well-known figures as Eric Portman, Jack Warner, Sally Gray (again), Herbert Lom and Dennis Price, are available for film-by-film hire, or theatre work.[40] The situation encapsulated here dominated British film history, its cinematically debilitating consequences in the studio age underlined in the many negative replies given to Brian MacFarlane's question in his 'autobiographies' of British cinema, whether actors felt their early careers were guided.[41] In *The British Film Yearbook* stars list their agents. In a much earlier article (1936), 'Practical Star Building', Dwight Deering argued for the key role of such agents in advancing British stars, but that this could really replace the planned deployments of the studio is special pleading.[42] The passage in Durgnat's *A Mirror for England* on the 1940s and 1950s British cinema's 'extraordinary difficulty, not in finding, but in developing starlets, female, assorted, innumerable',[43] addresses the product of this situation, more extreme with female stars because of the decline of female-centred films in the 1950s, but true of male performers as well. At the breakup of the Hollywood studio system the roles of the agent and freelance star became the norm, in Hollywood leading to star power and economic demands unprecedented since Mary Pickford. British stars, though, except in the case of the Hollywood British, largely failed, as Alexander Walker notes, to benefit much from such changes (which led, for instance, to the star as producer), their position remaining similar to that before.[44]

Despite a number of the earliest native stars, such as Chrissie White and Alma Taylor, being created by film rather than theatre, the norm of dual theatrical and cinematic performers (with television the later third element) never fundamentally shifted. Low argues that this reliance on theatre performers held back the industry materially by making unnecessary more rewarding salaries for film actors, and aesthetically by retarding cinematic modes. 'It was easier to let the actors flutter and wring their hands, storm and stamp, clutch and gasp, than to work out incidents and shots which would convey feelings and thoughts with less absurdity.'[45] This critique, though, needs to be moderated by Burrows's evidence of early concern with naturalistic film acting,[46] and also by Low's assertion that circa 1925 new British film performers had emerged 'equally at home on the screen and on the stage'.[47] The latter is a key phrase, for her examples are followed by a long succession of major British film stars, whose screen charisma and acting abilities are undoubted, who, at the point where theatrical work ceased to be an economic necessity, remained, of choice, doubly committed to film and theatre, sometimes more to the latter than the former – Laurence Olivier, Vivien Leigh, Rex Harrison, Richard Burton, Peter O'Toole, Alan Bates, Glenda Jackson, Vanessa Redgrave and many others. The issues surrounding this tradition are complex, polemically driven either by deep cultural feelings about the theatre's superiority and greater demandingness as an acting medium or by strong cinephilic reactions. The latter may sometimes be as prejudiced as the former, as where one critic designates as 'screen phobia' Glenda Jackson's remarks about escaping the burdens of stardom while working theatrically in England,[48] or where John Ellis types the acting of some performers (Glenda Jackson again) as 'over acting', when all that is meant is that a code of self-conscious performance is activated rather than codes asserting unselfconsciousness.[49] Surveying an intensely disputed subject, enlightenment is perhaps most found in an admittedly undeveloped statement by Thomas Elsaesser where he sees the theatrical – television – film nexus of British film as one in which strengths and weaknesses are inextricably bound together.[50] Since the weaknesses (such as the notorious 1930s RADA voice, the West End's inability to produce physical heros) are most often foregrounded, we might look to Hollywood's use of British actors to highlight a few of the strengths in the tradition – self-conscious virtuosity, impersonatory skills, wit and irony, all often taken for granted and even somehow deemed uncinematic. (Even those rather class-ridden paeans to English voices of some of Mayer's respondents might be read as a thrilling to the foregrounded vocal, rather than just snobbery.)[51] While the theatrical tradition highlights impersonation, any over-simple posing of impersonation against personification as the key to British/Hollywood differences needs checking, for stars such as Ivor Novello, Trevor Howard, Celia Johnson, or Hugh Grant are as iconic, as serially recognisable from role to role, as any Hollywood stars, whatever other differences (different kinds of iconicity) may obtain. What also might be said is that while, for an expert performer, a career divided between stage and film should have no effect on film performance (for, as the theorist Barry King notes, 'the demands of stage acting can be scaled down whereas film techniques cannot really be scaled up'),[52] it probably makes cinematic star-building more difficult both because of the performer's divided audience and, consequent on long absences on stage, because of fewer films. Oppositely, too constant exposure on tv (technically close to film acting) may operate against the mystique of film stardom.

Low's second point related to the British cinema's difficulties in developing and publicising stars. In *Searching for Stars* Macnab quotes the film journalist E. L. Mannock's campaign through the 1920s and 1930s against the industry's ignoring of the 'systematic business' of star-making, even at the obvious level of the availability of glamour portraits.[53] A telling addendum to this can also be found in Noble's *British Film Yearbook 1949–50*, where Leslie R. Frewin, Elstree's publicity manager, wrote an article entitled 'British Film Publicity – the New Renascence', basically publicising a four-day shoot of Patricia Roc, for publicity portraits for home and international distribution, which he presents as a unique venture heralding a new publicity age for British stars.[54] That Frewin could write this with any degree of plausibility certainly justified Mannock's perennial complaints. Publicity portraits, however, became a mainstay of Rank publicity in the 1950s, for the writer, in Auckland aged 12, was among the reputed sixty thousand a week who applied for personalized photos – receiving not only Dirk Bogarde's but one signed 'Sincerely Yours, Diana Dors'– which were lodged in an autograph book between the 1954/5 MCC Touring Party and the 1955 Lions in South Africa. Again there is an overdetermination of reasons for this backwardness in 'booming' stars. Strong cultural attitudes towards the vulgarity of self-display played a deep-seated part in inhibiting publicity. Celia Johnson's famous explanation of her dislike of being interviewed – 'One doesn't talk about oneself, does one?',[55] – may now feel anthropologically distant from the tabloid culture of the present, but it expresses attitudes that ran deep in British middle-class life, in the British cinema and its stars, and on whose apparent complete extinguishing it is too early to comment authoritatively. But in thinking about inhibited publicity, one also cannot ignore the fundamental economic reality of a small unstable production base in which few film-making concerns regarded stars as their own investments rather than commodities to be picked up for occasional use. Developing 'bankable' stars, is, of course, a way to render production less unstable, but the histories of the concerns that did this most successfully – Korda, Gainsborough and Rank – demonstrate that the production of stars within the British cinema tended to raise problems pertaining to the consistent use of them. When stars were adeptly developed, as Olivier, Oberon, Harrison and others were by Korda, through a highly organised cluster of film parts over a short period,[56] the problem could easily emerge that not enough substantial films were produced by the studio to use the star to greatest advantage, thus leading to problems of consistent casting. Certainly (though the issue is complicated by the decline of the 'woman's picture' at the end of the 1940s) first Gainsborough/Rank, then Herbert Wilcox, struggled to find adequate vehicles for Margaret Lockwood's later career. Other complicating factors were the strong presence of an 'impersonatory' ideology –no doubt intensified by the theatrical base – which led to feelings that major players should succeed across many genres (Lockwood, for instance, valued her comic roles), and the strong tradition of ensemble playing which prompted a veering away from the star vehicle. Only comedians and musical stars (such as Jessie Matthews and Gracie Fields), secure in a generic identity, were unlikely to suffer in this way. If performers were lent out to other concerns to make good the production shortfall, the royal road to stardom was to lease them to Hollywood, but, as was the case with Oberon, the success generated could lose the star to the larger industry.

One way around the problems of grooming stars, and simultaneously attempting to penetrate an American market resistant to non-Hollywood British stars, was to star Americans: a long-lived strategy, from Cutts's £1000-a-week use of Betty Compson in *Woman to Woman* (1923) to the long roll-call of 1930s, 1940s and 1950s (mostly) minor Hollywood stars in British films, to the recent uses in *A Fish Called Wanda* (1988), *Four Weddings and a Funeral* (1993) and *Notting Hill* (1999) of, respectively, Jamie Lee Curtis, Kevin Kline, Andie MacDowell and Julia Roberts. These last films, all notably successful in America, are, however, unrepresentative historically, of a strategy where successes have been outnumbered by failures, or at least a majority of cases where it would be hard to prove the strategy's efficacy. Indeed Michael Balcon, who actively promulgated the policy in the 1930s, later admitted that it was a costly mistake.[57] The deployment of American (and indeed a smaller but substantial number of European) stars, though there may be occasions where there are economic and/or aesthetic justifications, hardly constitutes an answer to questions of stardom in the British cinema, particularly since its consistent use militates against the development of local stars and has inevitable and narrowing consequences upon the kinds of films made.[58]

Low's third point concerned the exodus to Hollywood. In the American silent cinema, in which stars of any Western nationality could function, even if they spoke little and heavily accented English, British stars' chief advantage over European stars was that they could easily graduate to film from the New York stage. This near equality changed with sound, and the linguistic circumstance that made penetration by the Hollywood cinema easier in Britain than elsewhere, gave British stars a much greater advantage. While Hollywood also desired European stars, their more obvious difference made them more narrowly deployable and in smaller numbers. French stars could only be French, but British stars might be used in ways that accentuated their Britishness (usually Englishness), as with Herbert Marshall or David Niven, or – as has happened from Cary Grant to Minnie Driver and Gary Oldman, diminished it so that they pass, all, or some of the time, for Americans, impossible for Europeans who could play only first generation immigrants.

The British migration began with theatrical rather than film performers, often via the American stage, for example the comedienne Flora Finch (co-star of the American comedian John Bunney from 1911), H. B. Warner and C. Aubrey Smith (both in US films from 1914) and the most famous cases of Charles Chaplin and Stan Laurel. The screen diaspora began slightly later, with Ronald Colman, Basil Rathbone and Clive Brook. In the 1930s Madeleine Carroll, Herbert Marshall, Charles Laughton and George Sanders emigrated. Even in the 1940s, at the height of British postwar film production optimism, James Mason, Stewart Granger and Deborah Kerr left, followed by Jean Simmons and Audrey Hepburn. Important later exiles include Sean Connery, Michael Caine, Julie Christie (for a significant period) and Julie Andrews, and some contemporary instances are Daniel Day Lewis, Minnie Driver and Gary Oldman. Looking over this abbreviated list, several points ask to be made. First, there have always been major exceptions, stars coveted by Hollywood, such as Robert Donat, Leslie Howard and Jessie Matthews, who worked entirely or mostly in Britain for reasons more personal than professional. Second, there have also been major stars, particularly comedians, too local in meaning to travel well, such as George Formby, though, very surprisingly, Gracie Fields did make some Hollywood films. Third, the theatre, often oversimply cast as the villain in the story of British film, kept numerous performers (most obviously Olivier) substantially within the industry's orbit. By the 1960s, however, the conditions governing the flow to Hollywood changed significantly with the decline of the studio system, meaning the end of the long-term contracts which had made going to Hollywood an irrevocable long-term break with the British industry. Though, as noted previously, this change, by which freelancing became the international norm, failed largely to benefit most home stars, at the highest levels of stardom British Hollywood performers, with perhaps optimistic portents for the twenty-first century, could now work both sides of the Atlantic when projects and finance were right, a pattern highly visible in Michael Caine and Bob Hoskins, for instance, but earlier evident in the careers of James Mason and David Niven.

Hollywood's uses of British actors to represent a heightened Britishness (usually Englishness) are fascinating, but largely outside the reaches of this book, except as they touch on discussion of its subjects Kerr, Andrews, Mason and Connery. The paradox that the most influential representations of Britishness/Englishness are in a foreign cinema, filtered through American stereotypes, is obvious. It would be over-simple, though, to see these archetypes as merely negative. Where, say, have the virtues of the English upper-middle-class ideal ever been as movingly embodied as in Ronald Colman? But, potent as these representations are, they tend to a static mythology, at the least slightly out of sync with reality, and this is as true of Hollywood's recent uses of British working-class toughness as of its traditional love affair with the gentleman or lady.

Acting out stardom

Such negative constraints on stardom are, for all their force, in part deceptive. Even the abbreviated list of stars above emphasises how many extraordinary film performers the British cinema has produced from its theatrical and, later, television and theatre base. Although, compared to studio Hollywood, institutional structures were lacking, identical mechanisms of inter- and extra-textual discourse in the developing media promulgated and sustained interest in stars. Circa 1918–22 many of these were attached to Violet Hopson, perhaps the first local star, as Low recorded, to be particularly noted for fashion.[59] A more modern figure than the Hepworth players, Hopson modulated their anti-urban qualities (see Burrows)[60] with more urbane ones (her type-castings as the 'dear delightful villainess' and the rich sophisticate),[61] and in this crossing of conservative and contemporary was a template for later stars. Accordingly her Broadwest publicity was more adept than Hepworth's, particularly in using photo portraits along with text,[62] and, rather than praising her acting, in claiming her (dubiously) as 'Britain's best loved star',[63] also in opportunistically connecting her with manufactured events in a way Hepworth's stars were generally not. For instance, *Picturegoer*'s search for a new female star in 1918 has a role in a Hopson film as the prize,[64] and another competition invites children to write an essay from Hopson's lucky Manx kitten's point of view.[65] The relatively prolific material about her circa 1918–22 is a compendium of British star publicity of that time, with at least fifteen micro-discourses discernible, fusing de Cordova's 'acting', 'picture personality' and 'star' discourses:[66]

1 biographical information: e.g. convent education, mother's objections to a performing career[67]

2 a classic 'discovery story' involving a chance visit to a film studio[68]

3 release of information about new films building up audience anticipation around her[69]

4 identification of the star with a particular genre, the 'sporting [i.e. horseracing] subject', as earlier she had been role-generically identified with the 'dear delightful villainness'[70]

5 stories of the star's daring on set, e.g. doing her own riding for a film[71]

6 human-interest stories, like her ring being swallowed by a calf during the shooting of *Widdicombe Fair*[72]

7 the suspense of The Star In Danger – her illness and then recovery in the South of France[73]

8 reports of the star's personal appearances, e.g. at Birmingham cinemas or 'the Public Hall at Canning Town' where she presented athletics prizes to factory workers[74]

9 early evidence, albeit minuscule, of recognition of fan following, where Hopson says she has received two letters from viewers of a film produced years ago[75]

10 a photographic glimpse of the star supposedly at home, appended to an interview 'As I am in private life', this suggestion of the personal furthered by her signature attached to some articles[76]

11 emphasis on the star's offscreen as well as onscreen glamour, as when she is noted wearing a distinctive 'Hopson hat' and getting into a big yellow Daimler[77]

12 the star as fashion authority giving her opinion on short and long skirts[78]

13 the star giving beauty advice to women, e.g. in a piece called 'The Care of the Hair'[79]

14 the star discussing acting – a very British star trait – in a piece called 'From Super To Star' where she advocates the sinking of the self into the part[80]

15 the (very modern) revelation of the star as businesswoman exploiting
    her own image in Broadwest's announcement (1919) of 'Violet
    Hopson' films made under her supervision, and her agent's
    announcement in 1921 that she is selling the rights of her films in
    'the biggest deal yet attempted by a woman in British film land'[81].

These micro-discourses, playing across the discourses of 'acting', the
'picture personality' and the star-specific discourse of publicised private
life, closely parallel the Hollywood paradigms that slightly precede them.
Each analysis is hardly visible at all. This can be said also of the analysis
of discourse surrounding British stars. Each of them becomes a convention, disseminated through developing media channels – the primitive
'for the favour of insertion' pieces sent out to newspapers and magazines;
the specialist popular film magazines (around in Britain by 1910) which
followed their American counterparts' quickly developing star-centred-
ness; the general (mainly feminine) interest magazines whose writing on
films based itself around stars; the popular newspapers which exploited
the desire for personality-based news (and much later employed new
kinds of journalists, the Donald Zecs, Peter Evanses and Alexander Walk-
ers, in symbiotic relationships with stars such as Peter Sellers and Laurence Harvey, specialising in breaking stories about them);[82] the radio,
then the television, and, today, the Internet. Hopson's 'discovery story' is
already a variant on Chrissie White's (with no film experience Chrissie
cheekily volunteered to replace her indisposed sister),[83] which was varied
in Mabel Poulton's discovery as a Lillian Gish lookalike,[84] and the composer Ivor Novello's photo being accidentally seen by a film producer.[85]
But though formally the same as Hollywood's discovery story, this micro-
discourse never attained the pre-eminence it had for American society in
which ideologies of mobility and progress dominated. Film stardom also
had lesser symbolic force as the site of the fulfilment of these ideologies
in Britain because the material rewards for British stars (unless in Hollywood) never went through anything remotely like the 1915–16 explosion
connected with Mary Pickford's renegotiating of her contracts.[86] Though
there have always been instances of British stars without theatrical experience, the theatre (later theatre and television) was the expected route to
film, making the American myth of accidental discovery less powerful in
the British context.

    In two of the micro-discourses (8 and 9) Hopson is involved both in
public appearances and in a glancing precursor of fan mail and fan clubs,
phenomena that escalated after the Second World War, with as perhaps
unlikely an object of mass desire as Richard Attenborough the recipient
of substantial fan mail (the subject of an article by Norah Alexander in

1947),[87] and fan club magazines such as *The International Patricia Roc Fan Club Magazine* relaying para-personal information to fans.[88] This period was notable for the development of public appearances and an attempt (of a kind Herbert Wilcox had pioneered in the 1930s)[89] to rival the razzle-dazzle of Hollywood premières with the institution of the first Royal Command Performance in 1946 as well as the cultivation of personal appearances by stars, most developed in Margaret Lockwood's two national tours.[90] In this period of the highest ever cinema attendances, related forms of star publicity (observable at lower intensity in the 1920s and 1930s) were correspondingly heightened; from the use of stars in advertising to the popularity polls, which had existed since 1914 and now flourished, particularly with the immediate postwar popularity of British stars, which all the polls registered, especially in the *annus mirabilis* of 1947 (from *Picturegoer's* to the research for the Granada cinema chain of Sidney Bernstein's survey).[91] These polls were, beyond whatever accuracies may be accorded them, another channel of star publicity, a key part of the fiesta of cinema, keeping cinema in the public eye through competitions amongst its stars and testifying to the centrality of stars in British popular film culture.

We may generalise (following Dyer) that British, like other, stars exhibit a 'structured polysemy',[92] have meaning in regard to dominant and subdominant ideologies, reinforce ruling values, sometimes articulate oppositional meanings, as they play out the culture's conceptions of individuality, masculinity and femininity. They also articulate, through the intersection of screen roles and (public) private lives, narratives of success, sex, love, marriage, leisure, consumerism, work, desirable lifestyles and what the culture prizes as national characteristics, hence the 'Britishness' ('Englishness', 'Scottishness', 'Welshness') or whatever of national stars. Further, they may also act out the darker implications of such thematics (Lillian Hall Davis's suicide,[93] Laurence Harvey's or Richard Burton's attempts to live out the fantasy star lifestyle[94]), as well as exemplary instances of the basic human inescapabilities of misfortune, ageing and mortality (Kay Kendall's early death, for instance). However, the intimate content of any of these is culture specific, in the case of Britain specific to a culture very different from the star paradigm culture of the United States. British culture was undoubtedly in the first half of the century more tradition-oriented, more class-bound and less materially wealthy. It was equally different in the second half of the century as it adapted with difficulty to its shrunken prestige, its loss of Empire but confusing new gaining of a multiculture, its middling economic power status and the apparent dissolution of a middle-class hegemony into an anxious fluidity. Here, in this last, it is difficult to know where to see abrupt dislocations, and where continuities, where the world of *Brief Encounter* and *In Which We Serve* may seem almost as distant as the tribes Margaret Mead wrote about, yet where British stars of the present such as Hugh Grant and Jeremy Irons suggest a surprising longevity in that broad archetype of the English gentleman. One might think this – in home terms if not Hollywood's – vulnerable to the point of extinction, that is if one did not see the type less as a simple reflection of sociological reality than a site of imagination, fantasy and nostalgia.[95]

With the 'discovery story' we have noticed a classic motif with less force in Britain than America, and something similar may be said of the micro-discourses of fandom and public appearances which have traditionally been played out with an ideologically meaningful reserve by British stars, so that, paradoxically, in their cases discourses of privacy are formulated through discourses of publicity. (Even a case like Richard Burton's exhibits subplots of anguish, intellectualism, irony, scepticism and the lure of traditional theatrical, literary and even hermetic scholarly values.) With Hopson, in micro-discourse (1), it can be seen that the invocation of the private life, at a time close to the full development of the 'discourse of scandal' in Hollywood, was extremely restrained, with no emphasis at all on romance, marriage and sex. This quickly changes, but until recently discourses of sex have been lightly played, dramatising different conceptions of the public and private to those articulated around many Hollywood stars, and ones in which scandal (give or take a few exceptions such as the Jessie Matthews, Evelyn Laye divorce case) has had only a minor role. (In the later tabloid efflorescence a special category of posthumous scandal has emerged, for instance revelations about Merle Oberon's mixed race and promiscuity.)[96] Clearly Morin's 'fiesta' of the star's private life was acted out less flagrantly in Britain, like other aspects of the star's life. To take one instance, the star's house, which, whether Alma Taylor's (part of a residence built for Anne Boleyn), Betty Balfour and her husband's 'The Old Dutch House' or the Oliviers' Notley Abbey, often seemed in its traditionalism the antithesis of the eclectic glamour of 'Pickfair'.[97] British stars largely represented a culture that did not see itself as 'a world in which material problems have been settled and all that is left is relationships'.[98] The education, the middleclassness of British stars, an intellectual society in which the cinema ranked low beside the theatre (it is only in the last twenty years or so that cinema has overtaken the theatre in intellectual glamour), all inclined British stars towards an anti-star inflection of stardom, which, despite major surfaces differences, covers stars as different as James Mason, Margaret Lockwood, Terence Stamp and Julie Christie, and which differed from the Hollywood anti-star's in being as close to dominant social ideologies as the rare American version's is distinct from them. The autobiographies of James Mason and Dirk Bogarde are particularly rich in acerbic comments distancing themselves from the illusions of publicity.[99] Perhaps the most extraordinary work of star biography ever produced, Roger Lewis's *The Life and Death of Peter Sellers*[100] is a summation of this tradition, expressing an almost Platonic revulsion at the consequences of becoming a commodity, an illusory self. From the mid 1950s, there are significant inflections in the self-presentation of many British stars, in tune with, rather than against, the culture of consumerism, and at first particularly embodied in two young female stars, Diana Dors and Belinda Lee, whose publicity narratives almost eclipse their screen careers, and form an extreme contrast to the publicity of the great 1940s actresses in whom glamour combined with work, marriage with career, and urbanity with vestiges of the long-lived pastoralism surrounding the Hepworth stars – all those country homes like the Flemings' (Peter Fleming and Celia Johnson's) 'Merrimoles', with their attendant menageries.[101] In such instances as Michael Caine's early publicity or Laurence Harvey's materialistic trajectory we may discern related defining changes, accelerating out of the 1960s with a pop culture stardom largely outside middle-class determinants, but these also modulate into unexpected traditionalisms:[102] Harvey's passion for stage performance, Caine's later purveying of actor masterclasses. And just as the forgotten Violet Hopson negotiated the early modern period with a mixture of modern and tradional traits, so British stars yet to come, including the stars of colour likely to emerge following stars and media celebrities in other fields, will probably reflect both a changing environment and elements of tradition in even the most apparently untraditional. (As where both Gary Oldman and Ewan McGregor are written of in terms of almost 'faceless' impersonatory abilities.)[103]

As regards future work on British stars, two kinds of investigation are vital. On the one hand, (1) an attempt to understand, in close relation to the socio-historical complexities of British society, the underlying typologies of stars that the British cinema has produced; on the other hand, (2) studies of the individuals within those genres, their differences and similarities. As (1) is pursued, it becomes evident that the typologies evolved for the Classical Hollywood Cinema – 'the Tough Guy', 'the Good Joe', 'the Pin Up' and other variants[104] – lack basic explanatory power in the British cinema (though 'the Tough Guy' and the 'Pin Up' have some late chronological resonance). Work such as Andrew Spicer's on patterns of male stars in the post-war cinema, in particular as related to the development of the meritocratic professional, and also to the rise of 'the Tough Guy' through the postwar crime film and the star Stanley Baker, suggests some of the possibilities in the first category.[105] Geoffrey Macnab's discussion of typologies in *Searching for Stars* is rather more directed towards typical occupational character types than star types, but his and Jeffrey Richards's discussions of 'the Gentleman' usefully explore aspects of a basic template.[106] The juxtaposition here of these antithetical social types of Tough Guy and Gentleman points also to the need to investigate the way in which modulating class realities have altered concepts of British film stardom. It is noticeable that, though there has been a small amount of significant work on individuals such as Dors, Fields, Matthews, Lockwood and Celia Johnson, little parallel investigation has been made of female star types, probably because British feminist critics interested in the mainstream cinema have worked more on Hollywood film than British, though this is in the process of changing.

Most of the seventeen chapters here pursue the possibilities of (2), exploring the individualities of stars in relation to specific British contexts. The part exceptions are where attention shifts to the uses of British stars in Hollywood films. These exceptions, where they also have substantial British careers, remind us that when native performers move to Hollywood there are losses as well as gains for their star personae. Because we know so well what is gained as they undergo quasi-universalisation, we often forget the former. To take one contemporary star to represent many: Michael Caine, who in fact (in the post-studio era) has worked very much between America and Britain. Here it is not a question of value judgements, of posing the British against the Hollywood cinema, but rather of seeing that what makes Caine so fascinating to a British, especially English, viewer relates intimately to a specific national, class, political and cultural environment. Here one is registering such elements as the touch of loucheness, the somewhat embattled arrogance, the insubordination in his slightly artificial casualness (in his early starring role in *The Ipcress File*, 1965, his superior reads him a report accusing him of being 'insubordinate, insolent, a trickster, perhaps with criminal tendencies'), and the rather ambivalent aura of escape from class restriction that (in line with the offscreen subtext of working-class escapee reactionary) often ends in shady entrepreneurial roles. This relates intimately to a specific national, class, political and cultural environment. For the Hollywood actor (except where a film such as Huston's *The Man who Would Be King* deliberately uses such elements) these meanings can figure only as a not quite decodable subtext. Again, this is not a simple statement of pluses and minuses. From one point of view you can see the Hollywood Caine as liberated from a lot of parochial baggage which does not signify outside the UK. But there is also a sense in which, whatever he, or other stars, mean in the larger cinema, they signify more complexly in relation to their original environment.

Stars in texts

Some recent influential star theory has adopted a rhetoric of imprison-ment towards textual analysis of stars in films, and even of the discourse surrounding stars – 'stardom as the effect of texts and discourse, but not practice'. MacDonald, concluding his summary of post-*Stars* criticism, continues: 'The privileging of discourse has led to studies of stardom becoming *"trapped in a realm of textuality"* (my italics).[107] Although the con-clusion to the piece asks for 'a pragmatics of star practice' to 'accompany a semiotics of star meanings', the rhetoric of entrapment suggests a more radical demotion.[108]

While not disputing the usefulness of such 'a pragmatics of star prac-tice' (and actually a wider one than the usual restriction to sexual subcul-tures), suggesting a cessation of textuality is both premature and misguided. Even within the greater volume of analysis of the Hollywood cinema, it is hard to feel swamped by significant textual commentary on stars, and what is true there is doubly true of the British cinema.

The chapters in this book were commissioned with only two instruc-tions - that individual stars should be treated, and treated so as to illumi-nate some larger question(s) of British stardom. That they do not seem to dwell on textual entrapment is, I suggest, less the result of a misreading of priorities than a recognition that the basic activity of the film star, on which all associated charisma, discourses and practices ultimately depend, is performance, and that the most fundamental difference between the film star and other kinds of stars – pop stars, sports stars, supermodels, television celebrities etc. – is the elision of the star persona with fictive characters within screen narratives, creating multiplicities of meaning in excess of those connected with other types of stars. It is because of this that, first, analysis of stars in films, and, second, the play of meanings in stars' extrafilmic discourse, are central to star study, espe-cially in the relatively unexplored British context. Social practices relating to the star (the buying of a Margaret Lockwood hat, the writing of a fan letter to the young Richard Attenborough, being happy about Kate Winslet's heftiness, being disappointed or understanding at Dirk Boga-rde's not 'coming out') are all meaningful, analysable parts of the totality of star effects, but not at the cost of the textual appearances and meanings which are the precondition of other meanings. When in a recent drama-tisation of star 'practice' we watch in *Trainspotting* (1996) Sick Boy and Renton discussing the meanings of Sean Connery, their conversation reminds us in its pastiche of Connery's accent and lines and the textual references to *Dr No*, *The Name of the Rose* and other films that the mean-ings which generate other meanings are played out on the screen.

Notes

1 J. P. Mayer, *British Cinemas and their Audiences* (Dobson, London, 1948), p. 54. Mayer's military audit clerk is no. 19 in 'Films and the Pattern of Life'.

2 'Stars are incomplete images outside the cinema: the performance of the film is the moment of completion of images in subsidiary circulation', John Ellis, *Visible Fictions* (Routledge & Kegan Paul, London, 1982), p. 91. 'We call stars movie stars no doubt because of the primary importance we attach to their appearances in films (we do not call them magazine stars)', Richard deCordova, *Picture Personalities: The Emergence of the Star System in America* (University of Illinois Press, Urbana and Chicago, 1990), p. 11.

3 Richard Dyer, *Stars* (BFI, London, 1979).

4 Paul MacDonald, in Richard Dyer, *Stars*, new edition with a supplementary chapter and bibliography by Paul MacDonald (BFI, London, 1998).

5 Edgar Morin, *The Stars* (Grove Press, New York, 1960; Seuil, Paris, 1957).

6 Dyer, *Stars*, p. 4.

7 Jackie Stacey, *Star Gazing: Hollywood Cinema and Female Spectatorship* (Routledge, London, 1994).

8 Section B of Stacey's questionnaire has four questions, 16, 17, 18 and 20, which allow respondents to cite British stars, but all evidence of answers disappears from the book.

9 Dyer, *Stars*, p. 4

10 See, for instance, Richard Brooks, 'Revealed: The Nation that Dare Not Speak its Name', *Sunday Times*, News, 4 April 1999, p. 1.

11 Reading along my shelf, Robert Murphy, *Sixties British Cinema* (BFI, London, 1992); Antonia Lant, *Blackout: Reinventing Women for Wartime British Cinema* (Princeton University Press, Princeton, New Jersey, 1991); Jeffrey Richards, *The Age of the Dream Palace: Cinema and Society in Britain 1930–1939* (Routledge & Kegan Paul, London, 1984); James Curran and Vincent Porter, eds, *British Cinema History* (Weidenfeld & Nicolson, London, 1983); Alexander Walker, *Hollywood England: The British Film Industry in the Sixties* (Michael Joseph, London, 1974); Raymond Durgnat, *A Mirror for England: British Movies from Austerity to Affluence* (Faber and Faber, London, 1970); Charles Barr, ed., *All Our Yesterdays: 90 Years of British Cinema* (BFI, London, 1986).

12 Charles Barr, *English Hitchcock* (Cameron & Hollis, Moffat, 1999), p. 6.

13 Thomas Gray, 'The Bard'; William Collins, 'An Ode on the Superstitions of the Highlands of Scotland, Considered as the Subject of Poetry', in Roger Lonsdale, ed. *The Poems of Gray, Collins and Goldsmith* (Longman, London, 1969).

14 John Hill, 'British Cinema as National Cinema: Production, Audience and Representation', in Robert Murphy, ed., *The British Cinema Book* (BFI, London, 1987); and *British Cinema in the 1980s* (Clarendon Press, Oxford, 1999), especially pp. 241–4. See also Celestino Deleyto on Deborah Kerr, Chapter 9 below.

15 'You've got your name above the title in your first film. Technically you exist as a star, my dear', Dirk Bogarde, *Snakes and Ladders* (Penguin, Harmondsworth, 1988), p. 118.

16 deCordova, *Picture Personalities*.

17 Jon Burrows quotes Hepworth from *Kinematograph and Lantern Weekly* (1 February 1912), in *The Whole English Stage to be Seen for Sixpence! Theatrical Actors and Acting Styles in British Cinema, 1908–1918*, PhD thesis, University of East Anglia, 2000, pp. 238–9. In fact most examples are from a marginally later date.

18 David Shipman, *The Great Movie Stars: The International Years* (Angus & Robertson, London, 1972).

19 Sue Harper and Vincent Porter, 'Cinema Audience Tastes in 1950s Britain', *Jour-*

nal of Popular British Cinema, 2 (1999), 66–82, 69–70.

20 Paul MacDonald, 'Star Studies', in J. Hollows and M. Jankovich, eds, *Approaches to Popular Film* (Manchester University Press, Manchester, 1995), p. 81.

21 The usages 'personification' and 'impersonation' are applied by Barry King, 'Articulating Stardom', in Christine Gledhill, ed., *Stardom: Industry of Desire* (Routledge, London, 1991), p. 168.

22 On Rutherford, see *New York Times*, 18 March 1984; *Daily Telegraph*, 13 April 1990; and *Independent on Sunday*, 10 May 1992. On Terry-Thomas, see *Daily Mirror*, 18 January 1984 and 9 December 1988, and *Sun*, 9 January 1990. On Sim, see obituaries: *Daily Mail*, 21 August 1976, *Sunday Times*, 22 August 1976, *Observer*, 22 August 1976.

23 Martha Wolfenstein and Nathan Leites, *Movies: A Psychological Study* (Free Press of Glencoe, Glencoe, 1950).

24 Rachael Low, *The History of the British Film 1929–1939*, vol. VII (Allen & Unwin, London, 1985), especially pp. 145–9.

25 Mayer, *British Cinemas and their Audiences*, pp. 22, 52, 71.

26 John Sedgwick, 'The Comparative Popularity of Stars in mid-30s Britain', *Journal of Popular British Cinema*, 2 (1999), 121–7; and 'Cinema-going Preferences in Britain in the 1930s', in Jeffrey Richards, ed., *The Unknown Thirties: An Alternative History of the British Cinema 1929–1939* (I. B. Tauris, London, 1978), pp. 1–35.

27 *The Bioscope*, 23 May 1912, quoted by Burrows, *The Whole English Stage*, p. 155.

28 *Pictures and the Picturegoer (P&P)*, 18–25 July, 1918.

29 Chrissie White is on the cover of *P&P*, 5–12 October, 1918; and Hopson is on the *P&P* cover of 11–18 January, 1919.

30 See Jonathan Burrows Chapter 2 below.See also Byron Rogers on Joan Morgan in *Classic Images* (March 1990) on the idea of her as 'the English Lillian Gish', and Morgan describing herself as 'the Mary Pickford type', *Sunday Times*, section 10, 11 June 1998, as well as Kevin Brownlow's noting of the generally felt resemblance of Mabel Poulton to Lillian Gish, *Independent*, 30 December 1994.

31 Geoffrey Macnab, *Searching for Stars: Stardom and Screen Acting in the British Cinema* (Cassell, London, 2000).

32 Rachael Low and Roger Manvell, *The History of the British Film 1896–1906*, vol. I (Routledge, London, 1997; reprint of 1948 edition); Rachael Low, *The History of the British Film 1906–1914* vol. II (Allen & Unwin, London, 1950); *The History of the British Film 1914–1918*, vol. III (Allen & Unwin, London, 1950); *The History of the British Film 1918–1929*, vol. IV (Allen & Unwin, London, 1971); *The History of the British Film 1929–1939* vol. VII (George Allen & Unwin, London, 1985).

33 Low, *passim*, but especially IV, pp. 72–106.

34 E.g. Low, II, pp. 133–8; IV, pp. 33, 263–4.

35 E.g. Low, II, p. 124; III, pp. 57–8; IV, pp. 264–5, 301.

36 E.g. Low, II, p. 134; III, pp. 48–52; IV, pp. 215, 251, 304.

37 Low, IV, pp. 266–7, 303.

38 Burrows, *The Whole English Stage, passim*.

39 Director-producers, such as the Boulting Brothers and Launder and Gilliat, sometimes employed stars on a fairly extended basis, as the former with Ian Carmichael and the latter with Alastair Sim.

40 P. Noble, ed., *The British Film Yearbook 1949–50* (Skelton Robinson, London, 1949).

41 Brian MacFarlane, *60 Voices: Celebrities Recall the Golden Age of British Cinema* (Methuen, London, 1992), and *An Autobiography of British Cinema* (BFI, London, 1997).

42 Dwight Deering, 'Practical Star-building', *Picturegoer Weekly*, 25 April, 1936, 21.

43 Durgnat, *A Mirror for England*, pp. 184–5.

44 Walker, *Hollywood England*, p. 93.

45 Low, IV, p. 261.

46 Burrows, *The Whole English Stage*, pp. 155, 166–79.

47 Low, IV, pp. 264–5.

48 Sarah Street, *British National Cinema* (Routledge, London, 1997), p. 142.

49 Ellis, *Visible Fictions*, p. 105.

50 'Stylistically, the weaknesses of the British cinema are intimately connected with its strengths: the close alliance with the theatre – whether one thinks of acting, writing or directing – and now the quite inextricable dependence of both theatre and cinema on television, which of course is mutual and a three-way relationship', Thomas Elsaesser, 'Images for England (and Scotland, Ireland, Wales ...)', *Monthly Film Bulletin*, September 1984, 267–8.

51 Mayer, *British Cinemas and their Audiences*, pp. 77, 157.

52 King, 'Articulating Stardom', pp. 170–1.

53 Macnab quotes *Kinematograph Weekly*, 14 November 1929, in *Searching for Stars*, p. 29.

54 Leslie R. Frewin, 'British Film Publicity, the Renascence', in Noble, ed., *The British Film Yearbook 1949–50* (Skelton Robinson, London, 1949), pp. 136–7.

55 *Guardian*, 24 April 1982.

56 For instance, with Korda, and as a loaned-out star, Rex Harrison made successively *Men Are Not Gods* (1936), *Storm in a Teacup* (1937), *Over the Moon* (1937), *School for Husbands* (1937), *St Martin's Lane* (1939), *The Citadel* (1939), *The Silent Battle* (1939) and *Ten Days in Paris* (1940).

57 Michael Balcon, *Michael Balcon Presents ... A Lifetime in Films* (Hutchinson, London, 1969), p. 59.

58 European stars used in the 1930s included Peter Lorre, Oskar Homolka and Annie Ondra (by Hitchcock), Annabella, Tullio Carminati, Richard Tauber, Maurice Chevalier, going on to Brigitte Bardot and Mylene Demongeot in the 1950s.

59 Low, vol. IV, p. 263.

60 Burrows, *The Whole English Stage*, pp. 230–1. On Hopson's being 'vamped up' by Broadwest, see pp. 239–42.

61 *P&P*, 7–14 September, 1918, 246.

62 Compare the ad for *A Turf Conspiracy* in *P&P*, 31 August–7 September 1918, 239, and the one for four films, 19–26 October 1918, 399, with the Chrissie White ad in *P&P*, 2–9 November 1918, 447, and one for Alma Taylor in *P&P*, 26 October–2 November 1918, 423.

63 'The British cinema star supreme' in ad for *A Turf Conspiracy etc.*, *P&P*, 19–26 October 1918, 339, and 'the most popular British Film Actress' in the ad *P&P*, 31 August–7 September 1918, 239.

64 *P&P*, 31 August–7 September 1918, 222, and *P&P*, 7–14 September 1918, 246.

65 *P&P*, 26 October–2 November 1918, 25, 'The Young Picturegoer's Page'.

66 deCordova, *Picture Personalities*, p. 146.

67 See '"Days Before the Movies" No. 2 Violet Hopson', unattributed; 'Violet Hopson', Billy Bristow press release, 10 December 1919; '*Cheerio!*', p. 9 (all BFI Hopson microfiche).

68 Bristow press release, 10 December 1919 (BFI Hopson microfiche).

69 Bristow press release, 13 December 21 (BFI Hopson microfiche). See also the ad noted above, *P&P*, 19–26 October 1918, which lists four films shortly to appear.

70 Release of 13 December 1921 (on *The Scarlet Lady*), release of 31 January 1922 (Butcher's Film Service) and release by Butcher's, 17 January 1922 (*Kissing Cup's Race*).

71 Bristow press release, 13 December 1921 (BFI Hopson microfiche).

72 'The Golden Calf', Amalgamated Press release (BFI Hopson microfiche).

73 Bristow press release, 14 December 1922. (BFI Hopson microfiche).

74 'Violet Hopson Productions', 'Vi and the Factory Girls' (BFI Hopson microfiche).

75 'You have, of course, all seen Miss Violet Hopson on the Pictures, but probably have never heard her speak', 'Cheerio!', 31 May 1919, 9 (BFI Hopson microfiche).

76 'Cheerio!', p. 9, photos captioned 'As I am in private life' and 'Good-bye, I must be going now' (in truth, both pretty formal studiolike portraits).

77 See the 'Cheerio!' piece above.

78 A piece in relation to the film The White Hope (dated 1922, BFI Hopson microfiche).

79 'Health and Beauty Series No. 19', 'The Care of the Hair' by Violet Hopson, Walter West publicity release (BFI Hopson microfiche).

80 'From Super to Star: The Artiste's Art of Forgetting Self', unattributed (BFI Hopson microfiche).

81 'The Most Successful Woman of British Film Land. 2 Years Output Sold by an English Actress', Bristow press release, 8 November 1921; and 'Violet Hopson Films: Popular Star Enters the Managerial Chair', unattributed (both BFI Hopson microfiche).

82 On Peter Sellers's cultivation of such journalists as Peter Evans of the Express and Alexander Walker of the Evening Standard, see Roger Lewis, The Life and Death of Peter Sellers (Arrow Books, London, 1995), pp. 879, 888. See also Donald Zec's invocation of his closeness to Harvey in his obituary, Daily Mirror, 27 November 1973.

83 Hepworth Picture Player, 3, 3 February 1916.

84 Macnab, Searching for Stars, p. 51.

85 Ibid., p. 38.

86 Richard Koszarski, An Evening's Entertainment: The Age of the Silent Feature Picture, 1915–1928 (UCLA Press, Berkeley, 1994), p. 266.

87 Norah Alexander, 'Frustrated, Lonely and Peculiar', in John Sutro, ed., Diversion: 22 Authors on the Popular Arts (Max Parrish, London, 1950).

88 Vol 1, no. 1 of The International Patricia Roc Fan Club Magazine is held in the BFI Library on the Patricia Roc microfiche and relays biographical information in parasocial form, as well as information about British films in 'Pat's Chatter' and 'Gainsborough Spotlight'.

89 Picturegoer Weekly, 18 January 1936, 39.

90 One of the most interesting parts of Lockwood's autobiography is her account of her second national tour, its six weeks of travelling and appointments (in her six suits, eight everyday dresses, ten afternoon and cocktail frocks, and twelve hats), Margaret Lockwood, Lucky Star: The Autobiography of Margaret Lockwood (Odhams Press, London, 1955), pp. 137–40.

91 In Picturegoer's 1947 poll, where British and American stars competed, though Gregory Peck (in Spellbound – votes were linked to specific performances) headed the male list, Regrave was second, Wilding third, Portman fourth, Rains, Richardson and Harrison sixth, seventh and eighth, and Trevor Howard and Mason tenth equal; with the women Neagle was first, Johnson second, Leigh fourth, Lockwood eighth and Kerr tenth equal. In the 1946–7 Bernstein Film Questionnaire Mason and Granger were first and second, with Mills, Olivier, Milland and Redgrave in the top eleven, while with the women Lockwood topped the poll and Calvert, Garson, Roc and Neagle were fourth, fifth, sixth and eleventh respectively.

92 Dyer, Stars, pp. 3, 72.

93 On Lillian Hall Davis's suicide, see Daily Herald, 29 October 1933, and Evening News, 26 October 1933.

94 On Harvey, see obituary, Daily Telegraph, 27 November 1973, and Donald Zec, 'Life, Love and Larry', Daily Mirror, 27 November 1973; and on Burton, Melvyn

Bragg, *Rich: The Life of Richard Burton* (Hodder & Stoughton, London, 1998).

95   See Julian Petley on Jeremy Irons in 'Reaching for the Stars', in Martyn Auty and Nick Roddick, eds, *British Film Now* (BFI, London, 1985), pp. 225–41.

96   The Matthews–Laye scandal, was resurrected at the end of the 1980s. See *Evening Standard*, 7 June 1988 and 12 July 1990. Material about Merle Oberon's race and promiscuity surfaced around the same time. See *Daily Mail*, 4 June 1988.

97   'To their apogee on the screen corresponds the apogee of the mythico-real life of Hollywood stars. Sublime, eccentric, they build themselves pseudo-feudal chateaux, houses copied from antique temples, with marble swimming pools, menageries, private railroads. They live at a distance, far beyond all mortals.' Morin, *The Stars*, pp. 15–16. On Pickfair, see Larry L. May, *Screening Out the Past* (University of Chicago Press, Chicago, 1980), p. 145. On Alma Taylor's domicile, see Burrows, *The Whole English Stage*, p. 231, and Chapter 2 below; on Betty Balfour's 'Old Dutch House' see *Star*, 1 March 1938; on the Oliviers' Notley Abbey, see Roger Lewis, *The Real Life of Laurence Olivier* (Arrow Books, London, 1997), pp. 263–5.

98   See Dyer on the universe of the American film fan magazines, *Stars*, p. 51.

99   See Dirk Bogarde, *Snakes and Ladders*, pp. 141, 168–9; and James Mason, *Before I Forget* (Hamish Hamilton, London, 1983), p. 192.

100   Roger Lewis, *The Life and Death of Peter Sellers*.

101   For Dors, see, for example, *Guardian*, 5 October 1954; *Daily Mail*, 21 July 1956; *Daily Mirror*, 17 July 1956 (the famous comparison of Monroe's and Dors's statistics). For Lee, see *Sunday Dispatch*, 2 February 1958 ('My career means more to me than marriage'), and *Evening Standard*, 14 March 1961 ('I just want to live to have a good time'). To compare with 1940s stars, see Chapter 7 below. Also, on Roc, *The International Patricia Roc Fan Club Magazine*, vol. 1, no. 1; on Calvert, *Daily Graphic*, 9 March 1950, and *Evening News*, 3 April 1950; on Celia Johnson, *Leader*, 29 March 1942, *Evening Standard*, 3 January 1976, and *Guardian*, 24 April 1982.

102   For Caine, see Roderick Mann, 'Big Money has Altered my Life, says Mr Caine', *Sunday Express*, 25 July 1965; *Daily Telegraph*, 21 September 1977; and *Daily Express*, 2 September 1977. For Harvey, see note 94 above.

103   See on McGregor, *Guardian*, section 2, 13 September 1996, and 'Have You Seen this Man?', *Time Out*, 2 September 1996, pp. 18, 20, and on Oldman, 'Roll Over, Beethoven', *Daily Telegraph*, 12 July 1994, 'Oldman on the Edge', *What's On in London*, 19 June 1991, and 'Gary Oldman, from Sid to Ludwig', *Guardian*, section 2, 16 March 1995

104   Dyer discusses these, which come from Orrin E. Klapp, *Heroes, Villians and Fools* (Prentice-Hall, Eaglewood Cliffs, 1962), and other types, *Stars*, pp. 53–66.

105   Andrew Spicer, 'Male Stars, Masculinity and British Cinema, 1945–1960', in Robert Murphy, ed., *The British Cinema Book* (BFI, London, 1997), pp. 144–53, and 'The Emergence of the British Tough Guy: Stanley Baker, Masculinity and the Crime Thriller', in Steve Chibnall and Robert Murphy, eds, *British Crime Cinema* (Routledge, London, 1999), pp. 81–93.

106   See Chapter 13, 'The Romantic Adventurer: Robert Donat and Leslie Howard', in Jeffrey Richards, *The Age of the Dream Palace* (Routledge & Kegan Paul, London, 1984), pp. 225–41, and Macnab, *Searching for Stars*, pp. 104–17.

107   Paul MacDonald in Dyer, *Stars* (1998), p. 200.

108   Ibid.

JONATHAN BURROWS

'Our English Mary Pickford': Alma Taylor and ambivalent British stardom in the 1910s

2

Not yours the air of high romance,
The flashing eye, the burning glance,
The haughty look of cold disdain,
The pass'nate mouth and raven tress –
But rather the shy comeliness
Of Springtime in an English lane.
Those placid brows and peaceful eyes
'Mind me of lakes 'neath summer skies;
The sweet half-smile, tip-tilted nose,
A certain look of wistfulness,
Your girlish grace and form, no less,
Of some wild wind-kissed English rose.
Not yours the stage where blood is shed,
And Passion rampant stalks: instead,
Fair English scenes, and ways apart,
And art that lies in artlessness –
English are you, and I confess,
Alma, you have my English heart.
                    (May Herschel-Clarke, 'Alma'[1])

The quotation in the title of this chapter comes from the British fan magazine *Pictures and the Picturegoer*.[2] The phrase refers to the Hepworth Manufacturing Company's biggest star, Alma Taylor, and was provided by a reader from Huntley in response to a query the magazine had posed on its cover in May 1917: 'Is there an English Mary Pickford?' The editorial staff were not looking for strict personality correspondences between Pickford and local players, but merely to determine whether any British film stars could be said to inspire a comparable degree of affection and popularity as 'America's Sweetheart'. Historians of early British cinema have tended to answer this question in the negative. Rachael Low, for example, categorically states that here lay a most important difference between English and American producers. It is fair to say that hardly any of the English film players were stars on the American scale. There was probably as great a desire for the star system among British film makers as anywhere else, but little trouble was taken deliberately to build up the personality of native film stars by publicity.[3]

Certainly, British stars in the 1910s never matched the *international* profiles generated by their transatlantic peers. But on their home turf, British producers were not quite as straightforwardly lax as has often been assumed. Cecil Hepworth himself spared little expense on publicity for stars like Alma Taylor – who had no previous theatrical background which might have helped to familiarise her name with British audiences – in the pages of popular mainstream magazines, as well as specialist film trade and fan periodicals. And his intensive campaigns seem to have struck a chord with very responsive native cinema goers. One of the most obvious signs of this was the result of an extensive poll conducted by *Pictures and the Picturegoer* in 1915 to discover who the most popular British-born film performers were amongst its readership. Alma Taylor came out at the top, having received 156,800 votes and comfortably beaten Charlie Chaplin into second place.[4]

Another lay organ, *The Picture Palace News*, ran its own polls in 1916 which contain data of possibly even greater interest, since they counted votes for British and American favourites collectively. Their 'Films Beauty Contest' asked readers to nominate their most-cherished female stars. Alma Taylor was again crowned as the most popular British star of the era, and managed a creditable third place overall with 142,571 votes. She was only narrowly pipped by the American Mary Fuller (142,635) for the runner-up spot, although Mary Pickford was a predictably convincing claimant of the top position, and amassed 185,910 votes.[5]

Despite this degree of success and popular acclaim, though, I would still partly agree with posterity's sceptical verdict about British film stars in this decade. The question of whether or not there ever was an 'English Mary Pickford' cannot be answered in the affirmative without some equivocation. I will go on to demonstrate here that, in the promotion of Alma Taylor as a star, Hepworth did effectively imitate American publicity techniques to maintain a consistently high profile for her in the marketplace. But I will also argue that Hepworth was equally concerned to produce a representatively *national* style of film-making that distinguished itself from American imports. Where Taylor was concerned, this resulted in an attempt to be faithful to certain privileged icons and ideals of British womanhood and local cultural traditions in fashioning her star persona. I hope to make it clear that these nationalistic caveats lead to a great many discursive contradictions and ambivalences in the content of Alma Taylor's star image.

Star qualities

Writing on American cinema, Richard deCordova has suggested that the phenomenon of film stardom first began to achieve clear definition around 1914. The differentiation between a true film star and a popular performer appearing in films is seen to lie in the fact that the star's existence *outside* his or her work in films began to assume an importance for fans which was at least equal to their onscreen activities and performances. Details of the private lives of the players – sometimes true, sometimes fabricated – were constituted as an important commodity for audiences to consume alongside film viewing. There was a proliferation of information about the stars' childhood backgrounds, fashion tastes, marital status and choice of motor car, which helped to stimulate a major new publicity industry.[6]

Alma Taylor. 'Fair English scenes, and ways apart. And Art that lies in artlessness – English are you, and I confess, Alma, you have my English heart.'

PC. 2   Alma Taylor
Hepworth Picture Player.
"The Girl Who Believed."

In many of the press bulletins which Hepworth issued to help popularise Alma Taylor, the product offered to fans is not simply performance skill or acting ability but raw, authentic *personality*. The promise is repeatedly held out that the consumer will be able to experience something beyond pretence or simulation, something deemed to be more palpable and real than mere acting. In several respects the kind of personal information that was circulated about Taylor was systematic and sophisticated. Much of her press copy was very similar to the extrafilmic narratives which authenticated the personae of American stars. Hepworth clearly understood this kind of discourse, and knew how to deploy it to incite and increase audience interest.

In 1915, at the tender age of 20, Taylor's life story was serialised in ten weekly instalments by the Scottish women's magazine *Home Weekly*. Numerous tales of her childhood were divulged in these articles, and particular formative incidents (such as playing on barges or with steam engines) were seen to foreshadow activities that she would later undertake in her films.[7] Authentic life experiences could thus be seen to have fed into her screen work and could be retrospectively read into it to create deeper levels of meaning and significance.

In a more extreme sense, the details of Taylor's early screen career were depicted as what one can only (loosely) describe as an Edwardian forerunner of the premise behind *The Truman Show* (1998). Portions of her childhood were said to have been effectively recorded by the cameras in a substantially unstaged and psuedo-documentary fashion. A frequently repeated anecdote revealed that Taylor made her screen debut for Hepworth at the age of 12, and was repeatedly filmed there without her being in any way conscious that she was 'performing'. In her own words,

> I thought these studios were chemical works of some sort! ... I told mother that I had been invited to a big party at the chemical works – for I really thought it was going to be a party! ... The next day, clad in the smartest frock, I took part in a little scene, having to jump into a large hamper. I did not notice the camera, and still did not realise that I was taking part in a moving-picture. I just considered it as a new sort of game. After I had been to the studios several times I was given money. I couldn't understand this a little bit! What were they giving me money for? I asked.[8]

This story was endlessly circulated as emblematic proof of the unique levels of sincerity and intuitive spontaneity with which Taylor was 'educated' in the art of film acting, and it earned her the publicity nickname of 'The Girl Who Believed'.

Very few of the films which Taylor made in the 1910s seem to have survived, and these are nearly all short one-reelers from the first half of the decade rather than any of the feature film productions that she went on to headline. This scattered evidence does give us some indication of what the formal performative indices of her famous spontaneity and artless probity were, though. *An Engagement of Convenience* (1914), for example, seems at times to be carefully trying to direct and organise the viewer's intimate and privileged bond with the actress. It dictates an interpretation of the resonances of her performance, so that this can be seen as something more than a piece of acting. Taylor plays Nancy, a young secretary who is enlisted by her employer Fred (Cecil Mannering) to act as if she is his bride-to-be, so that he can fulfil the marital conditions attached to an inheritance from his Aunt Rosemary (Marie de Solla). Two brief shots can be read as a mini-allegory on the nature of star performance. In her diegetic role as the phoney fiancée, Nancy accompanies Fred to meet Aunt Rosemary at the station. Taylor's Nancy stands apart from them both to signify a degree of awkwardness, and as they exit left (in both shots) she makes three nervous half-glances to the right of the screen to further betray her unease. One does not need to read between the lines to understand that she is distinctly uncomfortable and unconvincing precisely because she is consciously *acting*. This state of affairs does not last. By her next appearance, genuine affections have outpaced and superseded pretended ones. There is no need to simulate strong feelings for Fred because they have come true, and what we get is character revelation rather than affectation.

Unfashionable femininity

This pattern seems very close to the ideals of star performance celebrated in American publicity discourse of the period. But on closer examination, it becomes increasingly clear that Hepworth maintained a schizophrenic and apologetic attitude towards his roster of stars – and Alma Taylor in particular – which manifests itself in the articulation of three different categories of supposedly nationally reflective qualities through which Taylor was increasingly defined. These can be identified as ideas about class, female comportment and cultural respectability.

One of the logical upshots of the idea that a film star did not really act but passively offered authentic ontological being to the recording apparatus instead was a popular conception that anybody could become a successful screen player. One Los-Angeles-based trade publicist, Fred Goodwins, encouraged this perception when he informed British manufacturers in 1918 that

The demands of the screen are not nearly as exacting as those of the stage. A stage find is indeed a *rara avis* – screen 'discoveries' are made in America almost every month of the year. Now it is up to the British producer to get out his line and tackle ... 'All the world's a stage, and all the men and women merely players'; rather, to my mind, all the players are merely men and women, so far as pictures are concerned. You will find your future stars, Mr. Producer, in choruses, shops, workrooms, factories, restaurants, just as Mr. American Producer found the majority of his.[9]

Goodwins's portrait of the American star system depicted it as a microcosm of democracy in action, distinguished by absolutely unfettered social mobility and the erasure or obliteration of conventional class distinctions:

You may have the poise of a guttersnipe and an accent like a Covent Garden porter, and still you may register on screen a perfect interpretation of a part that is the quintessence of refinement ... Bobby Harron was Griffith's errand boy; Monte Blue ... was driving stakes in the studio when Griffiths [*sic*] 'found' him; Mildred Harris is the daughter of Ince's late wardrobe mistress, and so you may go along the line. The first thing that strikes you on meeting a batch of 'movie' folk is their lack of poise, their Bohemian freedom of manner, and you marvel that they, the poiseful, impressive creatures you have seen with your own eyes upon the screen, can really be these folks whom the carpenters call by their first names and 'skylark' about with.[10]

This kind of image seems to have filled certain sections of the British film industry with horror. Even native fan magazines warned their readership against excessive adulation of the American stars they otherwise helped to promote on the grounds that they were 'drawn from all classes', and probably used language 'that would offend the average girl's ears'.[11] Cecil Hepworth was noticeably concerned that no such fears could be provoked by the likes of Alma Taylor and her stablemates. Whilst his players may not all have possessed established stage reputations or experience, he was none the less keen to insist that 'they will be drawn from the same *class* as at present provides the theatre'.[12] This, I would suggest, betrays the intention to cultivate a noticeably different image from that of the stock company stars promoted by his transatlantic rivals. In numerous articles it was strategically revealed that Taylor had grown up in 'a grand old house where Anne Boleyn used to live', no less.[13] Thus, the garden tree under which young Alma played cricket with her friend Bertie had once sheltered Henry VIII on a regular basis whenever he came courting.[14] Clearly, the Alma Taylors of this world could not be easily picked up in a trawl for pretty faces through factories or restaurants; they were hand-picked from English Heritage country!

This conservative emphasis upon lineage and social distinction was also matched by, and arguably wedded to, an equally pervasive attitude affecting gender issues in the content of Taylor's star image. It is a mistake to assume that regressive ideas about female desires and codes of behaviour were inevitable in this period. Janet Staiger has recently argued that the American cinema of the 1910s stimulated, encouraged and participated in several progressive debates about the 'New Woman' that were being produced by a series of cultural upheavals in US society. Many films sometimes worked to explain, sanction and even vindicate the flouting of Victorian conventions strictly regulating female sexuality and reinforcing gender restrictions, as part of the drive to create a new kind of desiring female subject for a new kind of consumerist economy.[15] Richard deCordova has also uncovered a complicity between the star image and new economic ideals which meshes neatly with this thesis. Because the spectacular fame and success which the new breed of stars were beginning to enjoy was based on neither inherited wealth nor economic exploitation, they provided apt advertisements for the democratic access to new forms of pleasure and leisure-time consumption which a remodelled commercial sector promised:

> The star was worshipped as a creature completely free to express him or herself by pursuing the pleasures afforded by the emergent consumer culture ... First, a number of articles appeared throughout the teens and early twenties that demonstrated the star's taste and extravagance in fashion. Players such as Florence Hackett and Norma Talmadge were presented as models for the way the women of the country should dress. Second, stars began to appear in advertising in the teens, even more explicitly promoting the joys of consumption. Female stars appeared, for instance, endorsing beauty products.[16]

As the scholarship of Erika D. Rappaport has shown, debates about changing standards and ideals of femininity were simultaneously taking place in Britain. Shopping was celebrated as an important leisure activity for women, who, by their increased investment in, and definition through, the rituals of consumption, became more active and visible in the public realm.[17] But this dimension is not just absent in the composition of Alma Taylor's star image, it is actively resisted. She is instead configured as someone who manifests a complete distaste for the emergent culture of consumerism. A reporter for *Nash's* magazine found her material desires to be almost non-existent: 'When Miss Taylor goes to London, which she does very infrequently, it is to do some simple shopping, for her wants are few.'[18] 'Movie Margerie,' a fan magazine correspondent who wrote exclusively on stars and their fashion tastes, recorded the following heretical statement when she took Taylor shopping down Oxford Street:

'No, I'm not frightfully fond of clothes,' she assured me ... 'At home, I enjoy myself in the oldest things I can find. Do you remember the little spotted frock I wore in *Comin' Thro' The Rye?* Well, that's my favourite garden frock, though it's pretty well on its last stitches now. I shall make another just like it next year'.[19]

In making her own clothes, Taylor is painted as an absolute non-consumer rather than just a reluctant one. Her avowed favourite pasttime involved nothing less than an escape from the exoticisms of sensual purchasing pleasures, in favour of 'a good long walk in a pair of brogues that claim no connection with "fashion"'.[20]

There is evidence to suggest that the very distinctive codes of dress, behaviour and national representativeness with which Alma Taylor's star persona was imbued did strike a real appreciative chord with many British fans, and were sometimes even seen as preferable to the prodigal spending and ornamentation associated with American stars. One admirer from Worcester wrote in to *Pictures and the Picturegoer* to note how 'disgusted' she had been at the amount of gaudy, 'superfluous' makeup worn by the archetypal American screen 'vamp' Theda Bara. She complained that 'practically all the American artists spoil their work in the same manner'. It correspondingly fell to the British to keep standards of mien high: 'to see a film featuring Alma Taylor one would never notice anything of this sort; she always appears perfectly natural'.[21] Another subscriber was privileged to see Alma in the flesh, and noted with approval that she was as unostentatiously dressed offscreen as she was on in a 'simple cotton costume', and thereby stood as 'the embodiment of charming, unspoilt, British girlhood'.[22]

Such confident statements of national pride should not deceive us into imagining that there was a wholesale consensus of opinion on this issue, however. F S. from Worthing spoke up for dedicated followers of fashion by suggesting that Hepworth had a lot to learn from their US counterparts: 'I was advised to go and see *Comin' Thro' The Rye, Molly Bawn, The Cobweb* ... I was delighted with them all – but I am sorry to say that the English actresses can't dress like the Americans, which adds to a woman's appearance, and to the picture.'[23] The disappointingly outfitted star of all three of these films was Alma Taylor.

Wider repertoires and lingering prejudices

The third component of Taylor's star persona, clearly designed to enhance her appeal to certain kinds of native audiences and to distinguish her from American stars, was a new emphasis upon her acting range and candidacy for taking on more demanding, canonical roles. Having initially worked hard to paint her as someone congenitally incapable of acting in the conventional sense, Hepworth now sought to bathe her in the reflective glow of the British stage. He started casting her in famous Victorian and Edwardian plays opposite distinguished visitors from the theatrical firmament such as Henry Ainley and Albert Chevalier. This change of emphasis in the career plan which Hepworth drafted for his young star is particularly evident in the leading roles she was granted in three heavily publicised adaptations of classic plays by Sir Arthur Wing Pinero, one of Britain's foremost playwrights of the era. These were *Sweet Lavender* (1915), *Iris* (1915) and *Trelawny of the Wells* (1916). Hepworth declared that his aim in securing the rights to such works was to accelerate 'the task of attracting strongly that large class of "non-goers" who have hitherto claimed that their ability to pay theatre prices relieved them of the necessity of attending "crude" cinemas'. Seeing Pinero on the screen would theoretically prove to be an ideal attraction to 'interest [...] the new type of picture-goer'.[24]

In repackaging Alma Taylor for this prospective cultured middle-class demographic, Hepworth began to cast her strategically against type. Few seem to have found this metamorphosis convincing. In an era when any hint of a popular success story for the British film industry usually generated reams of effusive praise and enthusiasm from the trade press, the series of harsh and derogatory reviews which met many of her performances in these and various other film versions of famous plays comes as something of a surprise. *The Bioscope*'s critique of *Iris* set the ball rolling:

> Where acting is concerned, *Iris* is very much a one-part play. A great deal of its success depends upon the actress in the title role ... Accomplished and experienced as Miss Alma Taylor is, we are not quite sure that we think her perfectly fitted for the character of Iris. We have had from her so many inimitable studies of the fresh, frank, ingenuous English girl, that it is, perhaps, difficult to accept her at once as this tragic victim of weakness and passion. All such prejudices apart, however, we do not think she quite succeeds in responding to the many emotional changes demanded by this complex character. For Iris was not merely weak and indecisive. Her nature contained deep wells of passion ... In brief, Miss Taylor does not bring her audience quite closely enough into touch with the character she represents ... [T]he film loses a little by Miss Taylor's failure to reveal this psychological action with quite the flexibility and sharpness that one might have wished for.

Identical disappointment was voiced by *The Film Censor*'s critic, who suggested that 'Alma Taylor plays "Iris" prettily, but ... we should like to have

seen her show more fiery passion', and the bad notices continued to mul-
tiply with each new ambitious role.[25] When Hepworth's next Pinero adaptation, *Trelawny of the Wells*, was released it was suggested that Taylor
could not 'quite realise the strong-minded determination and glowing
vitality of Rose's character'; in an adaptation of Sidney Grundy's *Sowing
the Wind* (1916) she purportedly 'hardly responds to the full emotional
demands of the part and is inclined to lack expressivity and vitality'; and
similar terms of disparagement were used again to debunk her performance in *Merely Mrs Stubbs* (1917): 'Alma Taylor is a beautiful, if rather
insipid, Edith'.[26]

I would argue that the tone of such reviews can be read as evidence of
a dissatisfaction with, and cultural snobbery towards, the whole concept
of stardom and its foregrounding of young, untutored, raw personality.
To the degree that the star system encouraged a concomitant relegation
in the discursive importance of traditional histrionic principles which
judged performance by the criteria of successful *impersonation*, and over-
coming the limits of inherited identity, it was often viewed as being
extremely detrimental to artistic accomplishment.

The censoriousness of trade critics was effectively mirrored by the
defensive and almost apologetic tone coming from within the Hepworth
camp itself, in the way that it increasingly sought to wrap its young stars
in an aura of culture and national tradition. The result was that at times a
star like Alma Taylor seemed to be neither one thing nor the other: she
was no evidential thespian when judged by certain theatrical standards,
but yet was still constrained from becoming a fully branded and com-
modified modern media personality in turn. The frequently skirted concomitant danger was that her appeal would be stranded between the two
constituencies, never fully satisfying critics or fans. For example, in 1917
Hepworth commissioned the playwright Herbert Pemberton to construct
an original scenario for Taylor which placed extra demands on her acting
dexterity. The resulting film, *Nearer My God to Thee*, was a twenty-year
saga in which the star had 'to interpret various parts in her character of
Joan, the heroine'.[27] In the first section of the film she appeared as a
young student teacher, in the second a harassed wife and mother, and in
the third an old lady and widow. The reaction from *The Bioscope*'s critic
was predictably mixed. The first section of the film, set against a rural
backdrop and with a character not at all dissimilar from earlier Taylor
incarnations, was viewed as highlighting 'her charm and freshness in
these beautiful pastoral scenes'. But the latter portions occasioned yet
more disappointment and regret that Taylor was 'compel[led] ... to
assume the disguises of middle age', which was done with such a noticeable deficit of skill that 'these later scenes seem to us less convincing than

the preceding ones'. A review in the *Kinematograph and Lantern Weekly* concurred that 'in the later and more dramatic scenes she is not quite so much in her element. It is more of an effort.'[28]

Significantly, and symptomatically, these judgements are not so far removed from one recorded reaction from Taylor's loyal fan base. 'Olben' of Liverpool wrote in to *Pictures and the Picturegoer* to vociferously register her own complaint about the film: 'to my mind Alma Taylor is too beautiful to be wasted on that awful old woman part'.[29] What to one dramatic connoisseur was too great a strain on the performer's talents was to this devoted admirer an unnecessary obstacle in the path of a previously untrammelled acquaintanceship. A staff writer in *The Picturegoer Monthly* (a temporary variant of the same fan magazine) felt it necessary to warn and remind Hepworth in 1921 that Taylor's 'charm lies particularly in her appealing simplicity of manner, and too much variety in her choice of rôles certainly weakens her hold upon the affections of her many admirers'.[30]

The tendency to ignore this fact, along with several other nervous equivocations in the presentation of Alma Taylor's star persona, is indicative of what seems to have been an ingrained prejudice within the British film industry against the new cult of the personality. *The Bioscope*'s regular pseudonymous columnist 'Observer' even went so far as to predict – rather shortsightedly – the imminent demise of the star system, as a result of the absence of notable dramatic qualifications amongst its chief beneficiaries:

> The time is near when the public will not designate as star any actor or actress who is not finished in histrionic art. Because motion pictures are comparatively new with the people of this country they have come to regard the player frequently as an old acquaintance. In the absence of a large number of truly capable players these actors and actresses of mediocre abilities have gone on appearing in picture after picture until they have acquired a certain vogue, which they and producers and others also mistook for stardom.[31]

In reality, the public's taste remained far more stable and consistent. The same was also true with regard to Alma Taylor's general appeal, because viewer polls confirmed her status as one of Britain's most popular film stars right up to the dissolution of the Hepworth Company in 1924.[32] Innumerable fan testimonials, like the reader's poem reprinted at the beginning of this chapter, indicate that her carefully constructed *difference* from American stars was at least partly responsible for her success with local audiences. Nevertheless, the *lack* or *absence* of a more universally representative icon of ordinary modern British femininity was frequently felt and articulated, and 'two flapperettes' from London who wrote in to *Pictures and the Picturegoer* in 1916 were undoubtedly not alone in feeling 'that [working] girls in America have heaps more chances of becoming cinema actresses than we English girls', and also in wondering if 'there are no English business girls with beauty? Or are they never to have a chance?'[33]

Notes

1   *Pictures and the Picturegoer* (hereafter *P&P*) 2 May 1917, 134.
2   *P&P*, 2 June 1917, 206.
3   Rachael Low, *The History of the British Film 1914–1918* (Allen & Unwin, London, 1950), p. 59.
4   *P&P*, 3 July 1915, 246. It should be noted that these figures, along with those of the *Picture Palace News* polls which follow, do not necessarily represent the number of voters, since each coupon allowed participants to vote for several stars in order of preference.
5   'The Beauty of the Films –The Battle of the Marys' *Picture Palace News*, 24 April 1916, 578.
6   Richard deCordova, *Picture Personalities: The Emergence of the Star System in America* (University of Illinois Press, Urbana and Chicago, 1990), pp. 98–114.
7   'Alma Taylor: Britain's Premier Picture Player' *Home Weekly*, 27 November 1915, 232.
8   'The Girl on the Film, No. 10: Miss Alma Taylor' *P&P*, 4 July 1914, 442.
9   Fred Goodwins, 'The American Way: No 4. Of Actors Generally', *Kinematograph and Lantern Weekly*, 26 December 1918, 46.
10   Goodwins, 'The American Way', p. 46.
11   *P&P* 14 February 1914, 603.
12   'Men of the Moment, in the Cinematograph World: No.3 – Mr. Cecil Hepworth', April 1912, *The Cinema*, 22 emphasis added.
13   *The Hepworth Picture-play Paper*, December 1915.
14   'Alma Taylor, Britain's Premier Picture Player', pp. 231–2.
15   See Janet Staiger, *Bad Women: Regulating Sexuality in Early American Cinema* (University of Minnesota Press, Minneapolis, 1995), *passim*.
16   DeCordova, *Picture Personalities*, pp. 109–10.
17   Erika D. Rappaport, *Shopping for Pleasure: Women in the Making of London's West End* (Princeton University Press, Princetown, New Jersey, 2000), *passim*.
18   'Alma: A Cinema Genius', *Nash's and Pall Mall Gazette*, May 1915, 328.
19   'Pink and Periwinkle: An Afternoon's Shopping with Alma Taylor', *P&P*, 15 September 1917, 329.
20   'Alma Taylor Betrays Some of the Secrets of Success', *P&P*, 13 December 1919, 690.
21   'Letter from A.W.W.' *P&P*, 22 September 1917), 351.
22   Vera Tremayne, 'Alma Taylor: A Reader's Appreciation' *P&P*, 21 September 1918, 301.
23   *P&P*, 11 January 1919, 63.
24   *The Bioscope*, 24 February 1916, 761.
25   *The Film Censor*, 10 November 1915, 2.
26   See *The Bioscope*, 9 March 1916, 1005; 18 May 1916, 728; 5 July 1917, 105, respectively.

27 *P&P*, 3 November 1917, 486.
28 *The Bioscope*, 8 November 1917, 56; *Kinematograph and Lantern Weekly*, 8 November 1917, 19.
29 *P&P*, 31 August 1918, 234.
30 *The Picturegoer Monthly*, May 1921, 50.
31 'Matters of Moment' *The Bioscope*, 31 January 1918, 29.
32 *The Bioscope*, 17 April 1924, 14.
33 *P&P*, 4 November 1916, 111.

LAWRENCE NAPPER AND MICHAEL WILLIAMS

The curious appeal of Ivor Novello

3

> I believe in beauty in the Theatre – I believe that in the Theatre lies a road
> back to sanity ... I want to give the people the chance to dream again – and
> I want to show them that there is an art beyond the reach of mechanical
> devices and black and white shadows chasing each other round a white
> sheet.[1]

This statement, placed in the mouth of one of the characters of his 1933
play, *Proscenium*, has been interpreted by Ivor Novello's biographer, W.
Macqueen-Pope, as a final declaration of allegiance. 'In it,' suggests Macqueen-Pope, 'he threw over films, and swore complete loyalty to the Theatre'.[2]

Such a statement perhaps does not seem a very promising place to
begin discussion of Novello as Britain's foremost film star of the 1920s,
particularly in the context of a national film industry generally accused of
over-reliance on theatrical sources and methods. In this cchapter we consider Novello's 1920s film career as an essential element in his creation
as a star of both screen *and* stage, looking at the way he himself controlled
this star persona through his own creations – most successfully his theatrical and cinematic role as the 'Rat'. The textual and extra textual activities of the 'Rat' provide an antidote to the simple assumption that
theatrical sources and players make for retrogressive cinema. Novello's
early career would appear in fact to be a shining example of the appropriate symbiosis which pertained between the British cinema of the 1920s
and various other entertainment media – the theatre, the popular press,
the wireless and the music industry – making Novello a star of modernity
itself, over and above his cinematic or theatrical status.

Not surprisingly, as a theatre historian, Macqueen-Pope resists such
discussion altogether. Throughout his biography, he treats Novello's film
career as a mere adjunct, a lucrative but irrelevant sideline, 'I do not think
it necessary,' he opines, 'to give much space to descriptions of those pictures and their making. They were silent films and now a thing of the

Ivor Novello posing as the 'Rat'. 'A knowingly provocative and uniquely modern star image.'

past. They will not keep their place before the public – for obvious reasons – as well as his plays and his music.'[3]

Writing shortly after Novello's death in 1951, Macqueen-Pope's neglect of the film career is perhaps excusable, for from the early 1930s onward Novello's star persona was increasingly dominated by his theatre work, particularly the overwhelming success of the spectacular musical shows he conceived for the vast stage of the Theatre Royal, Drury Lane. These shows – *Glamorous Night, Careless Rapture, Crest of the Wave, The Dancing Years, Arc de Triomphe, Perchance to Dream* and *King's Rhapsody* – not only starred Novello, but were also written and composed by him. Their lush scoring, opulent Ruritanian settings and visual extravagance achieved such immense popular success that by the time of his death Novello's earlier film career was so overshadowed as to be barely mentioned in his obituaries.[4]

Today, economics and cultural taste have ensured that the Drury Lane shows of Novello's later career can no longer be revived professionally. In contrast, attention is being paid again to his silent film work, with critics recognising its importance in the history of the British film industry. Novello was indisputably the most popular British star of the 1920s Michael Balcon remembered him as 'an ambassador for British films' and 'a star of the first magnitude'.[5] His films, particularly those made at Gainsborough, represent some of the most successful efforts of that industry, both commercially and aesthetically.

In this light, Novello's 1933 declaration in favour of the stage appears much more equivocal than Macqueen-Pope would have us believe. 'I have been harshly criticised ... for ... the phrase about the stage being so much more satisfying than the watching of "black and white shadows chasing each other across the silver screen".' He admitted to F. Leslie Withers in a *Picturegoer* interview clearly designed to calm the fears of film fans that he had become 'superior':

> Friends and others in the film world have pounced on me as a sort of back biter, considering my extensive film work and the cash that has accrued therefrom. Never mind, I stick to my statement. I *do* stand up for the stage. But that's no reason whatever for assuming that I dislike films. Give me the right kind of roles and I can be perfectly happy in the film studio.[6]

The article implies something more calculated than Macqueen-Pope's language of romantic love ('threw over ... swore loyalty'). The fact that Novello edits his own description of cinema from 'a white sheet' to 'the silver screen', as well as his careful language of 'concern' over his film future and his declaration of a desire to continue in cinema if he can get better parts, suggests not a romantic following his heart but rather a shrewd businessman making informed decisions about his career in response to a rapidly changing industrial context. Indeed, extending Mac-queen-Pope's romantic metaphor, one might suggest that Novello is not so much forsaking one lover in favour of another, as being simply promis-cuous. It was a habit he maintained throughout his life, working consis-tently across media – film, music, theatre – to maximise exposure of his multiple talents.

It was Novello's 1950s image as anachronistically 'safe' and 'bland' that Hitchcock drew on in the ubiquitous 1966 Truffaut interview. Excus-ing his use of an unambiguously happy ending in *The Lodger* over thirty years previously, Hitchcock suggests that Novello's presence in the title role was to blame: 'He was a very big name at the time. These are the problems we face with the star system. Very often the story line is jeopar-dised because a star cannot be a villain.'[7]

There is a typical disingenuousness in Hitchcock's assertion that the star presented some kind of obstacle of naive 'innocence', that he could-n't 'get his way' with Novello on screen, for, although the Novello of the 1950s was associated with the safety of nostalgic theatrical camp, in 1926 he was famous for being *less* than safe. Indeed, his popular identity was founded upon the modernity of cinema itself, coupled with the villainy and deception he perfectly embodied in his most famous persona – that of Pierre Boucheron, the 'Rat'.

Novello had started out neither as a film star nor as a theatre actor, but rather as a composer of popular tunes. He was born in Cardiff in 1893, the son of the already celebrated singing teacher Clara Davies. She was to dominate much of his early career. It was in 1915 at the age of 22 that he first captured public attention as the composer of *Keep the Home Fires Burning*, possibly the defining popular song of the First World War. He remained writing songs for various stage revues until his picture was spied by the French director Louis Mercanton who, legend has it, decided to cast him for the star of *The Call of the Blood* (1919) on the basis of his profile alone. Further film contracts followed: *Miarka* (1920), again with Mercanton, *Carnival* (1921), *The Bohemian Girl* (1922) both directed by Harley Knoles and *The Man without Desire* (1923) directed by Adrian Brunel. In 1923, he went to America to star for Griffith in *The White Rose*, where he discovered for the first time what an efficient publicity machine could achieve, and found himself compared with Novarro and Valentino before he had even begun work with Griffith.[8] The film itself, however, did not live up to its advance publicity, and Novello returned to England.

By this time Novello's reputation as a film star was clearly established alongside that of his musical compositions. In fact he continued writing songs and sketches for revues throughout this period, and began acting on the stage from 1921 onwards. His image offscreen was of the charming, urbane professional, balancing the demands of his several careers, but still finding time for intensely glamorous, if childish, amusements. Leslie Withers sums up the appeal perfectly when he describes Ivor at their interview, 'clad in a gaily-hued dressing-gown and ignoring a box of Turkish cigarettes to plunge his hand frequently into a bag of sweets'.[9] Indeed, in contrast to the more rugged American stars, Novello belonged, one might argue, to a particularly British interwar male celebrity tradition. Asked in a fan magazine as late as 1934 why 'All British actors are effeminate?' Herbert Wilcox, producer at British and Dominions, suggested that 'the effects of the war must be taken into account here ... nobody would be more pleased than I if we could develop over here men with the appeal of Clark Gable, Robert Montgomery or Gary Cooper'.[10]

The nearest equivalent might have been the stiff lips of Clive Brook, or the elderly good looks of Stewart Rome. Whether or not in a traumatic reaction to the war however, the British taste of the 1920s generally eschewed such dourly earnest masculinity in favour of an altogether more glamorous and exotic bird. Moving with ease between film and theatre acting and writing, composing and popular journalism, this kind of British male celebrity generally owed his success to an ability to manipulate and negotiate the modern media. Ruthlessly ambitious, and tirelessly hardworking, the promiscuity we have already attributed to Novello was a defining characteristic.

Noël Coward possibly stands as the shining example of the versatile 'modern' male star of the 1920s – he was not a film star (that was to come later), but he had plenty of other strings to his bow – playwright, actor, composer, cocktail drinker – activities which ensured he was never out of the gossip columns of the popular press. Much of his appeal was based on youth, on his ability to create and perform, to consume conspicuously the glamorous goodies of modernity, but also to construct himself as an object for consumption. He was not alone. Reviewing Coward's autobiography in 1937, Cyril Connolly observed that his phenomenal success meant that 'from the pinnacle he can look down to where Ivor Novello and Beverley Nichols gather samphire on a ledge, and to where, a pinpoint in the sands below, Mr Godfrey Winn is counting pebbles'.[11] Connolly is, of course, slyly outing a homintern, and it is partly the ability and willingness of these figures to perform an unthreatening version of masculine charm for a female audience, coupled with the unarticulated suspicion of their real-life transgression, which ensured their success. Novello, Nichols and Winn all traded heavily on their youth and physical beauty, but also on their 'sophistication', as essential elements of their modern commodity status. Connolly jealously warns that such success can only be temporary – that the productions these stars are involved in are essentially ephemeral – 'the cream in them turns sour overnight'. The warning, however, is surely redundant, since immediacy, modernity and surface are precisely what these figures sought to market, what made them such quintessential figures of the 1920s.

This sense of active self-marketing, and shrewd business acumen defines these British media stars, and Novello is no exception. When Gainsborough renewed his contract in 1927, they did so with 'Ivor Novello Productions Limited', and indeed, Novello had behaved like his own production company from the outset of his relations with Gainsborough in 1924. His star image and the screen role which cemented it (the 'Rat') were not the result of decisions in meetings amongst anonymous studio executives over how best to market their new property, they were the brainchildren of Novello himself.

The Rat

Novello first conceived *The Rat* in 1923, when he presented it as a film treatment to Adrian Brunel, with whom he had just made *The Man without Desire*.[12] The basic plot traces the illicit activities of the eponymous rogue, an Apache of the Parisian underworld, who, after becoming embroiled in a rather perverse love quadrangle on the pretence of a jewel-theft (wealth thus providing the catalyst, rather than romance), attempts to prove the innocence of a young woman accused of a murder he in fact committed himself in her defence. Though Brunel recognised it as a 'frankly 'commercial' story' that might revive the struggling fortunes of the distributing company that he had set up with Novello in order to market *The Man without Desire*, the project failed to get off the ground for lack of investment.[13] Novello then proceeded to turn it into a stage play – *The Rat – The Story of an Apache*, which he wrote in collaboration with Constance Collier, and which opened with great success at Brighton's Theatre Royal in January 1924. It was such a success, indeed, that even before the play transferred to the West End Novello had sold the film rights, and British film-fan magazine *Picture Show* proudly announced that Novello's production was to be adapted for the screen.[14] Novello, it seemed, had discovered an ideal vehicle for his talents, and a lucrative one at that.

By July 1925, Rat-fever had run so high that, in addition to the success of the London run, and a national tour, there was the publication of 'The Rat Step', a new foxtrot written by Novello himself,[15] and companies touring across Britain, Europe and America. The ultimate homage, however, to the attractions of the Rat became apparent with *Picture Show*'s boast that when Rudolph Valentino had seen the play in New York, where it was in its eighteenth week, he had 'cabled an offer to buy the screen version, but he was too late'.[16] Too late indeed, for the W. & F. Film Service Ltd (Gainsborough) production was already shooting with Novello, who ecstatically explains the significance of the production for British cinema in the Press-book of the film: 'it has been a definite pleasure to turn down offers of $35,000, $45,000 and $50,000 for the American rights of "The Rat", as, having had the privilege of making the picture in *England*, with a *British* director, I know that our little play which has meant *everything* to me, could not have received better handling *anywhere*'.[17] Michael Balcon concluded: 'this production will mark the beginning of a new era in the history of British Kinematography ... [proving] once and for all that the British Film Industry could rise from the ashes'.[18] Two more films would follow: *The Triumph of the Rat* in 1926 and *Return of the Rat* in 1929, all under the directorship of Graham Cutts. But what exactly was the appeal of this 'Rat'?

Apaches, who did for the Parisian underworld what sheiks did for the Sahara, were nothing new to the British cinema screens of 1925. Even as early as 1922 there were enough 'Apache' films (in the wake of the craze for Apache dancing in the London clubs of the early 1920s) to allow *Picture Show* to carry a photo-feature on 'The Apache Dance of the Screen', which portrayed the motley denizens of the silver screen underworld, all wearing the same trademark cap and scarf later adopted by Novello.[19] The essential ingredient of the Apache drama was violence. But this was a mode of violence, following the fashion set by Valentino in *The Four Horsemen of the Apocalypse* (Rex Ingram, 1921), that was inextricably combined with dance: the type of exaggerated, ritualised and yet ambiguous sexual display discussed by Miriam Hansen and Gaylyn Studlar in reference to Valentino.[20] In Novello's hands, ritualised sexuality is transformed into a mode of theatrical camp contingent on a performance of his homosexuality.[21]

Ruminating on the popular appeal of his stage persona as the Rat, whose very name was perhaps intended to convey the 'untamed', animalistic passions outlined above, Novello predicts the nature of the rodent's appeal in the cinema:

> 'The Rat,' as you know, is a story of the underworld of Paris, and as – but ought I to say it, do you think? – I have seen some of that particular part of the world in reality, I hope I shall be able to reproduce it on the screen ... the curious mixed character seems to have made an immediate appeal to all kinds of audiences, for it is a curious blending of child, angel and devil.[22]

Far from the epitome of straightforward innocence Hitchcock claimed to have inherited, Novello's popularity was contingent on an inversion of social mores, and a barely concealed affinity with a lifestyle apparently less salubrious than the one with which he was more generally associated. As Novello put it a few years later, 'every bad young man I've ever played on stage or screen has proved a huge success for me'.[23] In the role of the Rat, Ivor Novello discovered the knack for 'getting away with' the queer sexuality of a knowing devil confronting his audience with the 'butter wouldn't melt' expression of a guilty child. As one critic put it, 'anyone with a face like Ivor Novello must apparently be forgiven everything!'.[24]

While Novello's 'Rat' of Montmartre can easily be viewed as a 'low-life', the star's extratextual status, gained through his theatrical and musical connections, afford him a necessary level of social 'respectability' that elevates him from seediness to an odd state of nobility, while simultaneously allowing other quarters of his audience to consume the same theatrical values as camp. In this respect, Novello's entrance in *The Rat* in 1925 anticipates his more famous star appearance in *The Lodger* the following year. The latter film revolves around our suspicions of Novello as a serial killer, heightened by the fact that his dubious presence apparently ignites the desire of a young blonde woman, Daisy. The *New York Times*, however, suspected that the heterosexual overtures coming from Novello were rather unconvincing. Of his famous entrance, its reviewer observed: 'There now enters Mr. Novello, looking pale and drawn and with a manner plainly saying that he very likely doesn't care for blondes at all.'[25] If a voice of the American establishment such as the *New York Times* can publicise the implicit display of Novello's homosexuality in his performance, it is exceedingly likely that such readings were available to gay audiences elsewhere. Part of the thrill of watching Novello in *The Rat*, therefore, is in the way these competing discourses and romantic claims on the star are consolidated into the persona of the Rat so as to solicit the interest of both gay *and* straight audiences.

Child, angel and devil

This split mode of address is apparent in the opening sequence of *The Rat*, which clearly establishes Novello as representing, with typical irony, the defining spatial co-ordinates of both desire and escape. The opening montage thus serves to establish the cosmopolitan setting of the film and celebrates, through many superimposed layers cavorting deliriously across the screen, hedonistic attractions of the city as a vibrantly sexual emblem of modernity. Moreover, as cultural historian James Gardiner argues: 'not only was it acceptable to be queer in Paris, it was *fashionable*'.[26]

After the elaborately illuminated title 'Paris', we are presented with an image of the Arc de Triomphe, then we cut to another 'tourist' view looking down over the Seine. The latter shot, however, is superimposed with the image of two lines of 'dancing girls', presumably from the Moulin Rouge; a contrast not just of stasis and movement but of public and private, night and day. Next, we are immersed into this nightlife, as champagne bottles pop their corks suggestively, spilling their contents in a close-up that is quickly supplanted by a vertiginous sequence of animated neon signs, which spin and blur into one another in the vortex. A dissolve introduces a key, which opens the door of an extravagantly furnished apartment and heralds the intertitle – 'a bored woman looked at her luxurious world and found it wanting'. Anticipating the presence of Novello, we, the audience, realise just who will be required to satisfy Zelie's 'craving for sensation'. Thus the trajectory of this montage constructs Novello as a force that magically attracts both desire and wealth.

While the next two scenes in the sequence reinforce the persona of the Rat as something of a 'vortex of desire', the possibilities for such conjugal aspirations rapidly become problematic. As soon as the unfulfilled desires of Zelie de Chaumet (Isabel Jeans) solicit the star entrance of Novello, we cut to a shot of the banks of the Seine where a dissolve to the image of a rat entering a hole then dissolves, in (reverse) anthropomorphic fashion, into the image of the Rat himself, who is also running to ground in order to escape the unwanted attentions of the local gendarmerie. Boucheron's rebellious attitude to the status quo is swiftly confirmed as he casts a 'two-fingered salute' in their direction before taking refuge underneath the cover of a nearby drain. There, dwelling luminously in the gutter, the shadows of the grille above cast upon his face, Novello cuts a length from the lace of the shoe of the gendarme who stands above, oblivious to the close proximity of the Rat.

We might include the institution of marriage in this equation, for in the final part of this establishing montage Novello appears amid the daydreams of Odile (Mae Marsh, with whom Novello had starred in *The White Rose*) as she tends a stove in an apartment they apparently share. Marsh's more pedestrian aspiration is to win the love of Novello, or, to be more specific, to marry him, as we learn in her daydreaming break from her domestic drudgery. Thus, as Odile gazes at her hand we dissolve to her, rather delusional, fantasy in which the Rat playfully wraps a blade of grass around her finger in the manner of a wedding ring. Needless to say, the daydream passes, and the Rat dismisses Odile's conjugal reverie with a laugh as he unwraps her finger. The formal whimsy of the scene with its soft back-lighting viewed through a hazy soft-focus, much in contrast to the 'brutal' aesthetics of the rest of the film, serves to convey the naive loyalty of his companion (and perhaps give an ironic nudge to the watching audience that Novello is not really the marrying kind), but nonetheless reasserts that in Novello, sandwiched between the desires of Jeans and Marsh, we have a figure who is constructed to support the desires of both 'high' and 'low' social strata, and their respective expectations of both excitement and stability.

Then, just as Odile prays to an effigy of the Virgin Mary for her dream of the Rat to come true, the identity of the man she so idolises is further exposed to the audience as a mere façade by the device of a closed door, which prevents her from seeing that the Rat that swaggers into her apartment, emburdened with affected machismo, is quite unlike the Rat that the camera discovered climbing the stairs outside a few moments before. The mincing gait performed by Novello outside the door as he swishes, cigarette in hand, up the stairs is, perhaps, no more camp than the butch swagger he enacts, after adjusting his dress, once inside the room, for they are both the *performance* of a queer sexual identity, or as one publication, reviewing the play, unwittingly put it, quoting a line of Novello's stage dialogue, 'when he is sober he is savage; when drunk he is gay'.[27] The difference is once of audience. For Odile (as if representative of his legion of female admirers), Boucheron becomes the Rat, the epitome of contemporary heterosexual masculinity (*à la* Valentino), violent and sexually aggressive. In private, behind the door, we witness the 'real' Boucheron, which, in being closer to the star's theatrical public persona, can be simultaneously perceived as both a glimpse of the 'authentic' Novello, at ease in the wings as if before a stage performance, while also accommodating a reading of this deliberate expressive incongruity as camp.

It is only in the labyrinthine catacombs of the White Coffin club, however, that the Rat and his fellow denizens truly find their transgressive playground.

The White Coffin

Created almost simultaneously with his own real-life club, the 'Fifty-fifty' in Soho (which achieved some minor notoriety when raided by the police in February 1926 for licensing offences[28]), and decorated with the same stylish art-deco caricatures, Novello's White Coffin club is as ingenious a creation as that of the Rat himself. Indeed, at the height of the success of 'Ivor Novello's Bohemian play' in 1924, his entire company decamped from their theatre, to the delight, of the 'social notabilities [who] insist on seeing our latest matinée idol' and strolled, fully costumed, into the Café de Paris.[29] Here, at one of London's premier night spots, Novello would 'reproduce the 'White Coffin' atmosphere' as a "Rat" gala night'.[30]

While Gainsborough's *Rat* could not imitate the impact of Novello's coup at the Café de Paris, it none the less managed to bestow a sense of immediacy to the star's camp theatricality. *The Times* considered Hal Young's camerawork to be 'disconcerting',[31] however, Michael Balcon celebrated its 'brilliant innovation', whereby 'the old limitations of the camera lens have been completely overcome' in favour of a 'smooth, unbroken, continuous flow'.[32] Whether 'smooth' or 'disconcerting' the camera movement in the White Coffin sequences breaks down the proscenial boundaries of the film set, perhaps best evidenced by the scene in which a brawl between the Rat and one of his rivals is watched by Zelie and her table, through a coffin-shaped opening on to the floor below. As they watch, the camera is close behind them, framing the action with their enthralled gaze, but as the fight draws nearer, actually climbing the stairs and spilling into the space in which they are seated, the camera rushes back, emphasising the close proximity of the object of their voyeurism.

Not only is the immediacy of such display emphasised – and shortly to become incredulously over-played in the wild 'Rat-Step' sequence that follows – but the immediacy is accompanied by an ironic sense of excess, as if such proximity were a dare to question the theatricality of the scene or even that the spectators (and here Zelie and her companions function as surrogate filmgoers) were players on the stage themselves. The nudge and wink from Novello that might accompany such a proposition is perhaps figured in an earlier sequence set in the club, as the star, framed between the faces of two women whom he holds in each hand by the hair, dubiously induces them to perform a lesbian kiss before the audience's eyes. The bizarre artifice of this gesture is further underscored by a repeated intercutting between these antics of the White Coffin and those of the Folies Bergère, at which Zelie gazes. The implication is that we are viewing one performance of sexuality after another, both of which will be witnessed through the figure of Zelie, thus implicating Novello's ironic, and decidedly queer (in every sense), mode of theatricality. As *Queen* magazine perceived, 'they must have written *The Rat* with tongue in cheek all the time'.[33]

Novello would continue to capitalise on the perception of this ambiguously transgressive facet to his image in his subsequent films of the silent era such as *The Lodger*. Here, as the *New York Times* review suggested, Novello's equivocal Lodger, whose amorous intentions towards Daisy we are encouraged to suspect, trades upon contemporary, extratextual innu-endo regarding Novello's relationship to women *per se*. This sexual Oth-erness came back into play in *Downhill* (Hitchcock, 1927) a year later, another self-penned role that relies on our belief that he *didn't* get the woman from 'Ye Olde Bunne Shoppe' pregnant, an act for which he is nevertheless expelled from public school, thus providing an excuse for more dubious continental adventures in which Novello ultimately becomes a prostitute. The dubious tone was maintained in *The Vortex*, based on the play by Novello's good friend Noël Coward, where, although it is made explicit that his character, Nicky Lancaster, is a drug addict, it is left up to the audience's, no doubt fertile, imagination to deduce that he is also homosexual.

Novello's knowingly provocative and uniquely modern star image in the role of the Rat and his other films from the mid-1920s is, perhaps, dif-ficult to reconcile with the wistful nostalgia of 'dear Ivor', reassuring his Second World War audience that 'We'll gather lilacs in the spring, again' (*Perchance to Dream*, 1945). Perhaps the 1933 shift in his career announced on the set of *Proscenium* marked an expedient move in response to the coming of sound, a recognition that his voice – the weak-est instrument in his armoury – had not the depth and range to live up to the promise of his profile. Indeed, already in 1930, Gainsborough had run a competition in collaboration with *Film Weekly* to establish what kinds of sound properties they might produce. Respondents were asked to nomi-nate both a story and a star which they felt would combine to produce a good talkie. Unsurprisingly Novello was named more often than any other star, and there was an overwhelming opinion that he should remake his silent successes. Gainsborough's scenario editor, Angus Macphail, was not impressed. Reporting on the results to Balcon, he concluded that, despite his indisputable and undiminished popularity,

> the bulk of his admirers are drawn from the more illiterate and least intel-ligent of the female competitors. Mostly their reason for recommending him is his good looks alone: their judgement tends to become curious when they seek other reasons ('Ivor Novello's quiet but virile acting').[34]

Novello did produce a few talkies, notably, *A Symphony in Two Flats* (Gareth Gundry, 1930, adapted from his own play) for Gainsborough, and *Autumn Crocus* (Basil Dean, 1934) for ATP. He also worked with slightly more disreputable film companies, particularly Julius Hagen at Twicken-ham for *I Lived with You* (Maurice Elvey, 1933, based on another of his own plays) and a remake of *The Lodger* (Maurice Elvey, 1932). Novello was now a pastiche of himself, still playing the romantic interest, but in films such as *Autumn Crocus* endowed with a wonderful pan-European accent and clad in lederhosen. There was very little room left for the kind of sexual frisson associated with *The Rat*.

As we have suggested, the tactical retreat to the theatre did not mark a point when Novello *started* to become theatrical, for he had always been that way inclined. In the 1920s, his mannered style, combined with a hint of nostalgia persisting from his 'Home Fires' days, had functioned to give the radicalism of his performance a commercially expedient veil of respectability. As he explained to the *New York Telegraph* in 1924, 'the more essentially modern you are, the more old fashioned you can afford to be'.[35] As he and his fans grew older, the nostalgic element of Novello's appeal would come to subsume that radicalism. Turning his back on the modern 'mechanical device' of the cinema enabled him to revitalise his star image, ensuring the longevity of his name on the West End stage. It was, however at the cost of the 'essentially modern' persona that brought us the devilish frisson of the Rat's butch swagger and gay exoticism of the White Coffin.

Notes

1 Novello, *Proscenium*, quoted by W. Macqueen-Pope, *Ivor, The Story of an Achievement* (W. H. Allen, London, 1951), p. 298.
2 Ibid., p. 298.
3 Ibid., p. 219.
4 Geoffrey Macnab, 'Looking For Lustre: Stars at Gainsborough', in Pam Cook, ed., *Gainsborough Pictures* (Cassell, London and Washington, 1997), pp. 99–117.
5 Sir Michael Balcon, 'Man of the Theatre – and Screen: Novello the Ambassador of the British Film', *Daily Film Renter*, 7 May 1951, 7; Michael Balcon, *Michael Balcon Presents ... A Lifetime in British Films* (Hutchinson, London, 1969), p. 36.
6 *Picturegoer*, 23 September 1933, 8.
7 François Truffaut, *Hitchcock* (Paladin, London, 1984), p. 45.
8 Peter Noble, *Ivor Novello a Man of the Theatre* (The Non-fiction Book Club, London, 1951), pp. 96–7.
9 *Picturegoer*, 23 September 1933, 8.
10 *Film Weekly*, 4 May 1934, 14.
11 Patrick Higgins, ed., *A Queer Reader* (Fourth Estate, London, 1993), p. 344.
12 Adrian Brunel, *Nice Work – Thirty Years in British Films* (Forbes Robertson, London, 1949).
13 Ibid., p. 102.
14 *Picture Show*, 12 April 1924.
15 Sandy Wilson, *Ivor* (Michael Joseph, London, 1975), p. 124.
16 *Picture Show*, 11 July 1925, 3.
17 'The Rat's Beginning by Ivor Novello', Introduction to the Press-book for the 1925 Gainsborough film.
18 Michael Balcon's conclusion to the Press-book of *The Rat*.
19 *Picture Show*, 11 February 1922, 14.
20 Miriam Hansen, *Babel and Babylon – Spectatorship in American Silent Film* (Harvard University Press, Cambridge, Massachusetts and London, 1994); Gaylyn

Studlar, *This Mad Masquerade – Stardom and Masculinity in the Jazz Age* (Columbia University Press, New York, 1996).

21 For a discussion of camp see Moe Meyer, ed., *The Politics and Poetics of Camp* (Routledge, London, 1994).

22 *Picture Show*, 30 May 1925, 18.

23 *Picture Show*, 9 July 1932, 7.

24 *Horse and Hound*, 14 June 1924.

25 *New York Times*, 11 June 1928, 27.

26 James Gardiner, *Who's a Pretty Boy Then? – One Hundred & Fifty Years of Gay Life in Pictures* (Serpent's Tail, London and New York, 1997), p. 64.

27 *New York Times*, 11 June 1928, 27.

28 *Illustrated Sporting and Dramatic News*, 12 July 1924.

29 Reported in *The Morning Post*, 14 April 1926, 9.

30 *The Star*, 21 June 1924.

31 *The Times*, 8 September 1925, 10.

32 *Daily Sketch*, 25 June 1924.

33 Cutting from a Novello scrapbook held at the Theatre Museum Store, Blythe House, London, attributed to '*Queen*' magazine, possibly *Harpers and Queen*, 18 June 1924.

34 'Prize Story Competition Report – Report re. Ivor Novello,' internal memo from Angus Macphail to Michael Balcon, 12 March 1930. Balcon Collection (envelope A/59), BFI Special Collections.

35 Marion Ryan, 'When Ivor Novello Is Not Tearing Around London with the Treasure Hunt Bunch He is a very busy "Rat,"' *New York Telegraph*, 31 August 1924.

MARCIA LANDY

The extraordinary ordinariness of Gracie Fields: the anatomy of a British film star

4

Gracie Fields is identified with the nation at large and specifically with Lancashire and the town of Rochdale. Not primarily associated with wealth, glamour or eroticism, the peculiar character of her stardom, her acting and musical performing style emerges against more conventional images of femininity associated with Hollywood and with other British stars of the 1930s. What accounts for her popularity with film audiences in the 1930s and 1940s?

Jeffrey Richards identifies Fields as a national icon and as 'consensus personified', because she 'preached a message of hope' and exemplified 'a robust and optimistic self-reliance'.[1] In a similar vein, Stephen Schaefer argues that Fields was the embodiment of 'traditional values and beliefs, however humorously portrayed'.[2] While descriptions of Gracie as a national icon are intrinsic to her success as a star and connect the milieu of the early 1930s to British cinema – the Depression, the exaltation of the virtues of family as exemplified by the monarch, King George V, the revival of British nationalism, and the pervasive cultural emphasis on a politics of consensus – they do not sufficiently account for the theatrical character of her acting, her musical performing style, and the meta-cinematic dimension of her films.

A close look at her films reveals that they undermine many pieties associated with Gracie's star persona. Her appearance, gestures, comic persona and relation to romance unsettle simplistic conceptions of her stardom. Gracie is not a diva; she is not an inaccessible goddess. Nor is she a figure of eroticism and mystery. She is a fusion of traits: ordinariness and extraordinariness, femininity and masculinity, self-sacrifice and self-aggrandisement, homosocial and heterosexual relations, a studied yet spontaneous sense of performance and a compromise between tradition and modernity.

Publicity, Richard Dyer asserts, is often taken to give a privileged access to the real person of the star. It is also the place where one can read tensions between the star-as-person and her or his image, tensions which at another level become crucial themselves to the image.[3] Fields's screen image as disseminated through publicity is tied closely to biographical elements that involve an accent on her working-class origins, struggles to succeed, rise to fame and fortune, and the obstacles that inhere in her remaining at the 'top'. Central to publicity about Fields is a mother with burning ambitions for her daughter, ambitions that the mother could not gratify for herself. The family narrative also involves a father determined to keep the daughter at home.[4] The mother's efforts prevail and Gracie sets out on a path that makes her one of Britain's major stars.

Gracie's rise to stardom involved several marriages: first to Archie Pitt who acted as her manager and who, it is reputed, was domineering and verbally abusive. Her second marriage was to Monty Banks, who was to direct several of her films. This marriage too ended in divorce as a consequence of his gambling and philandering. The relationship with Banks, an Italian, was to cause her fans discomfort during the war years. Her third marriage to Boris Alperovici was presumably a 'love' relationship, though marred by his resentment over her career and contempt for her friends and family.[5] However, her films do not generally foreground heterosexual romance: if present, it is often formulaic and subordinated to her struggles to survive or to her relations with other women. The one film that highlights romantic elements, *The Show Goes On* (Dean, 1937), presents heterosexual coupling beset by insurmountable obstacles – class conflict and opposition between domesticity and career. Her working-class lover is resentful of her success, and her relationship to her middle-class mentor and sponsor is paternalistic rather than romantic. The film does not resolve these conflicts, ending as it does with her failure to reconcile with her lover and with the death of her mentor.

Romance in her films is largely with her onstage and offstage audiences. As befitting the musical, the films include frequent crosscutting between the star and the audience internal to the film. Her musical numbers are characteristic of music hall entertainment. It was well known that in her live performances she improvised and would depart from the prescribed act without warning,[6] and her numbers in the films strive to capture this improvisational quality. The intradiegetic audiences in her films respond to her as if witnessing an impromptu performance. Her audiences are men in pubs, people on the street, men sailing off to war. In the films, the internal audience is invited to sing along with Gracie, creating the appearance of spontaneity central to her role as catalyst in the creation of community. The external audience is often treated to direct address on the part of the star, though her backstage musicals contain more conventional images of the star in the 'theatre'.

Her appearance was ordinary. Her makeup was modestly applied, her hairdos simply arranged with waves and end curls. However, her movements were not conventionally feminine: she strode decisively like a man and her gestures were broad and masculine. Unlike Jessie Matthews, Gracie's contemporary, Fields maintained a working-class identity and was not lithe and slender but sturdily built. Her costumes were generally conservative suits, dresses, ruffled blouses and, when occasion required, house dresses. However, she made ordinariness seem extraordinary through her comic impersonations, cross-dressing, posing as opera singers and parodying high-society figures. In her character incarnations she was willing comically to get doused with flour or dunked in water. Her performances were a mixture of pathos and clowning that relied on miming, frequent resort to disguises and impersonations, and an improvisational quality. Her contralto voice was powerful and her style of belting out a song reminiscent of such singers as Fanny Brice and Sophie Tucker.

Her first British film, *Sally in Our Alley* (Dean, 1931)[7] sets forth the particular combination of ordinariness and extraordinariness that forms the basis of her persona throughout her films. Her ordinariness is evident in her appearance and her identification with a working-class milieu. Her extraordinariness derives from her ability to make the ordinary appear extraordinary through her energy, her humour, her versatility as a musical comedy performer, and, above all, the range and power of her voice. The film self-consciously sets up a contrast between conventional stardom and Gracie's image of a femininity outside Hollywood glamour.

The narrative is framed by Sally/Gracie's romance with George (Ian Hunter). The film opens with George and Gracie riding together on a cart, exchanging vows. George then disappears in the war, and the film develops Sally's character without romance complications. The narrative shifts its focus on to her relationship with a young woman, Florrie (Florence Desmond), who is beaten by her father and exploits others, including Sally. In this film, unlike many later ones, Gracie has no parents, and family plays a minor, even negative, role in the film.

A major reflexive aspect of the film centres on Florrie's character. Starstruck, she emulates hairdos and mannerisms of stars in the movie magazines that she reads as she sits before a mirror in Gracie's room. Florrie's attempts to resemble a Hollywood diva suggest theatricality, inauthenticity and melodrama, attributes contrasting with the Fields persona. Thus, the film introduces one version of the role of cinema and fandom – as escapism. Florrie's obsession with her mirror image and with glamorous stars is underscored in her rejection of Sally, her readiness to betray her by attempting to seduce a returned George. She rejects Sally's affection and wants, as she says, to 'smack' things.

Instead of turning against Florrie, Sally defies the young woman to follow her inclinations and 'smack' things. She watches as the girl breaks jugs and ornaments and a watch given Sally by George. Florrie seems to be enacting a form of melodrama identified with the extraordinariness of Hollywood stars. Gracie emerges as a counter-image, one that situates her as a maternal surrogate. This maternal image (or benign paternal image?) is a central feature of Fields's screen roles whether as Sally or Gracie in her British films or as Molly, the housekeeper, in her 1945 Hollywood film by Lewis Seiler, *Molly and Me.*

Unlike the stars in Florrie's magazines, Fields's physical appearance in the film is not feminine and glamorous. Her awkwardness is evident in her discomfort with the fashionable clothing she is called upon to wear while entertaining an upper-class audience. Dressed in a slinky backless gown, Sally tries to cover herself with a shawl. The dress is at odds not only with her appearance but with her performance as she sings a Lancashire song to a bored and mocking audience. Undaunted, she succeeds in cajoling the guests into singing with her and when finished is applauded heartily. However, when the ballroom dancing begins, she is ignored, and, even worse, she mistakes a waiter for a guest and dances with him, only to get him fired. This episode is one of the few times that the Fields persona does not triumph over adversity. The film seems to be testing Fields's audience appeal. While as an entertainer she can win over the aristocrats, she does not belong to their world.

At the conclusion of the film, a converted Florrie, seeking to undo her damage, rushes to George to keep him from sailing and to return him to Sally. The united couple embrace, only to discover that they are transported to a stage in the restaurant as the curtains part; she sings, and the community cheers the reunion. She has remained within her working-class milieu but the film has magically altered the terms of that world in her conversion of Florrie and in her role as entertainer. The transgressive aspects of her role that redeem it from mere sentimentality and propaganda reside in the de-romanticisation and de-sexualisation of heterosexual relations, and in the rejection of an exotic image of stardom.

Her later films will continue in this vein, focusing on her relations to women, downplaying her relations to men, but offering greater latitude to the protean nature of her character as exemplified in her talent for mimicry and impersonation. Fields's 1934 film, *Sing As We Go* (Dean), is considered by critics to be her most successful film, one that Andrew Higson identifies in his book on British national cinema, *Waving the Flag,* as a 'heritage film' in opposition to the Hollywood character of Jessie Matthews's musicals.[8] The Fields film is much slower moving, episodic rather than unified, more like the 'cinema of attractions', with its focus on spectacle rather than on narrative.[9]

This film allows Gracie a much wider scope than *Sally in Our Alley* to develop her versatile screen persona. When the mill closes on account of inadequate modernisation and loss of profits, Gracie, like other unemployed workers, seeks a job in Blackpool. The Blackpool carnival atmosphere is identified with working-class culture, holidays and leisure. This world allows Gracie to display her talents as an impersonator. She performs as a servant in a boarding house with obnoxious guests, accomplice and even stand-in for a fortune teller, song demonstrator, human spider and worker in an amusement concession. As matchmaker, she saves her young female friend Phyllis from a decadent life and unites her with the mill owner's son, Hugh. The film ends with the reopening of the refurbished mill and images of belching smokestacks and masses of workers returning to their jobs, singing as they go. Gracie's image is superimposed on the Union Jack.

Thus, Gracie's role can be reduced to simplistic cheerleader, offering workers hope of better days. However, unlike *Shipyard Sally* (Banks, 1939), Gracie's role is not the cause of the mill's reopening. Her contribution is elsewhere. She is an advertisement for the power of popular entertainment – not by making ordinary obstacles disappear but by acknowledging them and making them extraordinary through her skill at impersonation.[10] Gracie's persona is remarkable for its self-consciousness about performance. It is not the magic of the resolution that is believable but the star's ability to persevere while trying on different roles, including that of the star.[11] Her protean femininity encroaches on prevailing values associated with conventional images of romance, dependency and subjection.

Gracie's image seems more adult, accessible and ordinary than Jessie Matthews's. Gracie too projects an extraordinary talent at mimicry and singing, but, unlike Matthews's persona, Gracie can abandon success and material emoluments. In *Look Up and Laugh* (Dean, 1935) she plays the role of community saviour, suspending her theatrical career to save the ailing Plumborough market from the capitalist Belfer (Alfred Drayton) who seeks to supplant the market with a large department store. The market becomes a synecdoche for the world as stage and she the director of this theatre. The film is not a simple throwback to an earlier Britain: Fields's character dramatises a tension between tradition and modernity like the industry she seeks to save, and like the cinema industry that the film exemplifies.

Look Up and Laugh is not a backstage musical: it casts its net more broadly by extending the conception of entertainment to life.[12] Even when

Gracie is identified within the film as a performer, the world she inhabits becomes a stage. She brings theatricality into the ordinary world. Gracie is a figure of misrule, drawing on tradition when convenient and abandoning it when it proves to be constricting. Her impersonations parody venerated practices when they are pretentious. One of her impersonations in the film is as a buxom opera singer invited to entertain at Belfer's department store. Gracie locks the real diva in a room in her attempt to sabotage Belfer's efforts to draw customers away from the market. Padded and bewigged, she sings an aria from *La Traviata* and thus establishes her ease with opera as well as with popular song, an integral component of the film musical as it seeks to establish its primacy over pre-existing forms of art and entertainment.

As in most of her films, the carnivalesque prevails with the star as the agent who temporarily turns the world upside-down. The race between Gracie and the capitalist Belfer ends fantastically with Gracie descending on the mayor and his cohorts in an aeroplane with a charter from Edward III that protects the market's rights to maintain its operations. Gracie stops the firemen ordered by the mayor to hose the unruly shopkeepers quartered in the market (thanks to Gracie's plotting), but two men within light a cigarette and ignite leaking gas. The old market goes up in flame but a new market will take its place, and Gracie drives off 'singing as she goes'. Thus the old and the new are fused: tradition is preserved but enhanced by modern innovation, like Gracie's star persona that links tradition and modernity through the power of cinema.

Gracie acted also in backstage musicals. In *Queen of Hearts* (Dean, 1936) she is a performer who, after necessary trials, emerges as a star. In this film, too, she becomes a saviour of others as she sets about to rescue a bored theatre idol, Derek Cooper (John Loder), who is unhappy with his leading lady and has taken to drink. Gracie's persona is associated with clothing as Matthews is in *First a Girl* (Saville, 1935). She is a seamstress for the theatre, and many of her numbers self-consciously call attention to clothes. She has no designs on becoming a star, is ostensibly less driven by ambition than by her fascination with Cooper. By chance rather than conscious design, she reveals her talent to others.

In a madcap chase with Cooper drunkenly driving his car, she is dragged along on the fender and then in the rumble seat until she climbs inside and takes over the wheel with no idea of how to drive. A policeman charges her with driving a stolen vehicle. After many collisions, she brings Cooper home, puts him to bed and takes his jacket with her to mend – the pretext for her entry into the theatre. Meeting an old acquaintance in the chorus, she tries on a dress and fur stole in the dressing room. Looking at herself in the mirror, she comments, 'Even your own mother would not know you'. The theatre owner, Zulenberg, is waiting for a wealthy woman, Mrs Vandeleer, with theatrical aspirations. He wants her money but plans to frustrate her ambitions.

Mistaken for Mrs Vandeleer, Gracie performs, and Cooper is enraptured. He does not recognise her, and she does not reveal her identity. Still wearing the costume, she is berated by her mother for masquerading as a lady. Ironically, one of her musical numbers is about being a motherless child. The song burlesques melodrama in its emphasis on orphans and cruel alcoholic adults. Undeterred by her mother, Gracie continues with her impersonation, encouraged by her fellow seamstresses. However, her past pursues her as the policeman, who had earlier accused her of stealing Cooper's car, keeps reappearing and trying to arrest her.

Queen of Hearts climaxes in the predictable chase scene with Gracie pursued by police, but Gracie triumphs over numerous obstacles: family, representatives of the law and envious actresses. She emerges in a gown with spangles and puffy sleeves, performing a musical number that unites entertainment and life, transforming heterosexual romance into the romance of entertainment. The film provides a map for the making of a star. A poor girl, beset by indifferent or hostile forces but resourceful, she reveals that she can withstand whatever abuse is meted out (as for example in an Apache dance where she is thrown violently around the stage and eventually out of a window). Her musical talent sustains her. That her name is also Gracie in the film (as in other films) also contributes to fusing the screen image with the persona.

The Show Goes On (Dean, 1937) is a backstage musical melodrama, drawing on Fields's talents as a singer and as a serious actress. The film draws on the milieu of the music hall, identified with animal acts and with an older, benign generation of comedians, pitting this form of entertainment against West End, upper crust and cabaret entertainment. Parallel to these antithetical forms of entertainment are class oppositions – Mac who wants to keep Gracie within the working-class world and Martin Frazer who seeks to shape her into an elegant star. Her family is also divided, with an antagonistic father who also wants to keep her at home and a sympathetic mother who supports her daughter's aspirations.

Again, clothes play a crucial role in her transformation. When she goes to Frazer's apartment to audition, her friends dress her in fake fur and feathers that Frazer finds vulgar. Initially, Sally adheres to his advice for altering her clothing and performance style. Her transformation is evident in her appearance in a black velvet gown minus jewelery and in her restrained style of singing. Audiences receive her with little enthusiasm; but she is reluctant to confront Frazer with her failure. Finally when she appears before her own people – friends, family and Mac – she breaks loose and begins to chant, monologise and clown as she sings, 'I never cried so hard in all my life'.

Her career now burgeons, and Mac is left behind, she tries to abandon her career and join him, but chance intervenes when a letter she writes him is thrown into the rubbish by Frazer. He becomes seriously ill and she is determined to accompany him on a trip to the USA despite his urging her to remain in England and perform. In an extended sequence aboard ship intercut with images of men on a troop ship, chanting, 'We want Sally Lee', she sings a sentimental song about parting, inviting the men to join her in singing. This episode reiterates her intimate relation to her audiences.

The film's finale has her insisting, against the urging of others in the theatre, on maintaining a song in her act composed by Frazer who has insisted on her leaving him and accepting an offer to sing in Drury Lane. When she learns of his death, she sings his emotional ballad about hope and memory dressed in the costume of a Southern belle in a décolleté hooped gown, floppy hat and hair in long curls. A change of setting reveals her in a nightclub setting singing the same song in a faster tempo. The chorus kneels before her as she is carried down to the stage from one pedestal to another as the curtain falls and the film ends.

In keeping with the film's metacinematic character, Gracie is showcased in her rise to stardom with elements of her biography – parental discord, conflicts over class identification and her rise to fame and fortune at personal cost. The star is offered a musical career as compensation against death, illness and personal loss. The film capitalises on Gracie's musical talent but isolates her from her origins and transforms her into a more conventional image of the star persona who must inevitably sacrifice personal desire for fame. Perhaps this perspective can be attributed to the director, Banks, who shaped Gracie's career to Hollywood cinema. The film is also revealing of attempts to glamorise her starting in 1937.[13]

By contrast, another backstage film, *Keep Smiling* (Leeds, 1938), returns Gracie to a familiar milieu as facilitator of other people's good fortunes. The film begins with a stage performance and with Gracie dressed in a man's army uniform, miming Chaplin's walk as she sings, 'They call me barmy in the army.' The film focuses on her efforts to save a theatre troupe struggling to survive in the face of dishonest managers and unscrupulous performers. In order to save money, she takes the troupe to the country and to her grandfather's farm where they plan for the future. Gracie, in gingham dress and straw hat, blends into the pastoral landscape. In an attempt to mollify her grandfather, who is opposed to the troupe and wants them to leave the farm, Gracie takes the performers to church, where she sings 'Jerusalem' with the choir. She is filmed in close-up with occasional intercuts to the congregation, still another of her 'audiences'. Even the church becomes a stage.

Rene Siguro (Peter Coke), a classical pianist, is brought into the plot though his losing his dog (borrowed from the Hollywood *Thin Man* series). Shasta is found by the troupe, and Siguro decides to join the popular entertainers. His reputation as a concert artist enables them to find employment. The film ends with the reconciliation of Gracie and her grandfather, the expulsion of a member of the troupe who had sabotaged their performances, and the marriages of René and Avis (Mary Maguire) and Gracie and the pianist, Bert (Roger Livesey). Although there are several numbers highlighting Gracie's singing and miming, the narrative is diffused among several characters, and the focus is not on her rise to stardom but on the troupe's eventual success. The film makes clear that performers are exploited, that show business is competitive, and that entertainers need sponsors. *Keep Smiling* highlights Gracie's 'inspirational' qualities and her familiar role as maternal nurturer to the troupe. The romance elements do not directly involve her, though she is included in the heterosexual coupling that takes place at the end.

In Fields's last British film, *Shipyard Sally* (Banks, 1939), the world is again theatre, and Gracie adopts a number of impersonations to achieve an objective – the opening of the Clydebank shipyard. Among the many obstacles Sally confronts in her efforts to save the shipyard, her pretentious father Major Fitzgerald (Sydney Howard) is her greatest trial. He misrepresents his social and economic status and is addicted to gambling. She is an entertainer forced to abandon her career and run an unprofitable pub that her father has bought with her money and without consulting her.

Undaunted, Sally entertains her male clients by singing to them. She responds to their challenge that she can't sing Scottish songs by singing 'Grandfather's Bagpipes' and, of course, wins them over. The business thrives until work at the shipyard is suspended. Gracie carries on despite this economic blow and serves her customers with their paper IOUs. Her morose response is 'the Bonnie Brig is sinking and we're going down with it'. Her father is for escaping, but Gracie cannot accept this solution. She decides, after reading that the shipbuilding industry is under reconsideration by a select committee, to go to London and put the case for opening the shipyard to the head of a committee, Lord Randal. Armed with a petition signed by the yard workers, she sets off for London.

Sally is denied entrance to Lord Randal, and resorts to various disguises to get past his receptionist, amply displaying her talents for impersonation. As Lord Aldershot, wearing rented morning clothes, she swaggers into an exclusive club and makes contact with the members. With her hair sleeked down, her voice pitched low, and an air of bravado, she smokes cigars, takes down drinks in one gulp, and chats about hunting. Her identity as a woman is eventually exposed as various magical tricks literally jump from her costume – water sprays, African rope tricks and pineapples. Finally her jacket begins to inflate and explode, and she is unveiled as a woman. The episode reveals Gracie's versatility at comedy and cross-dressing and offers a spoof on the behaviour of upper-class males.

She is next thrown out of Lord Randal's house by the butler and collides with an American entertainer, Linda Marsh (Tucker Maguire), who has come to apologise for not being able to sing at the evening's entertainment on account of laryngitis. Pretending that she and her father are relatives of Lord Randal, Sally assures the woman that she will deliver her message. She gains entry to the house as Linda Marsh. She mimics the American singer and charms Lord Randal, who is as 'conservative in music as in politics'. The parallel between entertainment, politics and America, if not Hollywood, is thus clearly articulated.

A carnivalesque atmosphere reigns as Sally sings and encourages the guests to form a conga line through the rooms. Sally finally confesses to her impersonation but learns that the committee has decided negatively on opening the yard. This news becomes the occasion for an impassioned speech about the workers' loyalty to their country and how the nation owes them something in return. She leaves with her father in a taxi, only to learn that the driver is a 'communist' who hails Major Fitzgerald as 'comrad.' This allusion to communism is gratuitous, since the film presents Sally and the workers as immune to ideology, concerned only with their economic survival. When Sally and her father return to the pub, they learn that Lord Randal has decided in favour of reopening the shipyard. The film ends, as it began, with shots of masses of workers, a montage of smokestacks belching forth, images of ships, and Gracie singing 'Land of Hope and Glory'. The Union Jack is superimposed on a close-up of the star. More than other Fields films, *Shipyard* overtly links the star with the nation, with patriotism and with images of collectivity characteristic of British wartime cinema, a populist paean to the social productivity and solidarity.

This overview of Gracie Fields's British films reveals fundamental dimensions of her star persona. As befits a star of musical comedy, Gracie suffers the predictable vicissitudes in her climb to fame and success. She begins in obscurity and ends with community and national acclaim. The 'rags to riches' folklore is evident but tempered by the consistency of her identification with working-class life. The abiding aspect of her 'ordinariness' is stressed in her rapport with workers, her altruistic behaviour in the interests of others, her identification with street life and her physical appearance. Even when prosperous, she does not lose 'the common touch'. Her costumes and makeup reinforce her ordinariness – bland house dresses with aprons, gingham dresses, two-piece outfits, a short jacket over a blouse or dress, and often a tie or ruffle at the neck. She is identified with hats, decorated with flowers or feathers. When she wears long gowns, they are generally plain though trimmed in fur or ruffles and they are rarely associated with high fashion.

In her comic routines, she wears padding, men's clothes, a fortune teller's gown and turban, and she subjects herself to drubbing, drenching and hauling about the stage. While it has been claimed that she worked 'with few props, often without any',[14] her costumes and gestures serve as props. Her sharp chin, toothy smile, stockiness and strident walk enhance her comic persona, deflecting from her violation of conventional images of femininity. Her de-sexualised, even masculinised, character as organiser, entertainer and maternal figure makes her appealing to a broad audience. Her maternal quality (developed to the point of exaggeration in her Hollywood films such as *Holy Matrimony* (Stahl, 1943) and *Molly and Me* where she assumes the roles of governess and housekeeper), is a key element in the British films in enhancing her ordinary character and connecting her to the nation.

Through entertainment she invests the ordinary and familiar world with heightened significance. Her comment to an interviewer about herself, 'I'm ordinary ... don't raise me too high'.[15] can serve to acknowledge the extraordinariness of the ordinary persona she is called upon to perform in her films. Her films rely on the reflexive aspects of the musical genre and the star persona that serve to blur lines between life and entertainment. As Jane Feuer has indicated, the musical genre 'may be used to glorify its own musical form, identifying that form with folk relations'.[16] In the case of the British musical as exemplified by Fields, the self-referential strategies work to elevate the working-class world she exemplifies and transforms. Her star image serves to instil belief in the 'extraordinary' dimensions of ordinary life.

Notes

1 J. Richards, *The Age of the Dream Palace: Cinema and Society in Britain 1930–1939* (Routledge & Kegan Paul, London, 1984), p. 172.
2 S. Schaefer, *British Popular Films, 1929–1939: The Cinema of Reassurance* (Routledge, London, 1997), p. 200.
3 R. Dyer, *Stars* (BFI, London, 1996), pp. 69–70.

4 M. Burgess and T. Keen, *Gracie Fields* (W. H. Allen, London, 1980), pp. 9–21; D. Bret, *Gracie Fields: The Authorized Biography* (London Books, London, 1995), pp. 1–15.

5 J. Moules, *Our Gracie: The Life of Dame Gracie Fields* (Robert Hale, London, 1983), pp. 175–200.

6 Bret, *Gracie Fields*, p. 16. Fan letters and the press scolded her for abandoning England with headlines reading, 'Gracie you have let us down.' The papers questioned her finances, particularly the amount of money she was reputed to take with her to Canada and the USA during the war. She countered with the claim that the huge amounts she was earning were donated to the war effort and also laid emphasis on the tremendous physical toll taken by her tours while entertaining Allied troops.

7 The film was scripted by Miles Malleson and by Alma Reville, Alfred Hitchcock's wife. It was directed by Maurice Elvey and produced by Michael Balcon.

8 A. Higson, *Waving the Flag: Constructing a National Cinema in Britain* (Clarendon Press, Oxford, 1995), pp. 142–75.

9 T. Gunning, 'The Cinema of Attractions: Early Film, Its Spectator and the Avante-garde', in T. Elsaesser and A. Baker, eds, *Early Cinema: Space, Frame, Narrative* (BFI, London, 1992), pp. 56–63.

10 Schaefer, *British Popular Films*, pp. 56–87.

11 M. Landy, *British Genres: Cinema and Society, 1930–1960* (Princeton University Press, Princeton, New Jersey, 1991), pp. 337–8.

12 J. Feuer, *The Hollywood Musical* (Macmillan, Basingstoke, 1993), p. 24.

13 Bret, *Gracie Fields*, p. 66.

14 Moules, *Our Gracie*, p. 64.

15 Ibid., p. 97.

16 Feuer, *The Hollywood Musical*, p. 49.

'Britain's finest contribution to the screen': Flora Robson and character acting

5

There is something perverse about including a study of Flora Robson in a book on film stars. Robson was above all a woman of the theatre, who worked also in radio, film and television. Both her biographers concentrated on her theatre work more than her film work, as did most of her obituarists, and in delving into her career one is constantly struck by her commitment to the stage.[1] She actually appeared in more than sixty films, although few of them offered her starring roles. For a brief period from the mid-1930s to the early 1940s, efforts were made to promote her as a genuine film star, but in most of her films she had only small parts, while almost all of her roles were character parts – which is how Robson is best remembered in film circles: as one of British cinema's great character actors.

Born in 1902, her theatre career took off in the late 1920s; by the mid-1930s, she was regarded as one of Britain's leading theatre actresses, a reputation that was to last for many years. After a few small films in the early sound period, when cinema looked increasingly to theatre, she was taken up by Alexander Korda, one of the most powerful and creative producers in the British film industry in the mid-1930s. Korda played Robson primarily as the *'grande dame'* in a series of quality films at the prestige end of the market. He gave her her first major part in 1934, as the ageing Empress Elizabeth of Russia in *Catherine the Great* (Korda, 1934) – already, at the age of only thirty-two, she was playing the parts of mature women. Interestingly, on this occasion her character was identified as sexually promiscuous – before her first, magnificently theatrical entrance she is described as 'the most shameless rake that ever wore a petticoat ... If she weren't on the throne, she would be on the streets.' Promiscuity was rarely to be her role in later films – but the relation between female sexuality and power is raised time and again by her performances. Her acting in *Catherine the Great* is undeniably both powerful and theatrical, which is perfectly fitting in the circumstances: Elizabeth is a supremely accomplished performer on the stage of the court, with her courtiers as

Flora Robson as the Virgin Queen in *Fire over England*. 'A woman of action, and that is just the kind of woman I like best to portray.'

her audience. The grand gesture is thus perfectly in keeping with the masquerade of imperialism and the conceit of a woman ruling a patriarchal society.

Robson made three further films while under contract with Korda, *Fire over England* (William K. Howard), *Farewell Again* (Whelan) and the unfinished *I Claudius* (all 1937). She was well received in all three completed roles, but especially for her performance as Queen Elizabeth I in the extravagant and spectacular *Fire over England*. This gave her plenty of opportunities for grand entrances and speech-making in the theatrical tradition. Her most famous speech is Elizabeth's address to her troops at Tilbury, delivered on horseback and framed in medium shot, with the minimum of cutting. Again, questions of female sexuality and power are brought to the fore: 'I know I have the body of a weak and feeble woman, but I have the heart and valour of a king, and of a king of England too.'

Korda declined to renew Robson's contract when it expired. This was a sign of things to come: Robson was not destined to be the great film star with box-office pulling power. Although there was a fair bit of material in the trade press and the fan magazines in the latter half of the 1930s trying to build her up as a star, she lacked the conventional glamour, beauty and sex appeal required for such a role.[2] Even so, *Fire over England* had given her an international reputation as a fine actress who had made her mark with both audiences and critics. Inevitably, offers started to come in from Hollywood, initially to play the character part of Nellie Dean in Samuel Goldwyn and William Wyler's *Wuthering Heights* in 1939.

There is much that is familiar in this story for British cinema. First, Robson's career in films underlines the importance of high-quality character acting within British cinema. Second, it underlines the role played by theatre-trained actors in British film history, commuting to the film studios in the morning, returning to the West End in the evening, regarding the theatre as their most significant work and cinema as a mere money-spinner. It should be no surprise, then, to find Robson speaking in 1939 of turning down the part of the housekeeper, Mrs Danvers, in Hitchcock's *Rebecca*, partly because she wanted to go back to England and do more theatre: 'The people [in Hollywood] find it very difficult to understand the English actor's off-hand attitude towards the film industry.'[3] In fact, Robson took her film acting very seriously. Even if she disliked the mechanical quality of it, and was not always happy in front of the camera, she worked hard in the 1930s to get to grips with the different requirements of film acting. She retrained herself for the camera, sought advice from various people involved in film production, and developed a style of film acting that stood her in good stead for many years to come. These are matters to which I shall return.

The third familiar trait is Hollywood's role in the development of British cinema, poaching the best players and offering them more lucrative contracts than they could secure in Britain. Robson's relation to Hollywood was ambivalent, however: because of her commitment to the theatre, she never in fact accepted a long-term studio contract with any of the Hollywood companies. Thus in 1939, after *Wuthering Heights*, she returned to England and filmed *Poison Pen* (Stein), one of the very few films in which she played a genuine leading role and was given full star billing. Indeed, it was probably only *Fire over England*, *Poison Pen* and the modest 1945 film *Great Day* (Comfort) in which Robson was promoted as the star.

If *Poison Pen* gave her star billing, it also established a character role she subsequently repeated in different permutations on numerous occasions. As the unmarried sister of the vicar in a small English village, she is the image of polite middle-class respectability on the surface. But she turns out to be the author of a series of anonymous letters that have wreaked havoc on the village community and reveal her as full of pent-up, frustrated desires that eventually push her into malevolence. This was by no means the only occasion on which she was asked to play the part of an unmarried middle-aged woman deemed in some way abnormal or deviant because of her lack of a husband and because she does not play out the conventional roles of lover or mother allotted to women in patriarchal society.

After *Poison Pen*, Robson returned to Hollywood, where she made four more films, including a reprise of her role as Queen Elizabeth in the swashbuckling Errol Flynn vehicle, *The Sea Hawk* (Curtiz, 1940). Back in England in 1943, she proceeded to play often quite spicy parts in mainly Rank-sponsored films throughout the 1940s and 1950s, including *2000 Women* (Launder, 1944), *Caesar and Cleopatra* (Pascal, 1945), *Frieda* (Dearden, 1947), *Black Narcissus* (Powell and Pressburger, 1947), *Holiday Camp* (Annakin, 1947), *Saraband for Dead Lovers* (Dearden, 1948), *Malta Story* (Hurst, 1953), *Hightide at Noon* (Leacock, 1957) and *Innocent Sinners* (Leacock, 1958). In most of these films, she had relatively small character parts, but they were frequently memorable because of the quality and power of her playing and her undeniable screen presence. Such performances kept her very much in demand, so much so that she was still playing cameo roles well into her seventies.

The height of Robson's fame in films was undoubtedly in the late 1930s and early 1940s. Even after that, she was still well enough known to be able to insist that her name appear above the film title, even for very small parts, like the nun she plays in *Black Narcissus*. There is little evidence that the film trade ever really regarded Robson as a star in the box-office sense, however. What she was appreciated for was her ability to turn on a great character performance – in effect, her ability to act. Acting and stardom are of course by no means necessary to each other, with stardom depending as much on image as technique.

As a fan magazine commented in 1936, 'although she has a strong personality of her own, she has always kept the faculty, comparatively rare in film stars, of losing her own identity in the role she is playing. For this reason, she may never be a great star, in the ordinary sense. But her characterisations will live in your memory long after those of the more conventional type of screen star have been forgotten.'[4] Stars are usually discussed in terms of their persona, a sort of meta-character built up across several films, a star image that can be carried into each new film.[5] The film is to this extent precisely a vehicle, organised around the star image(s) of its central protagonist(s). As one of the selling points of the film, as one of its main attractions, the star needs to stand out from the narrative. Rather than losing his or her identity in their allotted narrative role, that identity remains relatively detachable. Character actors on the other hand are valued precisely because of their ability to create a character that is absorbed into and used up by the narrative work of the film. The capacity of character actors to lose themselves in the roles they play is what makes them significant. Whereas a strong extra-textual image is vital to the success of the star, it may be a hindrance to the character actor.

Even when Robson did receive star billing, promotional material still tended to focus on her acting, as in this comment about *Poison Pen*: 'The name of Flora Robson at the head of the cast is a sure sign that this is something very much more than a mere recital of horror and tragedy. This is one of the few opportunities the screen gives of seeing England's finest emotional actress.'[6] In other words, if Robson did have an image outside of the films she appeared in, it was precisely as a serious actress. A few years later, the London correspondent of an American trade paper noted in *2000 Women* 'a gem of a performance ... by Flora Robson. That woman, a body of connoisseurs this side [of the Atlantic] declare, is Britain's finest contribution to the screen.'[7] The implication of this claim is not only that she was regarded as a serious actress but also that her talents could really be appreciated only through the refined filter of connoisseurship. While the principle of mass adulation is central to the idea of stardom, for Robson it was the admiration of the knowing few that made her special.

The film *2000 Women* tells the story of a group of British women interned in Nazi-occupied France in the Second World War, one of them played by Robson. The film is of a type in which Robson excelled: the ensemble piece, in which there is no star role, no leading player above all others, but in which a range of characters are allowed to emerge. Other films in this category include *Farewell Again*, about a group of people on board a ship; *Frieda*, about how the various members of an extended family react to the German wife one of their number marries during the war; *Holiday Camp*, about the escapades of a group of people brought together for a week at a Butlin's-style holiday camp; and *Malta Story*, which details the reactions of various characters to the siege of Malta in the Second World War. In each case, Robson establishes a strong, thoroughly convincing and charismatic characterisation of a middle-aged woman defined above all by her often thwarted maternal instincts.

The titles I have cited begin to give some idea of another of Robson's strengths: her ability to make her performance work across a variety of genres, including woman's pictures, war films, period costume dramas, contemporary domestic dramas, light comedies, thrillers – and even a few horror films in the 1960s and 1970s. Kenneth Barrow identifies three recurring roles in her films: the *grande dame*, the sinister woman and the 'perennial spinster'.[8] This suggests that, even with character actors, there is often a strong sense of typecasting. In Robson's case, film producers clearly did establish certain images around here, then attempted to reproduce those images in a range of films. But it is a mark of her qualities as a character actress that Robson seems equally at home with each of these images and in all of these roles and genres, with the different performance modes they each call for.

The grandest of Robson's *grande dame* roles were the regal parts to which Korda assigned her in the mid-1930s. She returned to the role in later period films such as *Saraband for Dead Lovers*, a seventeenth-century costume drama in which she played Countess Von Platen; *55 Days in Peking* (Ray, 1963), set at the time of the Boxer rebellion in China, with Robson as the Dowager Empress Tzu Hsi; and *Alice in Wonderland* (Sterling, 1972), in which she played the Queen of Hearts. These aristocratic roles afford Robson the space and the character for theatrical acting on a grand scale, full of speech-making and dramatic gestures. As I've already suggested, the highly performative style Robson adopts for such roles is perfectly in keeping with characters for whom masquerade is part of their makeup.

In the late 1930s and early 1940s, Hollywood played Robson as sinister, evil, a villainess, even a murderess, in films like *We Are Not Alone* (Goulding, 1939), *Bahama Passage* (Edward H. Griffith, 1942), and *Saratoga Trunk* (Conway, 1945).[9] In roles such as these, Robson could turn on the full range of her abilities as a powerful melodramatic actress. By the mid-1940s, and for much of the Rank period, she had become the perennial spinster – that is, the independent, middle-aged single woman she plays in *2000 Women*, *Frieda*, *Black Narcissus*, *Holiday Camp* and *Innocent Sinners*. In many of these films, she plays good, decent characters, strong, full of integrity and compassion. In such roles, she aims for an impressively convincing realism. She becomes so thoroughly absorbed into her character that she no longer seems to be acting.

A good example is her first scene in *Holiday Camp*, as she settles into her room at the complex and gets to know her roommate. In an extraordinary ninety-second shot, Robson busies herself about the room, moving into and out of medium shot, unpacking her bag and hanging up her clothes, all the while talking in the most intimate but restrained manner about her austere life with her late mother. On the one hand, it is yet another long speech, in the theatrical tradition, preserved in its integrity by the long take. On the other hand, it is thoroughly naturalistic, with no extraneous gestures on Robson's part, as she talks about quite mundane things. It is an emotionally powerful scene, but its power comes not from any melodrama but from the script and Robson's highly controlled performance.

In *2000 Women*, Robson has a similar role, but this time is able to turn her performance into superbly understated character comedy. She plays Miss Muriel Manningford, another middle-aged, single, independent woman, interned by the Nazis with her equally respectable lady friend and hundreds of other women. In one scene, an airman who has been shot down by the Germans finds his way inadvertently into the bedroom Miss Manningford and her friend share. Again, Robson allows almost no outward display of her character's emotions in a scene that could have been played as either high-anxiety melodrama or low farce. Her speech deals in no-nonsense practicalities and is delivered with an authority that no one dares challenge. Although her gestures are more prominent, as befits the comedy of the scene, they are still tightly controlled and her body is held carefully in check, as she clutches her handbag to her chest and pulls her dressing-gown tight around her neck.

These three roles – the *grande dame*, the sinister woman, and the spinster – are by no means rigidly defined or mutually exclusive categories. On the contrary, they often blend into one another. As I indicated in looking at *Poison Pen*, the roles she was asked to play often overloaded the figure of the independent single woman with so many and such intense frustrations and neuroses that she was forced into the type of sinister villainy. This is in effect a demonisation of the independent single woman, a demonisation of her unmarriedness, her position outside conventional gender relations. On other occasions, certain attributes of the spinster image are reassembled to create what patriarchy sees as the 'normal' homely virtues of asexual motherhood, as in *Farewell Again*, *Invisible Stripes* (Bacon, 1939), *Great Day* and *Malta Story*.

In fact, these various characterisations play off each other, even depend on each other. The respectable dutiful homeliness of the middle-aged mother can be turned up a notch or two, can be theatricalised as it were, so that she becomes the grand lady, mother of the nation, as in *Fire over England*. The regal types, on the other hand, often quite 'masculine' in their authority and power, have their homely, vulnerable side or are themselves unmarried – so bleeding into the perennial spinster role. Underneath the respectable façade, behind the masquerade of gentility and the confidence of the privileged classes, complex passions rage, and, when they burst hysterically to the surface, the sinister role takes over.

In a scene from *Saraband for Dead Lovers*, for instance, the Countess Von Platen confronts her recalcitrant younger lover, who is now more interested in the princess than in her. As her respectable façade slips, she reveals both her vulnerability as an unmarried middle-aged woman and her villainous and sinister streak. Her pent-up emotions erupt melodramatically. First, she attacks her lover with the heated tongs she has been toying with, burning his neck, then she falls to her knees, clutching his body, pleading with him. Even here, though, it is notable that Robson keeps physical gesture to the minimum, conveying the emotion of the scene much more through her powerful voice and to a lesser extent her eyes (she is frequently shot in close-up this time).

The regal types, the queens, countesses and empresses that Robson performs, can be seen as career women, like the MP she plays in *Frieda*. They have, in patriarchal terms, forsaken their 'femininity' for their professional ambitions, and are presented as lacking true fulfilment, their emotional frustrations emerging as a rational coldness, as warped passions or as profound regrets. As the fan magazine *Picturegoer* put it in 1945, 'even in her more sympathetic roles she has usually been frigid, dignified and unbending'.[10]

What we have here is a whole roster of female character types that patriarchy finds it difficult to value positively. Whether they wield unaccustomed power or they exist outside conventional gender relations, these women come across as threatening to men – and Robson's characters were often formidable and forbidding, and perfectly capable of becoming quite terrifying or tyrannical. Her performances, the way she uses her body, the costumes she is given to wear and the lines she is given to speak play up this sense of authority and independence beautifully: as a performer, she could be quite awesome. In *2000 Women*, for instance, when the women arrive at the internment camp, they are confronted by an officious Nazi officer. Miss Muriel Manningford soon cuts him down to size, as Robson looks haughtily down her nose at him and summons up all the authority and clarity of the southern English upper-middle-class voice. There can be no argument with such a performance!

A modern feminist audience might of course read these roles much more positively than *Picturegoer* did, revelling in the strength, authority and independence of the characters. It is equally possible to see the responses of those around her as more the product of a patriarchal sensibility that finds such women problematic, rather than the product of the women themselves. There is plenty of scope for positive feminist readings of Robson's characters. In *Catherine the Great*, for instance, the all-controlling and imperial Elizabeth is horrified to learn that Catherine's husband has deserted her on her wedding night. Storming into the bedchamber, she both comforts Catherine and launches into a tirade against men. In one memorable shot, she stands, hands on hips, dressed in a magnificent gown, and pronounces to Elizabeth, crying in bed: 'There's only one way for a poor, defenceless woman to treat her husband, and that's to get the upper hand of him in the first five minutes, and to rule him.'

Robson herself evidently empathised with some of the women she played. In 1937, she wrote of how she saw the part of Elizabeth in *Fire over England*:

> Provocative, aggressive, possessive and perhaps a bit temperamental, Elizabeth was every inch a queen. She was essentially a woman of action, and that is just the kind of women I like best to portray. Whether they are characters of actual history, or folk-lore or of pure fiction, such women – women whose lives and work were more important than their loves – are much more in tune with our modern ideals and tempo of life than many of the silken sirens who have figured as the heroines of sexy and sentimental films in the past.[11]

This was shortly after Robson had played the name part in *Mary Read*, a play specially written for her by James Bridie, about the exploits of the eighteenth-century female cross-dressing pirate. More generally, the range of women that Robson played in her films, and the ways that she played them, point to the instability of traditional gender roles. There are no hard and fast categories; there is no pure feminine identity, distinct from a pure masculine identity. Identity is much more hybrid than this – women can be masculine, and masculine women can be compassionate and maternal. Gender identity is underlined precisely as performance by Robson's characterisations. The power dressing of the various queens, countesses and empresses, and the masculine attire of the various contemporary career women and independent single women, is precisely about dressing for the part, a form of masquerade. In the various ensemble pieces in which Robson appears, there is always a range of gender identities on offer, among which Robson's character provides just one possibility.

Nicholas de Jongh has written of the 'blazing emotional force and histrionic power' of Robson's theatre acting.[12] In her film work, she was perfectly capable of this dramatic force, but what is even more remarkable is her control, so that, when the passions are loosed, the outbursts are all the more impressive. In the 1930s, Robson spoke in interviews of retraining for the camera: watching lots of films, talking to actors, cameramen and directors, watching the studio at work and looking at the rushes. She even welcomed the idea of a film training school, which established theatre actors would have to go through before they tried making films.[13] She talked of learning the technique of the close-up, learning to relax, to stop acting in front of the camera, to underplay rather than overplay – in other words, she talked precisely of learning how to *control* the expressiveness of her acting for the cinema.

'The slightest touch of self-consciousness on the screen shows', she was quoted as saying in 1937. 'I've learnt that from bitter experience ... In the theatre one feels the audience. One overacts. But the camera, like a huge eye a yard away, snaps up everything.'[14] She talked of how the American cameraman Hal Rossen 'helped me to overcome the inevitable theatrical exaggeration and to eliminate certain small mannerisms of expression which, while perfectly natural on the stage, were little short of grotesque when translated to the screen'.[15] This was not just a matter of physical gestures, she realised, but of facial expressions too: 'I knew of course that the camera demanded much less emphasis of facial expression than the stage, but I had not realised that it required *under*-emphasis, that is, less than would be natural.'[16] In reworking her performance style for the camera, Robson thus tried to minimise all bodily and facial movement and expression. 'Everything like this has to be entirely eliminated for the camera, and you must even speak with as little lip movement as possible.'[17]

On screen, Robson did indeed hold her body extremely still, using only the most minimal and subtle movements. Of course, while this restraint and understatement may be good screen acting at one level, on another level it can be read as thematically important to the roles she is playing, where the physical control and restraint suggests the repression of emotion. It is also possible to read this performance style as typical of the tradition of English theatrical training that focuses on the voice and leaves the body stiff and inexpressive. It is certainly the case that Robson's voice was one of the vital tools of her screencraft, the eloquence, power and musicality of her voice contrasting with the stillness of her body. At the same time, her precise diction is suitable only for certain roles, and again implies great control over her performance, which may register as emotional restraint.

Her voice is deep and vibrant; it is capable of quietness but remains forceful; it has a hard-edged authoritativeness, but also a compassionate softness. The combination of the two can seem patronising, school-marmish, but again this is very often in keeping with the parts she plays. The control she exercised over her voice made her a very powerful speaker. Indeed, as I've noted above, one of her strengths is precisely to make speeches, in a theatrical manner. This is obvious in scenes like the Queen's speech at Tilbury in *Fire over England* or the election hustings in *Frieda*, but it is also there in less obviously theatrical settings. Thus one of Robson's specialities was to gaze off into the middle distance, avoiding eye contact with the person with whom she is conversing, affording her the psychological space in which to deliver a monologue, to make a speech. On other occasions, the camera creates that theatrical space for her, capturing her performance in real time and space, in long takes and mid-shots, rather than fragmenting it by cutting rapidly back and forth between close-up reverse shots of two interlocutors.

As Robson developed as a screen actor, we find her also very effectively using stillness and silence, conveying pent-up feelings as she steadfastly and relentlessly gazes into the distance, doing nothing, but hinting at layers of unexpressed or inexpressible emotions. There is little room for open emotionality in her carefully controlled performances. For the most part, it is squeezed out almost reluctantly, it seems, as maternal compassion, or it bursts out with great force. As has often been remarked of British films, they are often extremely good at dealing with emotional repression, especially where the actor has a theatre training, and this is particularly true of many of Robson's films.[18]

In 1938, Alfred Hitchcock wrote that 'the screen actor ... has to submit himself to be used by the director and the camera. Mostly he is wanted to behave quietly and naturally ... leaving the camera to add most of the accents and emphases. I would almost say that the best screen actor is the man who can do nothing extremely well.'[19] Leaving aside Hitchcock's gender-specific language, we might note that this is exactly what Robson aspired to. A traumatic scene from *Frieda* provides an object lesson in this idea of cinema and of film acting. Near the end of the film, Frieda's husband confronts her with apparent evidence of her Nazi sympathies. Nell, played by Robson, who believes that all Germans are Nazis, applauds him for his actions, but is challenged for failing to see Frieda as a human being. 'Can't you feel what she must be feeling?', she is asked. 'Very easily', she replies, 'but I'm trying not to let feeling blind me. I'm crushing it down.' Later, she watches almost impassively as Frieda walks past her, clearly bent on taking her own life. Robson's face has remained nearly expressionless throughout the sequence, while her body remains still and gestures are kept to the absolute minimum. Even as she realizes what Frieda is doing, her expression hardly changes. There is a narrowing of the eyes, a sharp raising and straining of the voice, but little else. Nothing more is needed, however, for despite the understated acting the sequence is one of high melodrama. The emotion and the drama are provided not by overwrought performances but by the combination of lighting, use of shadow, framing, cutting and music. Robson's achievement is to have recognised what it takes to 'submit herself to the camera', to recognise what is necessary in creating a character on the screen.

Notes

This is a revised version of a lecture delivered at Brighton University as part of the 'Dame Flora Robson Memorial Day', 21 May 1996. My thanks to Lawrence Napper for research assistance.

1 Janet Dunbar, *Flora Robson* (Harrap, London, 1960); Kenneth Barrow, *Flora* (Heinemann, London, 1981); among obituaries, see, for instance, N. de Jongh, 'Theatrical Sadness for Dame Flora', *Guardian*, 9 July 1984, 2.

2 See Anon., 'Catherine the Great', *Kinematograph Weekly*, 16 August 1934, 42; Press books for *Catherine the Great* and *Poison Pen*, held at the BFI National Library, London; T. T. Fleming, 'Elizabeth of Denham', *Film Weekly*, 8 August 1936, 10; M. Breen, 'The Star Nobody Knows', *Picturegoer Weekly*, 16 January 1937, 10–11; J. D. Williams, 'Is it Fame at Last for Flora?', *Film Weekly*, 22 April 1939, 9.

3 Williams, 'Is it Fame ...', 9.

4 Fleming, 'Elizabeth of Denham', 10.

5 See, for instance, R. Dyer, *Stars* (BFI, London, 1979).

6 Press Book for *Poison Pen*.

7 London review of 2000 *Women, Motion Picture Herald*, 9 September 1944.

8 Barrow, 'A Tribute to Flora Robson', National Film Theatre programme booklet, October 1981, p. 8.

9 See A. Fletcher, 'Lady Be Bad', *Picturegoer*, 23 June 1945, 8.

10 Fletcher, 'Lady Be Bad', p. 8 (the roles cited are those in *Fire over England, Catherine the Great* and *The Sea Hawk*).

11 F. Robson, 'My Film Future', *Film Weekly*, 2 January 1937, 8.

12 De Jongh, 'Girl who Never Quite Grew Up', *Guardian*, 9 July 1984, 11.

13 See Robson, 'My Film Future', 7.

14 Quoted in G. Roberts, 'Determined Lady', *Film Weekly*, 25 September 1937, 12.

15 Robson, 'My Film Future', 7.

16 Quoted in F. B. Lockhart, 'Elizabeth of Elstree', *Film Weekly*, 11 January 1935, 9.

17 Ibid.

18 See R. Dyer, 'Feeling English', *Sight and Sound*, 4.3 (1994), 17–19; and A. Medhurst, '1950s War Films' in G. Hurd, ed., *National Fictions: World War Two in British Films and Television* (BFI, London, 1984), pp. 35–8.

19 Hitchcock, 'Direction', in C. Davy, ed., *Footnotes to the Film* (Lovat Dickson / Readers' Union, London, 1938), 9.

Dangerous limelight: Anton Walbrook and the seduction of the English

Anton Walbrook was born in Vienna in 1900. The son of a famous circus clown, he was christened Adolf Wohlbrück. Training at the Max Reinhardt theatre school in his late teens, he worked extensively on the German stage and made his first film appearance in 1931. After making his name in a handful of European hits, he signed a contract with RKO and went, briefly, to Hollywood, then after one film changing his name and settling in Britain in 1937 to star alongside Anna Neagle in *Victoria the Great* and *Sixty Glorious Years*, and to remake the famous 1927 Ivor Novello success, *The Rat*. During the next twenty years he collaborated with Michael Powell and Emeric Pressburger. His other important British films were Thorold Dickinson's *Gaslight* and *Queen of Spades*, and the wartime sentimental romance *Dangerous Moonlight*. Returning to Europe in the 1950s, he scored memorable successes with Max Ophuls in *Lola Montes* and *La Ronde*. He died in 1967 near Munich.

A theatre curtain, when lowered, separates the carnival-space of fantasy and desire behind the proscenium arch from the quotidian realm before it. It graphically exemplifies bourgeois culture's wish to police a demarcation between the utilitarian and the excessive, the regulated and the riotous, between 'life' and 'art' (and Romantically to accord 'art' a privileged status). Abruptly emerging from behind such a curtain to expose himself to the accusing gaze of a playhouse spotlight, Anton Walbrook shrieks the formal announcement to the expectant audience that 'Miss Page is unable to dance tonight'. He looks impeccable, yet, as a close-up reveals, he shudders with erupting mania. The Walbrook persona is often so bedevilled. His brittle features – the upright body, the thin upper lip hidden beneath an unfeasibly precise moustache, the elegant manners: these mark a patina of civilised control threatened with disintegration when confronted with incursions of the irrational. The year is 1948. The film is Powell and Pressburger's *The Red Shoes*; the role that of Boris Lermontov, the autocratic impresario for whom ballet is 'a religion'. In this, the film's morbid clos-

Anton Walbrook, an Austrian star in British films, crossing 'otherness' with Englishness in this publicity pose.

ing sequence, Lermontov faces the consequences of his rejection of 'human feelings'. His protégée Miss 'Page' (a *tabula rasa* on whom both he and her husband Julian Craster have striven to inscribe their conflicting wills) has leapt to her death, finding herself unable to reconcile the artistic absolutism which Lermontov demands and the social conformity of marriage. The last shot of Walbrook finds Lermontov in the shadows of his private box, isolated and mortified as the ballet 'The Red Shoes' is performed, with keen pathos, *sans* its prima ballerina. This scenario is emblematic of an actor who, because of his exotic roots and despite his charming manners, embodies recurring tensions in British cinema of the period.

Embracing the alien

Despite important work with Thorold Dickinson and Herbert Wilcox, Walbrook's British career is particularly notable for his involvement with Powell and Pressburger, with whom he collaborated on four projects: the 'war' films *49th Parallel* (1941), and *The Life and Death of Colonel Blimp* (1943); *The Red Shoes*, and finally *Oh ... Rosalinda!!* (1955), their updated version of *Die Fledermaus*. Each draws on distinct aspects of Walbrook's persona, but wherever he appears his 'foreignness' is the common denominator. The British response to it is a commentary upon indigenous tastes and prejudices. Unable simply to accept Walbrook, they adopt one of three strategies. In 'war' films he is provisionally embraced to illustrate how generous the allied rhetoric of tolerant rapprochement is (differentiating it from its opposite, the rabid racism of Hitlerism). Here, the hegemonic project of the People's War downplays his alien status. Elsewhere his foreignness is the occasion for romance, and the continental charm of the star is celebrated. But sometimes, thirdly, that same exoticism is demonized, and the actor is given scope to vent his always present, but generally veiled, tendency towards mania.

Walbrook's flight from the European mainland in the 1930s closely mirrored Pressburger's, in whose scripts we find a fascination with crossed boundaries. As Antonia Lant has remarked, Pressburger's work is dominated by 'The masquerade of nationality ... and the difficulties of being alien but not enemy, of being non-national'.[1] With 1940s British cinema galvanised by a 'propaganda of communality', Walbrook tests its inclusiveness by playing a 'good German', an oxymoron within more simplistically constructed strands of wartime discourse. A film such as *Colonel Blimp* strives to recruit him to its overwhelmingly incorporative ideology, and posits an apparently easy transition into an idealised sanctuary. Yet, despite his fluent English, Walbrook continued to sound Germanic enough to inscribe his foreignness in a way that marked a resistance to the incorporative zeal of the times.

It was in a popular romantic comedy, *Maskerade* (Forst, Austria, 1934), that Walbrook first made his name.[2] This work's limited British release familiarised 'specialised' British audiences to him,[3] and, according to one typical review, 'his elegant, humorous and completely charming portrait of the philanderer made him just about the most popular member of the select group of Continental actors who are internationalists among screen artists'.[4] Fanzines later invoked this performance when marketing him here as 'a light comedian'.[5] The flurry of press coverage which greeted Walbrook's arrival in Britain in 1937 alluded to his earlier continental career and championed his status as 'a great romantic star.'[6] In Hollywood his name was changed from the brusque Adolf Wohlbrück to the semi-English-sounding, more romantic Anton Walbrook, although obviously the rejection of his first name is meaningful in the context of the 1930s. Early interviews also focus on his acquisition of English. Walbrook concedes, for example, that he 'would never attempt to play an English role'.[7] His accent would therefore determine the parts he could play. By 1940, a desire to be 'more English than the English' is admitted and he regrets that he feels unable to act his beloved Shakespeare: 'Ever since I came here I've tried to lose my accent, but I've still got it, you see!' he sighs in one interview.[8] Elsewhere, however, his effort to maintain it is noted. He 'very deliberately preserved the soft Viennese accent. Shrewdly he believes that a trace of accent appeals to English-speaking audiences.'[9] More recently Kevin Gough-Yates has quoted another contemporary account about Walbrook's voice-coach: 'When [Walbrook] came to Denham, to play opposite Anna Neagle in the Victorian pictures, he sent for a teacher, who while in Vienna had given him his first English lesson ... She has, in fact, been chiefly responsible for Anton's English developing into a most charming aspect of his screen personality.'[10] Whether a canny ploy or not, the accent remained (although his English became accomplished). Within British cinema it is the dominant expression of his difference.

The fact that Pressburger often wrote crucial set-piece speeches for Walbrook indicates the weight his oratory carried. Pressburger had drafted star roles to utilise Conrad Veidt for Korda in the late 1930s (*The Spy in Black* and *Contraband*), and the homage to Europe is perpetuated in his affinity for Walbrook. Always eloquent, Walbrook's voice is a subtly modulated and rhythmed tenor, tightening in moments of urgency into a guttural, strangulated rasp – a flicker of the barely submerged hysteria which would break loose in Walbrook's more histrionic moments. As Peter, the leader of the German Hutterite group in *49th Parallel*, Walbrook gives a keynote speech in which he strenuously denies any kinship with the Nazi invaders of his Canadian sanctuary. 'We are not your brothers,' he declares, 'Our Germany is dead!' Peter's disavowal of national identity is expanded in *Colonel Blimp*. The official and critical resistance to Walbrook's portrayal of the Prussian Theodor Kretschmar-Schuldorff (written specifically for him) is a measure of the blunt germanophobia to be found within elements of the British establishment at the time.[11] Again, a 'big speech' from Walbrook forms the crux of the film. The aged Theo's plea for asylum in Britain argues that national identity is to be subordinated to a sense of 'home' born out of personal affiliations, a fondness for the English countryside, and shared values united in their antipathy to fascism. *Blimp*'s assimilation of a 'good' German into its conscripted modern community problematises more energetically flag-waving wartime discourses, with Walbrook's status as a sympathetically accepted foreigner confounding the polarisation of 'us' and 'them'. That the intellectual weight of the film in its closing sequences is allotted to this alien voice marks how far its makers endorse the idealised rhetoric of wartime allied consensus. 'It's a different knowledge they need now', Theo tells Clive (the film's 'Blimp', personifying a redundant English mindset, also to be spiritually recruited into the British people's 'new model army'). 'The enemy is different ... If you preach the Rules of the Game while they use every foul and filthy trick against you, they will *laugh at you*!! ... You have been educated to be a gentleman ... but Clive, dear old Clive, this is not a gentleman's war.' It is only when Walbrook directly speaks of the Nazis' contempt that his voice loses its gentlemanly melodiousness. In wartime Walbrook can be identified as an ally, his persona partly assimilated into British culture. Yet this is accompanied by a constant awareness of his foreign origins. He remains an outsider, but, with Nazism reserved as the only significant 'other', he becomes unthreateningly different.

He is not always so domesticated. An alternative response to Walbrook fastens upon this very difference to maximise his exotic characteristics, a road which would lead to Lermontov, both denounced and lustily admired by Lady Nestor in *The Red Shoes* as an 'attractive brute' and later considered by her niece Miss Page to be a 'gifted cruel monster'. Much of the tension which Walbrook excites emerges from this ambivalent response to his 'otherness'. The exotic and the erotic can be coterminous and, in this sense, Lady Nestor's reaction is typical. Walbrook became established in the popular mind as a matinée idol, yet he is often coded as a stern autocrat, a dangerous, hypnotic anti-hero (and this darker dimension is traceable to a set of gothic characteristics predating his British career).

If the adjective 'charming' is the word most associated with Walbrook (by 1941, as Stefan Radetsky in *Dangerous Moonlight* he himself jokes self-referentially about his 'continental charm'), we should reflect on what that

word signifies. To be charming or fascinating is not simply to have the passive qualities of desirability or attractiveness. It is to cast a spell, to bewitch
and captivate. It is an expression of power. Walbrook's 'softer', more
debonair aspect was set to endure. 'Remember the Warsaw Concerto,'
prompts Walbrook's obituary in the *Daily Express* in 1967, noting that Walbrook 'became the idol of millions after his performance as the airman-
pianist in ... *Dangerous Moonlight*' (implying that, after his relatively
unproductive last decade, the star had been outshone by Richard Addin-
sell's hugely popular and gushingly Rachmaninovian score for that film).[12]
To the *Daily Telegraph* Walbrook was 'an actor of great charm' who 'made
his name in Britain in Herbert Wilcox's film *Victoria the Great*,[13] while the
Daily Mail considered him 'one of the last of the romantics' and noted his
'devastating effect on female hearts'.[14] Most of the tributes also record
important parts he played in the commercial West End theatre. He 'set
women sighing' in the early 1940s as the German anti-Nazi in Lillian Hell-
man's *Watch on the Rhine*. Appearances in the musicals *Call Me Madam*
(by Irving Berlin, 1952) and later in *Wedding at Paris* are also mentioned,
along with his 1939 London debut as Otto in Noël Coward's *Design for
Living* (an implicit association with 'sophistication' is clearly integral to his
public image – hence *Variety* magazine enthusiastically divulges that his
hobbies included such refined pursuits as painting, fencing and riding).[15]

Despite the 'matinée idol' status, only rarely in British films is Walbrook cast as a genuinely romantic lover. Where he is, menacing traits are
naturally downplayed. *Dangerous Moonlight* and his Prince Albert in
Wilcox's *Victoria the Great* (1937) and *Sixty Glorious Years* (1938) exploit
his Europeanness to negotiate tensions between national identity and
their 'romance plots' (if Victoria and Albert's relationship is readable as
the stuff of romantic film). These films are warmed by his charm. I shall
return to the 'Victoria' films in a moment, for it is with his performance
as the celebrated pianist and pilot Stefan Radetsky in *Dangerous Moonlight*
that we see the apotheosis of his more engaging side. Here, Walbrook's
charisma is ambitiously conflated with undimmed Polish national consciousness, with the determination to defeat Hitlerism, and with the uni-
versalised human aspirations suggested by Stefan's musicianship.
Embodying these strategically blurred messages, Stefan is an attractive,
vulnerable hero: with a quiet pathos, a close-up dwells upon a slight bite
of the lower lip and a single teardrop as, sorting through his friend Mike's
belongings after Mike has been killed in an air mission, Stefan reads his
own wife's letter addressed to Mike and learns that she too hopes for a reconciliation in their marriage. This is a rare moment of genuine empathy.
Walbrook emphasises the most inviting dimensions of his persona (and
downplays his voice's harsher register) to foster an easy identification

between the audience and the film's ideological purpose. The propaganda is predictably distilled into the tear-jerkingly climactic embrace between Stefan and his wife.

Romantic pedigrees – the 1930s

Walbrook romantically partnered (let alone singing and dancing, as he often did, on the London stage)? For those now familiar only with his more obsessively alienated incarnations this might seem improbable, yet it was familiar territory to him, with much of his early film career devoted to light-hearted comedy romances. Born in Vienna in 1900,[16] by the age of 16 he was playing minor roles on stage for Max Reinhardt, with whom he had trained. By the time of his first film, the circus picture *Salto Mortale* (Dupont, Germany, 1931), he had played in over two hundred stage productions (including Wilde, Shaw and Shakespeare).[17] His early film success *Viktor und Viktoria* (Reinhold Schünzel, Germany, 1933) was notable for its frivolous exploration of gender and sexuality. A comedy musical set primarily in London's theatre world, its premise, echoing *As You Like It*, is that Suzanne, a struggling female singer (Renate Müller) poses as a male drag-artist, 'Herr Viktoria', in order to advance her career; Walbrook, secretly aware of Suzanne's deception, plays her suitor. *Viktor*'s interrogation of masqueraded sexual identity is ripe material for queer readings, and Walbrook's portrayal of the romantic hero involved with the contingently regendered protagonist (in a semblance of a gay romance) may clearly be decoded with the hindsight of Walbrook's own homosexuality. This biographical detail was understandably erased at the time. While in the 1930s his image in Britain had been established as having a 'faint aura of reserve', and it was noted that 'unlike many actors, he will not open his heart to any casual acquaintance',[18] his sexuality remained covert. Later, Michael Powell, while acknowledging Walbrook's sexual orientation, would still reaffirm the star's 'enigmatic and elegant' persona.[19] The mystique of the romantic star is thus handsomely peddled, with the intrusive public gaze conveniently deflected from his private life. Most biographical sketches remain coy about Walbrook's sexuality. His *Times* obituary makes the starkly opaque conclusion that 'he was unmarried', while, as recently as 1989, David Shipman euphemistically narrates a sadly anonymous domestic drama with the cliché that '[Walbrook's] *friend of some years standing* killed himself shortly after his death'[20] (my emphasis). There is a clear if dubious temptation to meld biography with performance and naively to over-read the catastrophically splintered, narcissistic or haunted roles which Walbrook would later play as somehow expressing a warped or repressed aspect of his 'hidden' identity, and this is fuelled by the genuinely gay subtext to *The Red Shoes*.[21] For in contrast to the light musical-comedy fare there were always darker performances. Such roles, from his German remake of *The Student of Prague* (Arthur Robison, 1935), a Faustian tale of a student who sells his reflection and is tormented by his doppelgänger,[22] through *Gaslight* and *Queen of Spades* to Lermontov, are determined more by their traditionally melodramatic or supernatural narratives than by Walbrook's sexuality. In any event, the 'submerged' fact of Walbrook's sexuality is complicated by enigmatic reports in 1938 of his engagement to an 18-year-old actress, Maud Courtney (a marriage 'indefinitely postponed' because of Miss Courtney's age, because of her mother's disapproval and because he was still an Austrian citizen).[23] Whether such reports were a mere smokescreen I have been unable to ascertain.

Walbrook's early British films hint at how his image would be entertained by his host nation. The depiction of the inhospitable welcome meted to Albert in the 'Victoria' films reads immediately as an inauspicious castigation of British insularity (particularly in *Sixty Glorious Years*, which is metaphorically imbued with the immediacies of 1930s European politics). Stricken with bad weather on his journey here, Albert jokes that England is 'a country that's so difficult to get to'. The film presents a hostile British establishment, and it is perhaps significant that only where Walbrook plays an *alter ego* for the devoutly anglophile Pressburger – as Theo in *Blimp* – does he really fit snugly into the textual rendition of England. In *Blimp*, as elsewhere, Pressburger romantically idealises the island refuge, where for all its faults of woollymindedness and backward thinking Theo can be welcomed as a friend. Like Theo, Prince Albert nostalgically finds a sense of home in similarities between the British countryside and his native Germany, although his vigorous efforts to assimilate himself are doomed to failure. Hence the distracted paranoia of Albert's dying words in *Victoria the Great*: 'Don't leave me. They are waiting for me at the Tower. I've done my best.' To empathise here is to castigate British xenophobia.

The 'darker' side of Walbrook's persona begins to show itself in *The Rat* (Raymond, 1937). Considerable focus was given to this 'talkie' remake of Ivor Novello's silent film (Cutts, 1927), with comparisons to Novello echoing throughout Walbrook's career.[24] The changes between the versions exploit Walbrook's more romantically solitary traits. In Novello's film, a Parisian jewel thief (the 'Rat') is tricked into temporarily abandoning his platonic girlfriend Odile to the lusts of the melodramatically villainous Stetz. Interrupting the attack, Novello stabs Stetz. When Odile is arrested, Novello is helpless, passively resigned to the fates (part of the work's melodramatic conventions). Odile is later released, the case is dismissed and the pair are romantically united. Walbrook's 'Rat' lacks Novello's playful swagger and his feminine swooning. Although both are attractively cavalier objects of erotic fantasy, Walbrook possesses a degree of cool disdain, tempered only by moments of provocative flirtation (performative signs cannot be directly compared, of course, as Novello employs codes of physical gestures inherent to the semiotics of silent film). Walbrook is a loner, reluctantly charged to care for Odile by her imprisoned father. Less sympathetic at first, his reserve nevertheless softens, and he and Odile are drawn together. But ever chasing jewels, he begins an affair with Madam de Chaumon, and is with her when Stetz assaults Odile. Here, it is Odile who kills her assailant, although to save her Walbrook makes an impressive and heroic court-room confession (another narrative entrusted to his eloquence). Madam de Chaumon finally provides an alibi, commending Walbrook's 'lies and incredible chivalry'. He is acquitted, Odile is sentenced to one year's imprisonment and, acknowledging his love, he pledges to wait for her. The Rat's social aloofness is thus finally compromised. He is never really more anti-heroic than many other wayward rascals, yet Walbrook's Rat shows a misanthropic sense of alienation which is more than a mere Romantic pose.

Demonising the alien

What then of Walbrook at his darkest? It is rooted in his Germanic past. The German theatre of his youth descended from nineteenth-century Romanticism, and its foremost practitioner, Max Reinhardt (influenced by Adolphe Appia and Edward Gordon Craig), often shunned realistic staging. Appia's non-representational designs encouraged freely symbolic mise-en-scène, while Craig gave fervid expression to the rejection of bourgeois realism by envisaging an ideally 'actorless' theatre. Advocating a visionary theatrical aesthetic, Craig yearned with Nietzschean vigour for the 'Über-marionette' to replace real people on stage, calling for an escape from the constraints of the human body (which is biologically and inartistically bogged down in the aesthetics of naturalism). Emancipation from this corporeal bondage is available to the actors he envisages: 'To-day they *impersonate* and interpret; and the third day they must create. By this means style may return.'[25] The spirit's struggle to transcend human limits; the recourse to anti- or non-rational energies; the fractured identity of the alienated artist: the stuff of Romanticism which later fed into the abstract extremes of expressionism. Michael Patterson's account of expressionist theatre suggests that its 'hero' was 'constantly straining towards superhuman ecstasy', abandoning civilised restraint in favour of religious or spiritual or sexual fulfilment marked by a primitive aesthetic where just a scream ('der Schrei') became the exclamatory articulation of this radical psychological state.'[26] The extreme physicality preserved in German expressionist cinema is a mute indication of this profoundly non-naturalistic style.

Such techniques remained in Walbrook's repertoire. As *The Times* perceptively noted, 'he had not attempted on beginning to work in England to change his style radically, but he judiciously toned it down, while slyly drawing attention to its individuality at moments'.[27] His restraint dovetails into the lauded stiff upper lip which is synecdochal of English middle-class manhood and which would feed the understatement which characterised the dominant realistic aesthetic of 1940s cinema. But recontextualised into England, his 'moments' of 'individuality' strike violently at such values and render him monstrous. Wedded neither to the mannerisms of the West End stage nor to the trend towards cinematic realism, they become explosive. The schism between Walbrook's 'well-mannered' persona and his innate hysteria, in a small cycle of films, marks out those characteristics which proved unassimilable within British middle-class culture. With his foreignness paraded, he reminds us of boundaries, of border-crossings: a figure with all the schizoid tendencies which belonging to the margins can produce.

Louis Bauer in *Gaslight* (Dickinson, 1940), Hermann in *Queen of Spades* (Dickinson, 1949) and Lermontov are double-identities, tortured, obsessive, facing disintegration. They echo the gothically haunted *Student of Prague* pursued by his liberated mirror-image. Bauer, returning to the site of his crime to seek the jewels he murdered for, is recognised by Rough, the retired detective, as a 'ghost from the past'. Masked with a new 'respectable' identity (as Paul Mallen), Walbrook sadistically protects himself by psychologically torturing his inquisitive wife. *Gaslight* delineates the crucial fractures between respectability and vulgarity, sanity and madness, and Walbrook's split personae fight to contain these incompatible energies. Descended from the Victorian stage, Bauer is irredeemably wicked. Like James Mason in the Gainsborough melodramas, the historical costumery here grants him a licence to shock. And as George Turner has noted, *Gaslight* significantly de-anglicises him into a Teutonic villain: the original stage play's 'Manningham' is here renamed Bauer (and coded as a 'queer' foreigner).[28] Whatever the reason for the change, this is the only time Walbrook played a nominally German villain. He never gave us a stereotyped Nazi. Doubtless Walbrook might well be decoded in a vaguely psycho-social way as being the embodiment of a stereotypical German tendency towards hysteria and excess. Regardless, Manningham's name change suggests a paranoid tendency to cast 'otherness' nationalistically.

The façade Walbrook presents mirrors the narrative's clichéd treatment of Victorian hypocrisy. Thus Bauer remains charming when illicitly 'entertaining' his parlourmaid or enjoying the 'vulgar' delights of the music hall, yet when vexed by his wife there is the hint of a twitch about his upper lip, ominously suggestive of insanity. His monstrosity is linked to the mystery of his background, and it is his wife's suspicion about his real identity that most jeopardises her. As Rough tells her, 'You got into his personality, and that made you dangerous to him.' Secrets are integral to these Walbrook roles. They signify resistance to the shared ethos of 1940s 'communal' British cinema, and mark his difference (hence, layers of identity are concealed, just as Adolf Wohlbrück is kept buried by the good manners of Anton). A tense denouement here sees Bauer physically bound to a chair, deranged by the realisation that his wife has all along been in possession of the jewels he has lusted for. The ropes which now forcibly harness him supplant the psychic control which has abandoned him and serve as a visual expression of society's coercive power.

In *Queen of Spades*, an impoverished Russian soldier fixates on an ancient Countess's devilish secret for winning at cards. Insinuating his way to her via her ward Lizaveta, he terrifies the Countess to death before he can extract the key, although her spirit later divulges the mysteries of her Faustian pact with the proviso that he marry her ward. Rejected by Lizaveta, he risks his earnings on a game of cards. But fate cheats him of his fortune and he is left ridiculed, penniless and insane. Dickinson's highly stylised mise-en-scène is matched by performances from both Walbrook and Edith Evans which sustain the atmosphere of theatrical excess, role-playing and artifice. As with *Gaslight*, Walbrook's monstrosity is enacted on a fantastic stage – here displaced not only into the early nineteenth century but also to Russia. Seething with class resentment and material ambition, wary of his mirrored reflection and presented throughout as an unsympathetic victim of his obsession, Walbrook is again a monster. 'It was like looking into the eyes of Satan,' Lizaveta confesses, and a close-up of Walbrook writing masqueraded love-letters pans to a spider's web on his desk, dissolves to a grotesquely extreme close-up of the spider, and then superimposes this image on to Lizaveta's pillow as she sleeps alongside it. While the film proved too exotic for some reviewers,[29] one particularly commended Walbrook's 'two screams'.[30] These 'shock horror' moments, as Walbrook confronts the dead Countess, echo the primitive shrieks of the expressionist stage.

We are brought back to the 'attractive brute' Boris Lermontov, Walbrook's homage to the German stage, with Powell and Pressburger also stamping their own cosmopolitan credentials as they had done almost a decade earlier with Conrad Veidt. Specific allusion is made in *The Red*

Shoes to Walbrook's *The Student of Prague*. Having renounced Vicky Page because of her love for Julian Craster, Lermontov is found alone in his darkened room (vampirically, he is often in shadows). His fingers twitch nervously; he punches his fist into the palm of his hand; and grunting with fury he approaches his mirrored reflection and smashes his fist through the glass (*The Student of Prague* concludes with Walbrook shooting the reflection which has become his pursuing 'other'). Lermontov's partial collapse here anticipates his final ruin. Using all his mesmeric 'charm' to tempt her, Svengali-like, he lures Vicky back to the ballet. Lermontov coaxes Vicky to 'put on the red shoes': his arm behind her, she sits on his knee, like a ventriloquist and his dummy (throughout, he has insisted to his protégée that he 'will do the talking'). The young acolyte's acquiescence to the impresario's will is a metaphor, a warning to all those fans too readily seduced by the dubious charms of a matinée idol. Yet not at home either within marriage or within Lermontov's system, Vicky exits from the film by leaping balletically to her death. It is at this stage that a drastic inversion takes place. Lermontov's system collapses; the all-seeing impresario becomes the object of the gaze, onstage, transfixed by the theatre spotlight.

In an 'Afterword to the Actor' suffixed to his tragedy *Die Verführung* in 1916, Paul Kornfeld advocated a particular style of acting. The actor should 'dare to spread his arms out wide and with a sense of soaring speak as he has never spoken before in his life ... Let him not be ashamed that he is acting, let him not deny the theatre ... Let him abstract from the attributes of reality and be nothing but the representative of thought, feeling or Fate.'[31] This is the wild abandon Walbrook aims for. Devastated by Vicky's death, Lermontov becomes a figure of naked rage, every part the ecstatic 'hero'. As Powell memorably recalls: 'he was going to play the scene like a marionette, like the husk of the cool, confident, polished individual we had known ... his voice ... bleached, mechanical, like that of a ventriloquist's dummy.'[32] The crew of the film were nevertheless astonished at the electrified screech ripped from him, 'like an animal trapped in agony.' His voice's tone is the primeval, dehumanized howl of a tortured human spirit.

Dynamics of inclusion and exclusion characterise much of Walbrook's British film career. A figure of the margins, he is either semi-incorporated, romantically exoticised or fearfully demonised. But a further point needs to be made. In a sense with *The Red Shoes* he *necessarily* remains outside the narrative itself. Cast as an apparently godlike father-figure (and an *essence* of art), he transcends mundane reality. He is here the *alter ego* of the auteur (in its most stridently heroic guise). While in *Blimp* he simply reflects Pressburger's experience as an alien in wartime, here his role is more formally innovative: with the 'Ballet Lermontov' a metaphor for

Powell and Pressburger's 'Archers' production company, Walbrook's persona is Powell's self-reflexive comment upon his own film-making process. As the key device structuring the narrative, he embodies authorial confidence and willed-for authorial omnipotence: a projection into the work of Powell's own obsession with cinema. Lermontov's onstage address which concludes *The Red Shoes* is also an address directly to the cinema audience (while the spotlight fixing him to the theatre curtain reminds us of the directed beam from the projector behind us). Lermontov is formally lifted from the world of the film and assumes metanarrative proportions. This superhuman quality characterises Walbrook's last significant role as the protean compère guiding the proceedings in Max Ophuls's *La Ronde* (France, 1950). Another puppet-master, he is again the director's substitute (in one blatantly meta-cinematic moment, Walbrook is shown literally slicing out excerpts from the film we are watching). Transcending the signifying system of the film, he hovers above the embedded narrative(s) with customary well-attired charm. He remains free (bound only to an artistic heritage of romantic idealism, of impossible dreams and high-vaulting ambition). As he introduces his nameless 'character' to the camera, 'Am I the author? The compère? The passer-by? I am you, any one of you. The incarnation of your desire – your desire *to know everything*.'

Notes

1   Antonia Lant, *Blackout: Reinventing Women for Wartime British Audiences* (Princeton University Press, Princeton, 1991), p. 197.

2   To *Picturegoer Weekly* (3 August 1935), the film was 'an outstanding feature', and Adolf Wohlbrück 'excellent'. Magazine and newspaper clippings are collected on microfiche and may conveniently be consulted at the British Film Institute library in London. Where comprehensive references cannot be cited, articles may be found on the BFI file for Anton Walbrook.

3   Margaret Burrows, 'Vienna's Idol Follows in Ivor Novello's Footsteps: The Story of Three Lives', *Film Pictorial*, 14 August 1937, 12.

4   Leonard Wallace, 'Meet Anton Walbrook', *Film Weekly*, 7 August 1937, 14.

5   Tom Dysart, 'Anton Walbrook', *Film Weekly*, 25 January 1937, 21. For Dysart Walbrook is 'something between a William Powell and a Robert Montgomery', and he notes that Powell replaced Walbrook when *Maskerade* was re-made by MGM as *Escapade* (Robert Z. Leonard, 1935).

6   Tom Burdon, 'Welcome to Walbrook', *Picturegoer* 1 January 1938, 17.

7   Max Green, 'Acting is in his Blood', *Picturegoer*, 25 October 1937, 17.

8   Sylvia Terry-Smith, *Picturegoer*, 27 April 1940, 11.

9   Lotte Eisner suggests that German 'talkies' favoured Austrian actors too, where their 'softer speech' was more congenial than harsher German voices. See Lotte Eisner, *The Haunted Screen: Expressionism in the German Cinema and the Influence of Max Reinhardt* (Secker & Warlburg, London, 1973), p. 312.

10 Kevin Gough-Yates, 'The British Feature Film as a European Concern: Britain and the Émigré Film-Maker, 1933-45', in Günther Berghaus, ed., *Theatre and Film in*

Exile: German Artists in Britain, 1933–1945 (Berg Publishers, Oxford, 1989), p. 154.

11 For a fuller account of the reaction to *Colonel Blimp*, see Michael Powell and Emeric Pressburger, *The Life and Death of Colonel Blimp* (Faber & Faber, London, 1994), and Ian Christie, ed., *Powell, Pressburger and Others* (BFI, London, 1978). The most sustained and notorious attack at the time was from E. W. and M. M. Robson, *The Shame and Disgrace of Colonel Blimp: The True Story of the Film* (The Sidneyan Society, London, 1942).

12 *Daily Express*, 16 August 1967.

13 *Daily Telegraph*, 10 August 1967.

14 *Daily Mail*, 16 August 1967.

15 *Variety*, 16 August 1967.

16 Some accounts give his birth date as 19 November 1896.

17 Some doubt exists as to Walbrook's film debut: most accounts, including his own published in interviews, cite *Salto Mortale*. However, Nicholas Thomas, ed., *International Dictionary of Films & Filmmakers* (St James Press, Detroit, 1992), has his debut as *Mater Dolorosa* (1922). Nevertheless, it was with 'talkies' that Walbrook began to make any real impact.

18 Burrows, *Film Pictorial*, 12.

19 Michael Powell, *A Life in Movies* (Mandarin, London, 1992), p. 639.

20 David Shipman, *The Great Movie Stars: The Golden Years*, 2nd edn (Macdonald, London, 1989), p. 595.

21 The Vicky/Lermontov relationship is often seen as a heterosexual codification of that between Nijinsky and Diaghilev, and Powell concedes that Walbrook's performance is 'filled with passion, integrity and, yes, with homosexuality'. Michael Powell, *Million-Dollar Movie* (Mandarin, London, 1993), p. 279. As a marker of the gay appropriation of *The Red Shoes*, Mike Nichol's *Birdcage* (1996) has its camp drag star, Albert, hysterically repeating Walbrook's 'Miss Victoria Page will not dance tonight!'

22 Burrows, *Film Pictorial*, 12.

23 See two unlabelled news cuttings (dated 24 October 1938 and 24 November 1938) on the British Film Institute's 'Walbrook' micro-file.

24 Burrows, *Film Pictorial*, 12. The stage musical *Call Me Madam* was similarly publicised ('some of the old-time Ivor Novello matinee-magic is back in show business', *Daily Express*, 13 August 1952).

25 Edward Gordon Craig, *On the Art of the Theatre* (reprinted Heinemann Educational Books, London, 1980), p. 61.

26 Michael Patterson, *The Revolution in German Theatre, 1900–1933* (Routledge & Kegan Paul, London, 1981), p. 58.

27 *The Times*, 10 August 1967.

28 George Turner, 'Gaslight', *American Cinematographer*, 76.1 (December 1995), 93.

29 The *Evening Standard* (17 March 1949) found it 'a little too harassed and melodramatic', the *Daily Express* (18 March 1949) 'a gloomy film', while *The Observer* (20 March 1949) thought it 'overstylishly brought to the screen'. The *Sunday Graphic*'s reviewer (20 March 1949), noted Walbrook's 'particularly hysterical performance' but conceded reluctantly that hysteria is 'exactly what the part requires'.

30 *Sunday Chronicle*, 20 March 1949.

31 Quoted in Patterson, *Revolution*, p. 79.

32 Powell, *A Life in Movies*, p. 639.

'Queen of British hearts': Margaret Lockwood revisited

7

I touched her nob, I touched her nob

In her autobiography *Lucky Star* (1955) Margaret Lockwood described an encounter with fans on her 1945 personal appearance tour.

> Inside the cinema I had felt a most peculiar thumping at the back of my head as I had been escorted down the main aisle to go up to the stage. And then I heard an excited voice yelling, 'I touched her nob, I touched her nob' and one woman had been been patting me quite heftily, on the top of my head. After the appearance there were so many people waiting for me outside that it was impossible for me to reach my own car – a large Rolls which the studio had provided. I was carried off my feet, willy-nilly, away from the car – when I spied another one, driven by a chauffeur of a firm who often used to drive me. I appealed to him and he tugged me to safety. Then he began. 'People! There was a woman standing here for hours waiting to see you and she was holding a baby in her arms. When you came out and all the crowd surged forward she got very excited and went with them. Five minutes later she was back saying, "The baby, the baby, oh my Gawd I lost me baby. I 'ad 'im in me arms a moment ago".'[2]

She was Britain's most famous film actress, and her anecdote suggests the excitement she generated. Though the chauffeur adds a residual male-rescuing-female decoration to the narrative, the dominating presences, with their fervid fan devotion, are both females and clearly lower-class. That they were so enraptured by their icon, whom the *Daily Worker* critic described not unkindly as 'a thoroughly normal middle class woman, more strong minded than the average',[3] testifies to the acumen of the Gainsborough producer Edward Black's insight that 'Margaret Lockwood had something with which every girl in the suburbs could identify herself'.[4] 'The suburbs' is ambiguous. It might cover the upper-middle class (from a *nouveau* fraction of which Iris Henderson in *The Lady Vanishes*, Hitchcock, 1938, comes), the lower-middle class (Nurse

Catherine in *Bank Holiday*, Reed, 1938), and the working class (Jenny Sunley in *The Stars Look Down*, Reed, 1939), and Black, emphasising her popularity, no doubt intended the widest meaning. The 1940s were a great period for British female stars. Besides Lockwood there were Celia Johnson, Patricia Roc, Jean Kent, Valerie Hobson, Phyllis Calvert and Deborah Kerr, but only Anna Neagle rivalled her sustained popularity. Jackie Stacey's *Star Gazing* (1994) argues that 1940s British women film-goers invested their fantasies in the utopic otherness of Hollywood female stars rather than native stars associated with the constraints on femininity and consumerism in early postwar Britain.[5] Persuasive as this may be, it fails to register the kind of identifications Lockwood excited. Those low-achieving West Bromwich schoolgirls, cited in contemporary sociological research as imitating her, underwrite this.[6]

Lockwood's mass popularity, though, was in conflict with much criticism of the time which, in hindsight, can be seen as fearing a melodramatic feminisation of British cinema. Leonard Mosley's *Daily Express* piece is representative in its attack on the post-*Wicked Lady* (Arliss, 1945) star. 'I just cannot believe in Miss Margaret Lockwood as a femme fatale ... What I see is no wicked lady, but a nice ordinary girl, with looks and personality as apt to rouse heady admiration and racing pulses in me as a side view of the Albert Hall!'[7] Interaction between ordinariness and extraordinariness is accepted as a constituent of star personae, but here suggests a fraudulence which Lockwood's fans cannot see through, though the critic does. However, while reassessments of Gainsborough have left such tirades looking quaintly chauvinistic, later, more approving criticism has had its own unacknowledged tendencies to simplify, reducing the star's many roles to 'The Wicked Lady' and her complex connotations to an unlikely unity of transgression and sexual appetite,[8] whereas even the vulgar journalism registered, though it misinterpreted, a tension between the ordinary and extraordinary which, though demanding redefinition, is fundamental to Lockwood.

Those 1940s critics' sense of the disparity they mocked was sharpened by a paradoxical homeliness in the immense publicity surrounding the 'Queen of British Hearts'. Though she was constantly presented as an object of glamour by the recurrent discourse of fashion in and around her films (for example the typical press book of *Madness of the Heart*, Bennett, 1949, with its double-page spread 'Margaret Lockwood's Fashion story in "Madness of the Heart"'),[9] her private life was unremarkable, her divorce unsensational and the melodrama of her relations with her mother unknown till much later.[10] Even with her pre-eminence as the screen's representative of British fashion there was a contradiction, for she mostly presented herself as uninterested in glamour offscreen, even being ticked off by Maurice Ostrer for appearing in public casually dressed.[11] Screen glamour apart, publicity could only celebrate her professionalism, industry and devotion to her daughter.[12] Nothing in the autobiography contradicts the view of her unremarkable middle-classness, so what is interesting is the tension between that and those qualities in her (more her screen images than offscreen persona) that excited passionate cross-class female identifications. Or, to redefine it, it may be something in the very disparity between her screen roles and many of her offscreen, and even onscreen, significations that led her audience to discover in her so intensely reflections of both their own ordinariness and fantasies of extraordinariness.

Reappraisals of Gainsborough melodrama posit female audiences experiencing, especially through *The Wicked Lady*, the excitements of transgressive release. What are called here the White Queen melodramas (*Love Story*, Arliss, 1944; *Hungry Hill*, Hurst, 1946; *Jassy*, Knowles, 1947; *The White Unicorn*, Knowles, 1947; *Madness of the Heart*, Bennett, 1949) have been less discussed, but, like the Black Queen melodramas (*The Man in Grey*, Arliss, 1943; *The Wicked Lady*, 1945, and *Bedelia*, Comfort, 1946), these melodramas of suffering also primarily address a female audience and differentiate themselves from the mainstream of the period by their concentration on personal, and female, desire. A brief comparison with her longlasting rival, Anna Neagle, is instructive.[13] Neagle's later career mixed two genres inimical to Lockwood, society comedies and historical biopics – neither as popular across the classes as Lockwood's cultivation of the domain of the psychosexual and, often, the role of the outsider. The two stars meet obliquely on a terrain marked out by feminism, but whereas Neagle's feminism was self-consciously manifested in playing national heroines from Florence Nightingale to Amy Johnson, neither Lockwood's films nor her offscreen utterances suggest that she deliberately chose roles later applauded as subversive. Not only does Lockwood – associated with the costume film – not appear in historical biopics, but she plays a marginal role in the war cinema (a civilian Czech in *Night Train to Munich*, Reed, 1940), never appearing in uniform, and swiftly prevented by the narrative in *Love Story* when Felicity attempts it. (Fascinatingly she wears in the later part of *Night Train* an outfit cut in military style, but with floral insignia on the collar, and in heart shapes over each breast.) Ironically, Lockwood's indirections, related to no conscious star-as-auteur programme – her comments on her films are unenlightening and she was originally antagonistic toward two of her great 'bad girl' parts, Jenny Sunley and Hester[14] – have interested critics more than Neagle's explicit patriotic feminism. Margaret Lockwood is clearly a star of the type whose most interesting meanings come into play in spite of what we can recover of her feelings and opinions.

The perfect-spirited partner

Across a mixture of genres – adventure romance in *Doctor Syn* (Neill, 1937) and *Rulers of the Sea* (Hollywood, Lloyd, 1939); a musical in *I'll Be Your Sweetheart* (Guest, 1945); pastoral romance in *Owd Bob* (Stevenson, 1938); romantic comedy (family inflection) in *Quiet Wedding* (Asquith, 1941) and *Dear Octopus* (French, 1945); backstage drama in *A Girl Must Live* (Reed, 1939); a western/Shirley Temple vehicle (invidious prospect for a Hollywood debut) in *Susanna of the Mounties* (Seiter, 1939); thriller romance in *The Lady Vanishes* (1938) and *Night Train to Munich* (1940) – Lockwood rose to stardom as the number one young romantic heroine of British film. The role, mixing conventional with unconventional, was appealing enough to bear recapitulation in late variations such as *Highly Dangerous* (Baker, 1950) and *Trouble in the Glen* (Wilcox, 1954).

Lockwood's early characters are intelligent, high-spirited and rebellious, and, whether pursuing careers permanently like Edie Storey, the music-hall star in *I'll Be Your Sweetheart*, or, more likely, as a prelude to marriage, they are never feckless. Whatever variations she plays on the type, Lockwood also captures perfectly, in her class-coded body movements – like her speech patterns, middle-class but casual and democratic enough to have wide appeal – gestures redolent of, or aspired to across, that wide-ranging suburban audience Black saw as hers. Because she evolves differently in the mid 1940s as she becomes a woman's star first, and a star for male eyes second, it is important to note how, initially, she is presented as much for male admiration, the Perfect Spirited Partner, as for female emulation, when she adroitly adjusts her coat in the motion of sitting down to tea in *The Lady Vanishes*, balances with mundane, stork-like grace to fix her shoe as she and Geoff search for a hotel room in *Bank Holiday*, or embodies middle-class confidence in her exchanges with the hotelier in *The Lady Vanishes* ('Lead on, Boris!'). Such gestures help charmingly define a heroine possessing what Forrest Tucker in *Trouble in the Glen* admires as 'sand', later defined as 'spunk' and 'fighting heart'. In another late film, *Highly Dangerous*, the scientist heroine's entymology signals something similar about her which has frightened off boyfriends fainter-hearted than the hero (Dane Clark).

This heroine's trajectory may be conventional, but she exhibits multiple deconventionalizing traits, summarisable in six ways. First, putdowns of the hero. *The Lady Vanishes* and *Night Train to Munich* are full of these, not necessarily eleborately witty, but engagingly both slightly minatory and inviting (as where Redgrave's 'Do you like me?' gets the reply 'Not much'). Such fond but determined resistance to male egos suggest a desire not to be dominated. Second, she often has a complex relationship with her father – for example George Arliss's priest/pirate in *Dr Syn*, Will Fyffe in *Owd Bob* and *Rulers of Sea*, Orson Welles in *Trouble in the Glen*, and the paterfamilias in *Quiet Wedding*. Fraught but loving, this relationship suggests the heroine's uneasy father-fighting/father-emulating difficulties of definition in the wider patriarchal world. In the later melodramas (most forcefully in *The Wicked Lady*) the heroine will be more the mother's daughter, with Miss Froy in *The Lady Vanishes* a transitional instance. Third, often, without hurting her femininity, the daughter adopts male-reserved traits; for instance, Mary's determination in *Rulers of the Sea* to accompany the men to sea, and her rejection of the homebody's role of 'stroking the cat'; Imogene's bold look at Dennis during the church service that begins *Doctor Syn*, and the long egalitarian gaze with which the heroine returns Dallas's (David Farrar's) look at the wedding which ends *Quiet Wedding*. Fourth, her verbal aggression increases (via incidents like her tossing away of Gilbert's suitcase in *The Lady Vanishes*) to the 'temper' for which Edie Storey is known in *I'll Be Your Sweetheart*, where Michael Rennie describes her as Jekyll and Hyde, and escalates into the heroine committing minor violence on the hero. In *Doctor Syn* Imogene slaps Dennis's face when he misjudges her, something that leads her father to celebrate her as 'a chip off the old block'. In *Quiet Wedding*, after berating Dallas for being 'such a soppy little bore', she responds to the clergyman's wedding rehearsal direction – 'Come on, dear, give him your hand' – by slapping her fiancé's face. Such moments (like another in *I'll Be Your Sweetheart*) release suggestions of subterranean frustrations related to the extreme violences of the wicked ladies, and to the female-on-female attacks in both sets of melodramas, that famous serial face slapping between Lockwood and Patricia Roc in *The Wicked Lady*, *Love Story* and *Jassy*. Fifth, the tendency for even the early Lockwood to be presented as problematically split. So in *Doctor Syn* she is the daughter of both priest and pirate; in *A Girl Must Live*, *Girl in the News* and *Highly Dangerous* she adopts aliases; in *I'll Be Your Sweetheart* and *Quiet Wedding* she plays women ambivalently wanting and not wanting marriage; and in *A Place of One's Own* as Annette Allenby she is possessed by a ghostly victimised second self, Elizabeth Harkness, from a darker age of male oppression. Sixth, an associated tendency to juxtapose Lockwood significantly with other actresses, not just for contrastive definition, as when her median charms are placed against Peggy Ashcroft and Celia Johnson in *Quiet Wedding* and *Dear Octopus* respectively – two actresses whose profound but narrower appeal underlines the greater cross-class inclusiveness of Lockwood's popularity. More complex parallelisms look forward to the memorable pairings of Lockwood with the prefectorial Phyllis Calvert and the more tennis-clubby Patricia Roc, as two interesting actresses, Linden Travers and Margaretta Scott, both, in monochrome, bearing a strong part resemblance to Lockwood, create doppelgänger effects around her. Scott is the murderess with whom Lockwood is confused in *Girl in the News* (Reed, 1940) and the wealthy woman with whom Joe has an affair in *The Stars Look Down*, whilst Travers plays the lawyer's mistress in *The Lady Vanishes* and John Lodge's wife in *Bank Holiday*.

The most complex of these figures is Nurse Catherine in *Bank Holiday*, her narrative trajectory the least resolved. Advanced enough to consider herself 'justified' in spending a weekend with her boyfriend (and not to allow Geoff to assume she is sacrificing herself), she is also a devoted nurse deeply affected by the hospital death of the wife of a slightly older man, to whom she offers comfort. Her encounter with the elegant, grief-stricken Stephen (John Lodge) triggers discontent with her ordinary boyfriend, whom she leaves, returning London in order to prevent Stephen's suicide. At the end, she stands as nurse by his bedside. Riven, she has moved between two men, one of them prosaically embodying her own class restrictions, the other higher-classed and romantic. Maternal in her nursing role, she is also eager for sexual experience, but, like the heroine of *Quiet Wedding*, with her phobia of public imaginings of her wedding night, seems to resent the cruder processes of sexual objectification, at least those of her un-ideal boyfriend, whose gaze at her bathing-suited body upsets her. Such ambiguities, like the implied union with Stephen, are unresolved, the latter very tenuous indeed, given his bereavement only the day before.

Black Queens and White Queens

Bank Holiday is exceptional. Elsewhere the PSP achieves couplehood and the insider becomes outsider, for example where the secretary, Penny Fenton, in *Dear Octopus*, marries into the Randolph family. Sometimes these marriages are between class equals, occasionally the heroine even has an advantage, but usually she is discreetly allied with a more advantaged male. In *A Girl Must Live*, where the heroine marries the Earl of Pangborough, Lockwood is flanked by two mercenary beauties, Renée Houston, all flinty experience, and Lilli Palmer, all calculating charm, whose unabashed golddigging deflects observations that the heroine, though nicer, still participates in the manhunt. However, the role that directly prefigures the Black Queens is Jenny Sunley in *The Stars Look Down* (1939). If there are sometimes subterranean suggestions in the PSPs of motives more pragmatic than love, the opposite is true with

Jenny, where the harsh governing perspective is obvious in the presentation of her calculating selfishness, yet in a pathetic gesture like the imperfectly imagined upper-class refinement with which Lockwood offers her hand socially, her resentment of her entrapping environment provokes sympathy. 'I was meant to be a lady, not a skivvy for someone who's a rotten failure!' Mean-minded though her outburst is, it links her to Hester's compelling articulation of her desires in *The Man in Grey*, 'I never knew such unobtrusive comfort could exist, that flowers could bloom so sweetly in winter, or that fires could burn all day so recklessly for people who sometimes never come in' and to Barbara's famous assertion, 'I've got brains and looks and personality. I want to use them!'

With the PSPs Barbara's triad is always evident, but questions of use tend to dissolve into the romantic promise of the films' endings. In the post-1944 Black and White Queen melodramas, the obstructions to use become more serious and the dissolving of problematics in romantic love is doubted. In the Black Queen melodramas, the implication is that the obstructions are so extreme that only as amoral villainess can the heroine achieve her goals (temporarily), through deceit, murder and jettisoning romantic love. While romantic love returns as the ambivalent centre with the White Queens, the Black Queens pursue sexuality for excitement (Barbara) and for power (Hester and Bedelia, the latter serially murdering her wealthy husbands). Clearly the female sexual adventure and the forbidden sadism and masochism enacted in the Lockwood/Mason relationships in both *The Man in Grey* and *The Wicked Lady* were key factors in the films' appeal to female audiences, together with the having-your-cake-and-eating-it aspect of the moral and patriarchal endings, which, significantly in the more popular *The Wicked Lady*, is playfully ironised to the point of parody. At the furthest extreme from this, *Bedelia*, both film and heroine, offers the possibility of identification only 'against the grain' of the heroine's pathology and a narrative structure controlled by male investigative viewpoints, constraints only momentarily abraded by the anti-heroine's sudden outburst against men and the use of the word 'divine' – the last with its teasing suggestions of discontent with the 'divinity' of the patriarchal order.

Across the melodramas two kinds of splitting act out intensely the less dramatic fissures noted of the PSP heroines. The Black Queen films externalise internal contradictions by projecting opposing bad and good heroines, in *The Man in Grey* Hester and Clarissa (Phyllis Calvert), in *The Wicked Lady* Barbara and Caro (Patricia Roc). But, complicating this, the audience are not only invited to ally with the bad heroine as outsider and rebel/critic (and part-detached from the good heroine by her naivety and complacency) but also prompted to see that the opposition is also a rela-

Margaret Lockwood and James Mason. The British 1940s megastars in the Gainsborough sensation *The Wicked Lady*.

tion, and that Hester and Clarissa, Barbara and Caro (and, more vestigially, Bedelia and Ellen/Anne Crawford) are symbiotically linked versions of femininity.

The White Queens, contrastingly, fracture internally into the heroine's
multiple 'selves', to take a simple instance, Felicity and Lissa in *Love Story*.
Thus in *The White Unicorn* there are three Lucys – the older framing narrator, and, in the flashbacks, the younger selves of her two marriages,
with even a fourth in the alter ego of Charlotte Fontenelle, the fantasised
ghost who represents the heroine's romantic aspirations. In *Hungry Hill*,
these fracturings become almost dizzying, with Fanny Rosa becoming, in
foreshortened succession, over the family saga, almost every positive and
negative role open to women, from young girl to ancient matriarch, via
multiple marital and maternal roles, and extreme abjection at the loss of
them. At the least the succession of roles played out encourages the spectator to see these heroines as more than equal in complexity to the males,
but more disadvantaged in the often irreconcilable demands laid upon
them.

A moment in *The White Unicorn* crystallises how late 1940s Lockwood
as female alter ego outweighs Lockwood as object of male desire. During
Lucy's Finnish honeymoon an old maidservant takes her to the sauna.
Undressing, Lockwood is offscreen, so we see just the homely old
woman's response, as sole viewer of Lockwood's nakedness, which is to
look and murmer admiringly. The implications of this concrete rendering
of a privileging of the female audience (62 per cent in 1946; it became a
masculine majority after 1950)[15] permeate the later female-centred melodramas, something reflected in *The White Unicorn*'s structuring its narrative through female-to-female narration, as Lockwood and Joan
Greenwood swap biographies, mirroring the film's and the star's address
to their primary audience. The replacement of Mason and Granger by less
sexually charismatic actors such as Ian Hunter and Dennis Price further
foregrounds the heroine rather than the couple. In these films romantic
love, as woman's fascination and destiny, but also as transitory and even
perhaps delusory, is central. But only one of these narratives – *Love Story* –
ends rapturously, and even then the heroine is dying and the hero likely to
be killed, while the 'happy' endings of *The White Unicorn* and *Madness of
the Heart* are both replete with ambiguities for those open to reading them.

A (literal) light on Lockwood in performance

As nemesis overtakes Barbara in *The Wicked Lady* she confesses to Kit
(Michael Rennie). Shocked, he leaves, and she dies alone. Though I com-

ment on Lockwood's acting below, my primary interest here is in what is best described as a powerful technological mediation of her physical image, through an intense bleaching light which all but erases the dominating feature of her face, her darkly painted over-mouth, along with other marks of artifice, her arced eyebrows and the famous beauty spot (augmenting a natural mole), which are nearly as much diminished. Though this lighting can be recuperated thematically (the light of truth shining on Barbara), it sustains another reading connected intricately with Lockwood's physiognomy, and underlined by her scenic transformation from the outlandish (highwayman's costume, painted mouth further dramatised by the blood at the corner) to the mundane (her unadorned nightgown, sudden regret and almost naked features). However film performance, amid the ensemble of mediating elements, is defined, Lockwood projects complex thematics, despite 1940s critiques of her acting – for example the *Daily Mail's* declaration that in *Look Before You Love* she brought 'to Rio and Monte Carlo the practical passion of Miss Margate, 1948',[16] or the cavilling at the star's supposedly missing impersonatory skills in *Jassy*: 'Margaret Lockwood's informal relation to the parts she plays is not unlike that of the pantomime principal boy who as giantkiller, Robin Hood or Chinese boy, is in fact just herself.'[17]

In fact exceptional impersonations such as Nina's expansive Russian accent and un-English tactility in *Give Us the Moon* (1944) and her unerringly observed middle-aged ex-barmaid in *Cast a Dark Shadow* (1956) expand appreciation of Lockwood's virtuosity, but underline the narrowness of her usual performative terrain, how seldom she strays from the Norwood suburban and accompanying speech patterns, the latter, though, less affected than most of her contemporaries' (certainly a further aid to cross-class identification).[18] Although her sketchiest approximation of regional working-class speech in *The Stars Look Down* is hard to generalise from, Anna's lack in *Night Train to Munich* of any trace of Middle-European accent (barely rationalised by her statement that 'I was at school there', i.e. England), suggests that Lockwood's personificatory attractions often outweigh impersonatory requirements. This does not exclude many compelling elements of mimesis like her performances in *The Man in Grey* and *The Wicked Lady*, the first within parameters of psychological realism, the second cultivating caricatural comedy. In Hester's first appearance, dressed in black, almost dwarfed by her sombre bonnet, and working to great effect a rather frazzled bitter expression, Lockwood produces complex defensive aggressive nuances, half Jane Eyre, half Becky Sharp, in extreme contrast to the household prayers in *The Wicked Lady* where her hypocritical piety is displayed with genial hyper-ostensiveness in a wholly different gestural framework. But while it is important to establish Lockwood's mastery of impersonatory codes, the path I want to follow here relates more to the star's being 'just herself'.

Stars bring to their roles basic physical characteristics that underlie everything they do, capable of significant but limited modulation, for example the shock in *Cardboard Cavalier* (1949), or when Hester plays Desdemona in *The Man in Grey*, as the perennially dark-haired Lockwood goes blond. It is the raison d'être of stars to be gazed at, and Lockwood is no exception, her most protracted instance being the delirious piano-playing sequences in *Love Story*, which present a lyrically concentrated version of what close-ups give in the narratives and publicity photographs give extrafilmically, the fundamental features and kinesics that underlie all the star's impersonations.

If, remembering Roland Barthes's 'The Face of Garbo', one attempts to characterise 'The Face of Lockwood' in its 'infinite complexity of morphological functions',[19] paradox dominates, pairing elements of the exotic with the English. On the one hand, the dark, rather coarsely wavy hair framing the pale face, which actually can appear darker in monochrome, and the exotically painted mouth, are metaphorically consonant with her playing a (half) gipsy in *Jassy*, and with the hints of otherness in her names, Barbara in *The Wicked Lady* and Mrs Barbary – 'The Barbary' – in *The Man in Grey* (where she becomes the stage wife of the Moor), all of which touch the Karachi–Norwood axis of her childhood and the journalist's quip about Margate, Monte Carlo and Rio. Conversely, there are the many median elements – her features' neatness, the slightly prominent nose, the prettiness rather than sultriness – often cohering in movements of sensible, brusque charm – which give rise to those perceptions of suburbanness. All these – underwritten by two of her film titles, *Girl in the News* and *A Girl Must Live* – influence her presentation as the generic end-of-the-1930s English girl and her comfortableness in the upholstery of Edwardian costume, and abet that element of the anodyne sometimes in her screen presence, especially in *Madness of the Heart*, where she is almost frumpish. Either set of semiotic potentialities can be emphasised to inflect towards one pole of the antitheses Insider/Outsider, Domestic/Exotic, Heroine/Anti-heroine, with the famous artificial beauty spot occupying an ambivalent median position, exotic and decadent, but recalling a very English period, the Restoration; a mark of extreme artificiality, yet at the same time a common contemporary cosmetic device. These polarities do not constitute two separate masks since one tends to be vestigially present in the other, giving, in an actress whose technique and films are not noticeably reflexive, a constant feeling of role-playing (unsympathetically interpreted above).

But the dominating signifier of the facial ensemble is the mouth, its naturally thin lips by the late 1930s a construct enhancing the upper lip's thinness against a thickened lower one, while further elongating the upper by painting the arcs of the Cupid's bow not centrally but either side of a pronounced central gap. Additionally, asymmetry is cultivated, with either arc raised higher, occasionally with the fleeting suggestion of the after-effects of a minute stroke. A marker of individuality in Lockwood's beauty, it easily inflects (through her mouth's downward turn) into 'temper' in the PSPs, alienation (*The Man in Grey, Bedelia*), and even the gothic in *The Man in Grey* and moments in *Love Story*'s pianistic portrait gallery. The more sinister of these connotations are foregrounded in *Trent's Last Case* (Wilcox, 1952) where the portrait of Margaret Masterson /Lockwood, sketched by Trent (Michael Wilding), shows her caricaturally frowning and constricted, provoking dialogue about her resemblance to Lady Macbeth. But it is in *The Wicked Lady* that extreme elements are most overt, where a latent voluptuousness in Lockwood's facial features (glimpsable only in full face, and almost subliminally, in earlier roles, as when Leslie James reads her letter at the beginning of *A Girl Must Live* or when Iris, shot from a low angle, wakes up to find Miss Froy gone in *The Lady Vanishes*) is combined with an exaggeration of every element of arti-fice, but most of all the lips, no longer subdued by pale lipsticks but thick-ened to the point where Joan Crawford's 'postbox' mouth is inevitably invoked, and painted with such a dark gloss that they reflect points of light.

One last version of the predictable critique of Lockwood is made by Gavin Lambert in Stephen Frears's 'Personal [film] History of the British Cinema', *Typically British*, where, apropos of Barbara's death, he says that 'what was fun about the movie was that the whole idea of wickedness was so suburban, really'.[20] Again, the slight condescension hides something interesting. It is my contention that it is precisely what embarrasses the journalists and amuses the fastidious: the combination of the suburban with the exotic, the sense of ordinariness dressing up as extraordinari-ness, that, far from being the actress's fatal flaw, underlies all the other factors that constitute Lockwood's appeal to her 1940s female audience, making her, rather than any other actress, the necessary embodiment of the Black and White Queens. In her most extreme role in *The Wicked Lady*, the unmistakable allusion to Joan Crawford's lips functions less as a simple sign of secondarisation than as a dramatising of Lockwood's bonding with her audience, as if the star, in her most outrageous imper-sonation, was playing out a heightened version of her audience's everyday cosmetic and fashion transformations in accord with screen actress images (of which Crawford's mouth, with all its strange mixture of glamour and tortured aggression, was the most excessive) into imagined heightenings and extraordinarinesses. The wipe-off, the literal decosmeticisation performed by the death-scene lighting trope (whatever its meanings in the narrative), enacts dramatically the ordinary end of the ordinary – extraordinary, suburban – exotic polarity of the 1940s 'Queen of British Hearts'.

Notes

1 The rather compelling description comes from the *Madness of the Heart* Press-book held in the BFI Library.
2 Margaret Lockwood, *Lucky Star: The Autobiography of Margaret Lockwood* (Odhams Press, London, 1955), pp. 112–13.
3 Thomas Spencer, *Daily Worker*, 24 November 1955.
4 Alan Wood, *Mr Rank* (Hodder & Stoughton, London, 1952), p. 146.
5 Jackie Stacey, *Star Gazing* (Routledge, London, 1994).
6 Barbara Kesterton's Birmingham University PhD thesis is quoted by Sue Harper, *Picturing the Past* (BFI, London, 1994), pp. 138–9.
7 Leonard Mosley, 'Margaret is my Blind Spot', *Daily Express*, 15 August 1947. See also two defences of Lockwood: Eve Perrick, 'On Everybody's Toes', *Daily Express*, 3 December 1949, and Reg Whitley, 'This Girl Makes Me Scratch My Head', *Daily Mirror*, 25 July 1949, which both allude to anti-Lockwood criticisms.
8 Misleading generalisations from *The Wicked Lady* are common. See Janet Thumim's claim that Barbara is 'a typical heroine of the period', *Celluloid Sisters* (Macmillan, London and Basingstoke, 1993), p. 14, and Marcia Landy's description of Margaret Lockwood's 'usual role' as 'the headstrong female who is willing to violate convention in her quest for pleasure', *British Genres* (Princeton University Press, Princeton, 1991), p. 312. The three 'Black Queen' roles may be among her most memorable, but they are not typical, and even with them, except for Barbara, sexual pleasure is not the point. Bedelia wants money, Hester money and position, and if you observe Hester's face as she kisses Rohan, she looks distinctly sexually unmoved.
9 *Madness of the Heart* Press-book (BFI Library).
10 See obituary, *The Times*, 17 July 1990.
11 *Sunday Graphic*, 14 September 1955.
12 For instance, in *The White Unicorn* Press-book she is called 'Britain's favourite and hardest working star'; the *Madness of the Heart* Press-book says, 'she has few interests apart from her work'. An article purporting to be written by her in *Picturegoer* (9 December 1944), 'What's a Star to Do?', contradicts the accompanying cheesecake photograph by concentrating on purely professional matters.
13 See Sarah Street, 'Dover's White Cliffs', in *British National Cinema* (Routledge, London, 1997), pp. 124ff., for a discussion of Neagle.
14 See *Lucky Star*, pp. 76–7 and 98, and Hilton Tims, *Once a Wicked Lady* (Virgin, London, 1989), pp. 97–9 and 114–16.
15 These figures are quoted in Sue Harper and Vincent Porter, 'Cinema Audience Tastes in 1950s Britain', *Journal of Popular British Cinema*, 2, 67.
16 Quoted by Tims in *Once a Wicked Lady*, p. 153.
17 *Jassy* microfiche unattributed (BFI Library, London).

18 The *Daily Telegraph* obituary (17 July 1990), quotes the contemporaneous *Daily Telegraph* review of *Bank Holiday*.
19 Roland Barthes, 'The Face of Garbo', in *Mythologies* (Paladin, London, 1972), p. 64.
20 *Typically British* (BFI TV), first broadcast Channel 4, 2 September 1995.

James Mason: the man between

8

> In him inexplicably mixed appear'd
> Much to be loved and hated, sought and feared.
> (Byron, *Lara*)

No British film star has matched James Mason's blend of accursed beauty and doomed intensity. His career, as he himself remarked, resembled a three-act play:[1] the first act in Britain, the second in Hollywood and the third, by now no longer defined by leading-man roles, shuttling between Europe, the odd trip to Australia and America. The first phase sees him indelibly marked in the British cinema as a demonic lover whose appeal, establishing him as Britain's most popular male star in 1945, rests on a combination of romantic allure and Sadean fascination. In the second phase, this high-octane mix of flawed, irresistible charm makes him difficult to cast, as he drifts from heroic lover (*Caught*, Ophuls, 1948) to more characteristically troubled outsider (*The Reckless Moment*, Ophuls, 1949) to roles as dissenters and losers (*Julius Caesar*, Mankiewicz, 1953; *A Star Is Born*, Cukor, 1954, and *Bigger than Life*, Ray, 1956), parts that seem to reflect his own difficult offscreen adjustment to life in America. In the third phase, his age also by now disqualifying him from top billing, the cruelty of the persona is stretched to almost grand guignol dimensions in films such as *Mandingo* (Fleischer, 1975), and *Salem's Lot* (Hooper, 1979), though his dark humour and self-consciousness were allowed expression in late films such as *Age of Consent* (Powell, 1969) or *Spring and Port Wine* (Hammond, 1970).

Bigger than life

James Mason was born in Huddersfield in 1909. He was brought up in a well-to-do Yorkshire household, sent to one of Britain's top public schools, Marlborough College, and went up to Peterhouse, Cambridge to read architecture. While at Cambridge he took up acting and decided, despite the award of a first-class degree, to abandon architecture for the stage. After some work in the London theatre he was hired by Alexander Korda for his first film role in the 1934 production *The Return of Don Juan*. But this was a false start and he was eventually sacked from the film. This reverse was followed by a stint on the Dublin stage, where he played Brutus for the first time, in a production at the Gate Theatre, run by Michael Macliammoir, Hilton Edwards and Edward, Earl of Longford. Mason himself draws attention to Macliammoir's reference to his characteristically 'icy smile' and 'passionless voice',[2] highlighting what were to become key features of his screen appearances. After Ireland, he returned to England and eventually appeared in an insignificant film role, in *Late Extra* (Parker, 1935). This was followed by more negligible parts, but the importance in Mason's life of *Late Extra* was that it introduced him to the cameraman Roy Kellino whose wife Pamela would later become the first Mrs James Mason (1941). The daughter of Isidore Ostrer, head of Gaumont British, Pamela Kellino became one of the most influential figures in Mason's early film career. More negligible films followed before he teamed up with Pamela and others to form their own film company, a venture that led to *I Met a Murderer* (1939).

By this time Britain had already entered the war, but Mason refused to enlist in the armed services on the grounds of conscientious objection:

> The other thing that I wrote about in my statement was my abhorrence of war as an accepted means of settling international economic and political differences, institutionalised war in fact. I abhorred the glib acceptance in wartime of a totally alien code which we would quite properly condemn in the intervals of peace.[3]

The remarks are consistent with Mason's intelligent, thoughtful personality, but anxieties about his acting career cannot be discounted. At any rate these would probably not have been the sentiments of many of the characters with whom he had spectacular success in the next phase of his British career, the sadistic, psychopathic anti-heroes of his Gainsborough films (1942–47), such as *The Man in Grey* (Arliss, 1943), *The Wicked Lady* (Arliss, 1945), *Fanny by Gaslight* (Asquith, 1944) and *They Were Sisters* (Crabtree, 1945), co-starring the likes of Margaret Lockwood, Stewart Granger, Jean Kent, Phyllis Calvert and Patricia Roc. But even here, in what was arguably his most important moment in the British cinema (though *The Seventh Veil* (Compton Bennett, 1945) and *Odd Man Out* (Reed, 1946) were also hugely significant films), his knack for awkwardness led him into difficulties with influential people. There was, for instance, his undisguised contempt for producers, especially J. Arthur Rank. As he himself remarked: 'To me producers were men who polluted the artistic aspirations of writers, directors and actors; who responded only to the promptings of vulgar men in Wardour street; who were bad sports and bad losers.'[4] The clashes with producers did not go unnoticed by the press of the day ('Mason discovers it pays to be rude', wrote David Lewin in the *Daily Express*, 1948, 'Rank is the worst thing that has happened to the British Film Industry', quoting Mason).[5] A natural misanthropy mixed with a sharp eye for publicity probably caused these outbursts. Self-publicity was further pursued through writing, sometimes drawing on his reputation as a lady-killer or 'lady basher' to answer questions about his offscreen love life through journalistic pieces such as 'Yes, I Beat My Wife'.[6]

Like the Gainsborough melodramatic roles that fed off such self-publicity, his appearances in *The Seventh Veil* and *Odd Man Out* were equally successful, and eventually drew the attention of Hollywood's trade journals as well as *Time*, which eulogised his performance in *The Man in Grey*:

> It is possible the British matinee idol James Mason will be much better known hereafter. Swaggering through the title role, sneering like Laughton, barking like Gable and frowning like Laurence Olivier on a stormy night, he is likely to pick up many a feminine fan for himself in the US.[7]

Reviews such as this inevitably played a part in tempting Mason to America. He himself, though, gives as his reasons for leaving England the restricted number of quality productions in Britain as well as what he refers to as the 'wild sophisticated wit in many of the pre-war films and plays from America which had not yet been matched by anything that we had attempted in England ... I was powerfully influenced by thoughts of James Thurber, Robert Sherwood, Dorothy Parker, Preston Sturges, George Kaufman, Moss Hart, Herman Mankiewicz and many others'.[8] The stress on wit here indicates not only Mason's preference for roles with good dialogue but also his own slight air of detachment from the fictional worlds he helped create. There is a sense in which his whole career is surrounded if not by the aura of lofty ennui that characterised, say, the languid officer class mannerisms of George Sanders, then by an intellectual's cool distance from the melodramatic roles he traded in. Part of the excitement of Mason lies in his projection of intelligence, an arrogant scepticism towards not only his victims but also the very narratives in which he appears.

The move to America got off to a bad start. Mason became involved in a contractual dispute with an American producer, David E. Rose, and

offended the influential gossip columnist Louella Parsons, who did nothing to subvert his image as an uncooperative, awkward and swollen-
headed malcontent, an attitude that to further his own career Mason may
even have encouraged. After some work in the New York theatre, where
he played David in Jacques Devals's *Bathsheba*, and after winning the case
against Rose, he eventually landed in Hollywood, where his negative reputation duly preceded him. His first role here was in *Caught*, but the
attempt to redefine his screen villainy through a role that saw him rescuing Barbara Bel Geddes from the sadism of Robert Ryan was unsuccess-
ful, a venture that led to reassessment and some reversion to type in his
next film, also by Ophuls, *The Reckless Moment*, where the persona's dev-
ilry once more surfaced. The return to villainy was not, however, sustained in Hollywood, and he himself thought his career suffered as a
result.[9] He approved of Ophuls, and, whatever their shortcomings, these
films have proved with time to be significant episodes in his career.

Although there were several commercial flops during this period, as
Hollywood failed to decide how best to use him,[10] there are some films
that play an important part in Hollywood history, as regards not only
Mason's stardom but also the tradition of quality films in its classical
period: the divided patriot Brutus in *Julius Caesar* (Joseph L. Mankiewicz,
1953), the heroic loser in *The Desert Fox* (Hathaway, 1951), the Naziesque
villain in *The Prisoner of Zenda* (Thorpe, 1952), the tormented misan-
thrope in *A Star Is Born* or the fastidious, art-collecting saboteur in *North
by Northwest* (Hitchcock, 1959). A loser who dies in all of these films,
Mason projects life's underside. As in England, he offers his audience a
glimpse of their darker selves, the nightmare image of the average man.
In one of the many amusing sketches with which he decorates his autobiography, we see him appear in a self-portrait, 'Myself When Young',[11]
with a shock of dark hair, furrowed brow, raven-coloured eyes, toad-like
lips and jowl, a face falling, as he himself remarks, 'naturally into a
scowl',[12] looking like the gloomier side of George Gambol, the conventional Middle England family man cartoon character whose daily tribula-
tions appeared regularly in *The Daily Express* from the 1950s onwards. In
the caricature Mason looks like George Gambol after a dose of Dr Jekyll's
deadly potion, dressed, as so often in his screen roles, in dark clothes.

Eventually, in the third phase of his career, Mason returned to Europe
where, after 1960, he made over forty films. By now, following the collapse of his marriage to Pamela, and the birth of two children whose
unconventional upbringing and education often earned the disapproval
of the press, Mason drifted into a wide variety of character parts, many of
which, especially as the nymphet-doomed Humbert in *Lolita* (Kubrick,
1961) or the heartless slave-owner in *Mandingo*, allowed him to indulge

his repertoire of suave sadomasochists. Mason married his co-star in *Age of Consent*, Clarissa Kaye. He died in 1984.

Sadism

James Mason's appeal lay in a combination of looks and voice. The reviewer for Los Angeles television channel Z described him as 'one of the most beautiful men ever to grace the screen'.[13] The audience has little need of the remark made in *Caught* by the Robert Ryan character upon the discovery of the identity of his wife's lover (Mason): 'I might have known you'd be good-looking.' Ryan – whether in villainous or heroic mode – is tall, sturdy, rock-solid and powerful. Few would call him 'good-looking', much less 'beautiful'. James Mason, on the other hand, for all his pitiless treatment of his leading ladies, could indeed be said to be beautiful. In stature and physique not sturdy but slim, neither muscular nor hard but soft ('Do I look soft?' asks Johnny MacQueen in *Odd Man Out*), his facial features, when not scowling, bordering on femininity. Brooding eyes and thick waves of inky hair mark a face of almost Gypsy-ish swarthy beauty, a physiognomy as if modelled on his fictitious Yorkshire fellow countryman, Emily Brontë's Heathcliff, compromised by a cruel mouth whose fleshy lips and uneven teeth form the gateway to that legendary voice.

Characteristically soft and at times almost whispered, the voice is made of steely velvet. Sometimes coerced into foreign pronunciations (Irish in *Odd Man Out*, Deep Southern American in *Mandingo*, even Australian in *Age of Consent*), it is usually allowed even in the most unlikely circumstances, such as in the quintessentially American ambience of *Bigger than Life*, to retain its own idiosyncratic blend of Yorkshire and Cambridge respectability. Whether natural or affected, the voice never loses its menace, like a surgeon's scalpel slicing with words the futile defences of his interlocutors. The minatory potential of that instrument, so often remarked on by commentators,[14] is given perhaps its most grotesque expression in *The Pumpkin Eater* (Clayton, 1964), where in a succession of choker close-ups the camera focuses on Mason's mouth, its upper lip now decorated by a stockbroker's moustache, as it issues forth a stream of abuse at Anne Bancroft, spitefully informing her of her husband's adultery with his blonde bimbo wife. This volley of insults seems provoked as much by delight in upbraiding Anne Bancroft as by outrage at Peter Finch's involvement with his wife.

Like Milton's Satan, Mason, referred to as the Devil by Phyllis Calvert in *Fanny by Gaslight*, is a portrait of fallen beauty, predatory masculinity feasting on the frailties of nubile virgins or experienced doxies, attracted, in line also with Don Juan, more by the thrill of conquest than by the consummation of desire. Even, for instance, the romance between Captain Jackson and his wicked lady (Margaret Lockwood) rarely throbs with tender feeling or passionate ecstasy. Mason's demeanour, when not amused by his partner's antics, is one of detachment, as if bearing out the Byronic sentiment that 'man's love is of man's life a thing apart'. Undoubtedly, Mason's offscreen coolness towards Margaret Lockwood on the set of their films together did little to stoke the fire of their screen partnership: 'dour and uncommunicative ... generally to be found with his head stuck in a book, not a bundle of fun to anyone ... especially compared to Granger who was'.[15]

Ann Todd, on the other hand, draws attention to his trademark blend of softness and cruelty:

> There was something electric and at the same time very dangerous about James, which had nothing to do with conventional stardom in the post-war years. He was one of the few people who could really frighten me, and yet at the same time he was the most gentle and courteous of men ... what I always found so lovely and attractive about him was that sense of otherness, a sense that he would really have been perfectly happy, as he once said to me, living as a guide in the Swiss mountains.[16]

The Seventh Veil played to capacity audiences both in Britain and in America, leading to the overnight formation of Mason fan clubs in almost every US state in which it was shown. This mixture, noted by Ann Todd, of spikiness and softness, a struggle for supremacy fought by his feminine and masculine tendencies, is the source of much of his appeal. The Mason persona exemplifies the conflict in men between competing instincts, a struggle reaching its most dramatic climaxes in his various encounters with women.

His rude, hectoring anger seems sometimes directed as much against his own inner divisions caused by fears about his potential for softness, or femininity, as against the female victims, like Margaret Lockwood or Ann Todd, who became the screens on which was projected a self-directed rage. Mason's assaults on these women may be read in this respect also as the repression of his own femininity. Equally, for his female victims on and off screen, those bearing the brunt of his attacks onscreen, and those in the audience who vicariously delighted in their punishment, the popularity of an actor characterised by sadistic behaviour towards women raises important questions about spectatorship and masochistic audience identification.

Freud defines masochism in women as a tendency associated with sadistic feelings towards the mother. The process through which the desire for the father's penis must be transformed into a passive wish to have his baby is bound up with the need to become identified with the hated mother. But the suppression of sadistic feelings towards the mother, and ultimately as well towards the father, inevitably leads towards a return to passivity, masochistic drives and identification with the 'castrated' mother, like her converting penis envy into a wish for a baby. While, as many post-Freudians have argued, this is an extremely partial analysis of the development of masochism in the female, it nevertheless clearly illuminates at least some of the key stages through which a woman might come to accept a submissive role in private as well as in public life.[17] In this respect, the interesting issue from the point of view of the female audiences for James Mason's early films is their popularity at a time and place – 1940s Britain – when gender questions were formulated by predominantly traditional attitudes. The mass female audience in the UK and USA for these early films would have been drawn to Mason as much by awe and envy for his socially approved power and authority[18] as by his aura of fascinating sexuality.

The masochistic attraction to Mason, himself an enemy of submission, may well be conditioned to some extent not just by a desire to abandon control but also ultimately by a decision to accept submissive femininity as the price for social integration and acceptability. In some women spectators, as Stoller would argue, this attitude is in itself a form of control, an act of violence against the self as well as against the society that has created these conditions.[19] The sadomasochistic dynamic between the Mason character, his female co-stars and the audience is sometimes refracted through the perspectives of Pygmalion/Galatea narratives but, coming at a later stage in his career, these films begin to shroud the persona with pathos. There is a gradual shift from the early films and their attitudes of male supremacy, still to some extent in evidence in *Pandora and the Flying Dutchman* (Lewin, 1950), and films such as *The Story of Three Loves* (Reinhardt, 1953) and *A Star Is Born* or *Lolita*, where firmness is undermined by doubt. The confidence of the supremacist male is still relatively intact in *Pandora and the Flying Dutchman*, where right from the start the Mason character, still stamping his authority on the female, is beginning to show signs of wear and tear in a changing social climate. Nevertheless this may be Mason's last stand as the irredeemably unfeeling Gainsborough brute. When Pandora boards his ship, naked, still dripping with sea water, he avoids looking at her, not through embarrassment at her nakedness but through preoccupation with his brush strokes on a portrait of his long-lost love, the medieval beauty reincarnated in the twentieth century in Ava Gardner. He limits his interest in her to a command to look in one of the ship's cupboards for a bathrobe. This exchange is followed by a series of questions from Pandora issuing from another room that go coolly unanswered as Hendrick van der Zee remains absorbed by his work. Mason's melancholy is further reflected in the films that followed *Pandora*. *The Story of Three Loves* sees him playing the equivalent of Anton Walbrook's Diaghilev-clone in *The Red Shoes* (Powell and Pressburger, 1948), with Moira Shearer reprising her role from that film as an ultimately doomed ballerina. Mason's dialogue here is full of references to his reputation as a brute: 'Will you kindly stop pretending I'm an ogre'; 'I'm a very simple, ordinary, kindly human being'; 'you think I'm an absolute brute'. But these remarks lack the early Mason's resoluteness, undermined as they are now by doubt and self-pleading.

Doomed masculinity

Reviewing *A Star Is Born* for *Films in Review* in 1954, Henry Hart argued:

> Mason more than any other actor now before the public, knows how to project the neuroticism of contemporary human beings. His facial movements and the gulp in his throat, when he decides to commit suicide, so completely actualise the ineffable – the death of the ego – that they contribute one of the triumphs of the acting art.[20]

This screen angst seems to some degree born of an offscreen personality that, as Mankiewicz remarked, was also to some extent troubled:

> He always wished to be somewhere else, but could never quite decide where that somewhere was, or why he wanted to be there. He felt desperately unfulfilled by everything, and there was an inner man in him, as in all of us, only in him it was never struggling to get out, just to stay inside ... I knew that he was the Brutus I wanted ... because he was very complex and broody and unhappy, and that was precisely the Brutus I needed, a man who looked as though he belonged to a lonely battlefield.[21]

That link between private self and public persona was noticed also by Cukor, whose concept of Norman Mayne as John Barrymore was overridden by Mason's greater desire to base the role on himself.[22] But associations with doom were struck at the very inception of Mason's career. Frivolously at one point in his autobiography he cites his children's sad comment on the number of times he is condemned to die on screen. More seriously, as regards his British films, Mason seems to have exemplified in these roles the return of the repressed of a nation still in the

1940s and early 50s constrained by the conservative drives of a culture adjusting itself to the realities of wartime and postwar society. Never innocent of ideology, the Mason persona is, in its id-driven forms, a release of the libido as well as its punishment. Equally, the personal inflection Mason himself seems to confer on these contradictory images of masculinity represents a tension with accepted or idealised contemporary forms of male subjectivity. From one point of view, the eroticised violence of the early films exposes the dark side of the relations between the sexes. But, from another, Mason's aggressive sexuality – horsewhipping Margaret Lockwood, or caning Ann Todd – may be an outburst as much against a class-ridden, philistine culture as against the failures of a self entrapped by the demands of an official masculinity. An outsider and loser (for example in *The Wicked Lady*), he is also, to republicanism, an insider and hero (*Odd Man Out*), the arbiter of good taste (*The Seventh Veil*), his tantrums symptomatic of a malaise caused by the prohibitions and cruelties of a culture in crisis, of a society still governed by its conservative heritage, yet after the Second World War attempting to democratise itself and to readjust to post imperial realities.

This ultimately self-destructive, uneasy ambivalence at the heart of the Mason persona carries on into his Hollywood career. In *A Star Is Born* Norman Mayne remarks, prior to an unintended but nevertheless significant blow to Judy Garland's face, 'I destroy everything I touch. I always have.' The man with a genius, as he also later remarks, 'for doing the wrong thing' seems in this moment of self-awareness almost to comment on his career as a whole, in recognition of the persona's violence as fury both against the failure of women to surrender to their ideologised gender roles and against a self colluding with a system that demands fixed categories of human behaviour.

Beyond implications of a sexual-political kind, the significance of Norman Mayne's observation also raises what might be termed existential as well as psychological questions. From one point of view, as the doctor remarks in *The Upturned Glass* (Huntingon, 1947), the Mason persona often borders on paranoia. He recognises the Mason character's need for control, diagnoses him as a paranoiac and compares him to a cracked vessel:

> The vessel which we normal people use for imbibing experience is a stout, austerity model which doesn't crack. With others, like yourself, the glass, though of superior design, cracks quite easily. Now instead of leaving it upturned on the shelf a danger to all, it should be thrown away.

The reference to normality is ironic since the pontificating doctor has already been exposed as a cynic; the allusion to austerity is a deliberate acknowledgement of the meanness and cheerlessness of postwar British society. Normality and austerity are precisely what the Mason character attempts to evade. The film asks whether Mason's paranoia is the herald or consequence of austerity. The answers are to be found partially in psychological, cultural and historical contexts, but there is, too, a sense even here, though the point is more finely developed in *A Star Is Born* and *Bigger than Life*, of existential anguish. The Mason character's violence against self and others seems informed in a popularised way by contemporary existential angst mixed, in view of the violent peculiarities of the persona, with Sade. For secular forms of existentialism, in circulation through Sartre in the 1940s, the period of the emergence of Mason as a major star, the only certainty is death. Human beings live in a state of 'le néant', or nothingness, the sense of which can be grasped only through acts of will that will confer authenticity on the individual. Nothingness or 'absurdity' drives the Mason character to strike out, blindly and incoherently, for meaning in gestures that seem also indebted to Sade's account of existence as fatally flawed, a universe in which human beings are doomed to commit acts of horror and destruction – culminating in the Second World War – even as they attempt to construct a civilised world. Struggling for survival in a world where nature is at war with itself, the Mason character lashes out against lovers, family, strangers and self.

In *Bigger than Life*, the existential resonances are highlighted through Biblical references. The cortisone that Ed Avery is prescribed to relieve his bodily pain leads to a derangement of the mind that reveals itself in religious fanaticism in which he eventually becomes a modern Abraham intent on sacrificing his son. Like all the other Ray melodramas, the film attacks conformist 1950s American society, the medical metaphor hyperbolising the internal and external pressures on family life. But the film also breaks loose from generic constraint, going beyond psychology, culture and history to ask precisely through its religious allusions ultimate questions about existence. It is appropriate that these questions should be raised through a character played by James Mason. Ed Avery is another Brutus, 'with himself at war' not just because of a quirk of nature but through frustration at his failure to make sense of life itself.

Coda on Mr Van Damm

No plausible account of James Mason would be complete without some mention of his cameo in Hitchcock's great thriller *North by Northwest*. This was the film that made him aware of the end of his career as a leading man, where his performance of characteristic imperturbability was now, as his co-star Martin Landau perceptively observed, tinged with a certain sadness lending itself poignantly to his role as the saboteur and betrayer Mr Van Damm.[23] As in his treatment of Grant, Hitchcock helped develop various understated nuances of the Mason persona, especially his humour and dandyism, which are even discernible in the slightly asphyxiated and off-centre pronunciation of his vowels. Ernest Lehman's script calls for a professional bearing and appearance: 'In walks a distinguished looking man of about forty, professional in manner but definitely sexually attractive (to women), and only slightly sinister.'[24]

What Lehman neglects to mention here, something that Hitchcock himself picks up on, is the humour of the character: 'My dear Ernie ... let me say how much I enjoyed the 65 pages ... so amusingly written.'[25]

Mason's humour, as well as his sinister and sexually attractive aura, may be usefully compared to Grant's equivalent qualities and help explain why Grant, unlike Mason, continued to be romantic leading-man material. First, the history of their careers up to the making of this film saw Grant, never a screen loser like Mason, sometimes suspected of villainy (above all in *Suspicion*), but never actually guilty of it; Mason's past, unlike Grant's, deprived of purely heroic romantic comedy roles, was defined predominantly by romantic villainy. Second, Grant was always more athletic, even balletic, his every step across a room worthy of a Fred Astaire *pas de deux*. Third, Mason's physique was not exposed, like Grant's or other variant exemplars of the male form, as object of desire or wish-fulfilment fantasy for the delectation of the hetero- or homosexual gaze. Fourth, Mason did not age as gracefully as Grant, whose silvery hair, clipped and disciplined to millimetric perfection, contrasts favourably with the rather more unkempt, slightly less abundant Mason locks; Mason's occasionally hirsute roles (as in *20,000 Leagues under the Sea*, Fleischer, 1954) add to his aura of 'character actor', destroying the potential for clean-shaven boyishness that Hollywood often demanded in its leading men. Finally, though each had a natural gift for comedy, Grant's retained the wholesome qualities of his Screwball roles, lightening his sophistication in films as late as *Charade* (Donen, 1963), where in obedience to his farcical past he even takes a shower while still dressed in one of his characteristically smart Italian suits. Mason's humour is better suited to the slightly more stagy, intellectual play on words, and high-art milieux, exactly the sort of thing required by the actor who plays Mr Van Damm in *North by Northwest*:

> Has anyone ever told you that you overplay your various roles rather severely Mr Kaplan? First you're the Madison Avenue man who claims he has been mistaken for someone else. Then you play a fugitive from justice,

supposedly trying to clear his name of a crime he didn't commit. And now you play the peevish lover, stung by jealousy and betrayal.

Mason's performance throughout the film, here delivering Lehman's witty rebuke to Mr Kaplan through a voice oozing with honeyed venom, was the prelude to the last phase of his career, in which the theatricality of the man became his trademark even more than it did for Grant, whose persona as much as the part he was playing in this film is being self-consciously, and a little resentfully, satirised by Mr Van Damm. Played almost elegiacally, Mr Van Damm sees Mason in melancholy transition from a past where in its viciousness the persona bordered on what one reviewer defined as the Himmleresque[26] to a less swaggeringly defiant future.

Notes

1 J. Stott, 'The Rebirth of James Mason', *Guardian*, 26 November 1969.
2 James Mason, *Before I Forget: An Autobiography* (Sphere, London, [1981] 1982), p. 164.
3 Ibid., p. 164.
4 Ibid., p. 186.
5 D. Lewin, *Daily Express*, 16 December 1946.
6 Mason, *Before I Forget*, p. 209.
7 *Time*, 24 December 1945.
8 Mason, *Before I Forget*, pp. 206–207.
9 M. Hodgson, 'Star with Staying Power', *Sunday Times Magazine*, 15 April 1979, 37–9.
10 Sweeney quoting *Picturegoer* (20 May 1956), in Kevin Sweeney, *James Mason: A Bibliography* (Greenwood Press, London and Westport, 1999), p. 119.
11 Mason, *Before I Forget*, p. 113.
12 A. Eyles and L. Fitzgibbon, eds, *James Mason: Actor* (BFI, London, 1970), p. 1.
13 Sweeney, *James Mason*, p. 113.
14 V. Davis, 'Why Some Leading Ladies (and James Mason) are Glad He Doesn't Get the Girls These Days', *Daily Express*, 30 July 1974.
15 Sweeney, *James Mason*, p. 105.
16 Sheridan Morley, *James Mason: Odd Man Out* (Weidenfeld & Nicolson, London, 1989), p. 3.
17 Louise J. Kaplan, *Female Perversions* (Penguin Books, Harmondsworth, [1991] 1993), p. 216.
18 Jessica Benjamin, *The Bonds of Love: Psychoanalysis, Feminism and the Problem of Domination* (Virago, London, 1988), pp. 85–132.
19 Robert J. Stoller, *Sexual Excitement* (Karnac, London, [1979] 1986), pp. 3–35.
20 Sweeney, *James Mason*, p. 136.
21 Morley, *James Mason: Odd Man Out*, p. 99.
22 Ibid., p. 105.
23 Sweeney, *James Mason*, p. 123.
24 Ernest Lehman, *Alfred Hitchcock's North by Northwest* (Faber & Faber, London: 1999), p. x.
25 Ibid., p. x.
26 *New York Times* (24 June 1946), in Sweeney, *James Mason*, p. 110.

CELESTINO DELEYTO

The nun's story: femininity and Englishness in the films of Deborah Kerr

9

Sweet virgin, you have a spiritual face.
(Gabriel Pascal)

The above words, reportedly uttered by the Hungarian producer and director to Deborah Kerr when he signed her to play the role of Jenny Hill in his adaptation of G. B. Shaw's *Major Barbara* (1941), not only inaugurated her career as a film actress but defined, with surprising accuracy, the contours of her star persona in British and US films for the following three decades. A later account described her part in this film as 'the role in which she so often excelled, one whose moral fortitude was concealed beneath a delicate exterior'.[1] When, some years later, as a result of her long-term contract with MGM, the actress went to the US, and, in the opinion of her official biographer, Eric Braun, became 'the most enduringly consistent success story' of a British actress in Hollywood,[2] the phrases 'moral fortitude' and 'delicate exterior' continued to define her screen personality and began to be associated with her Englishness.[3] Press reviews, interviews and gossip columns described her time and again as 'a lady' or 'an English rose', definitions which were complemented with terms such as 'class', 'breeding', 'gentility', 'niceness' or 'delicacy'. Thus, C. A. Lejeune referred to her role in *Black Narcissus* (Powell and Pressburger, 1946) as one transmitting 'quiet, magnificent authority'[4] whereas, years later, French critic José Bulnes defined her as a 'petite pièce de porcelaine'.[5]

Outward delicacy and inward strength are, then, the initial characteristics of Kerr's star persona, a modernised version of the stereotype of the Victorian lady, a stereotype which, in terms both of its femininity and its Englishness, was revived in order to attempt to soothe postwar anxieties and frustrations through a fantasised return to the certainties and safe ideals of the past. The following quotation powerfully captures these meanings in the star: 'Miss Kerr smiles and you think of crisp summer

Deborah Kerr. An early pre-Hollywood portrait of Gabriel Pascal's 'Spiritual Face'.

linen and large sun-hats and the sound of lawn-mowers on Sunday morn-
ings. She is so English you'd rush to send a gunboat at her slightest dis-
tress.'[6] Even before Kerr went to Hollywood, the anonymous writer of
Time could define her as 'everything Englishmen mean when they
become lyrical about roses'.[7] Although written about *Black Narcissus*,
these words also describe her first important part in *The Life and Death of
Colonel Blimp* (1943), in which she plays the three women in the life of
Clive Candy (Roger Livesey), suggesting the idea that, at least in Powell
and Pressburger's powerful construction of male Englishness, 'Englishmen always fall in love with the same type of woman'.[8] If *Major Barbara*,
Kerr's first film, already anticipated a great deal of her future star persona,
Blimp, the film after which she became an established name, firmly
placed her as a figment of the male imagination, as an image of idealised
English femininity and one clearly attached to past models of womanhood. As Jeffrey Richards has recently argued, whereas Blimp becomes
'the embodiment of a chivalric ideal overtaken by the grim reality of
modern war',[9] the three characters played by Kerr are, in a very real sense,
'the same woman, the eternal, sensible, forthright, independent-spirited
British woman'.[10]

Yet the neo-Victorian stereotype did not embody the whole story of
British femininity in the cinema of the 1940s. Alongside films such as
Blimp or the very successful *Brief Encounter* (Lean, 1945), the popular
Gainsborough melodramas put forward a very different type of heroine,
one who, in the words of Richards, was 'independent, aggressive and
single-minded in [her] pursuit of wealth, status and sexual gratification',[11]
a heroine who, as played by Margaret Lockwood and others, was a reflection of important changes in women's sexual behaviour and attitudes
produced by the war. Clearly, the Victorian model of femininity, while
powerful and still attractive to audiences, was insufficient to encompass
women's gains in social and sexual independence. The differences
between the three Kerr characters in *Blimp* timidly point towards these
changes, but it would be in *Black Narcissus*, their second film with the
actress, that Powell and Pressburger would try to come to terms with
these fiercely opposed pulls in contemporary ideas of femininity. The
result was the creation of a complex, often contradictory female type that
would become the template for most of Deborah Kerr's films to come.
Therefore, although Hollywood immediately dubbed Kerr as the succes-
sor of Greer Garson in the role of 'English lady', the construction of her
Englishness was already well under way by the time she left Britain to star
in *The Hucksters* (Hornblow, 1947). For this reason, I will concentrate on
the ways in which *Black Narcissus* explores and consolidates the meanings
of Deborah Kerr as a star and then refer to other films as extensions or

derivations of her foundational role in this film.[12] In order to analyse these meanings, I will use, as part of my theoretical framework, Richard Dyer's recent formulation of the association between spirituality, race and the colonial project in *White* (1997).[13]

Dyer argues that the discourse of Christianity contains a productive contradiction between spirituality and embodiment. Christianity is extremely physical and body-minded: the body appears constantly as the basis of Christian imagery, for example in the Nativity and the Crucifixion. Yet, for all its emphasis on the body, what has made Christianity a powerful discourse is the mystery 'that somehow there is in the body something that is not of the body',[14] something we may call spirit, mind or God. This spirit is superior to the body, organises it and controls it. The precarious balance in which the spirit reigns superior but the body keeps returning both to incarnate the spirit and to threaten its authority was carried into colonial discourses of race: the white spirit organises white flesh and non-white flesh. The white man's 'natural right' to organise, civilise and possess is carried out through a linguistic slippage: Christian spirituality becomes colonial 'spirit', 'get up and go, aspiration, awareness of the highest reaches of intellectual comprehension and aesthetic refinement'.[15] It is this 'spirit' that helps the imperial subject both to master and to transcend the body, and sets it as the ruler of the inferior races. Whiteness aspires not only to invisibility in that it is the unmarked race, the race with no colour, but also in a kind of translucence: 'Those who can let the light through, ... those whose bodies are touched by the light from above, who yearn upwards toward it, those are the people who should rule and inherit the earth.'[16] However, this aspiration of purity, spirit and invisibility brings a further problem in the sphere of sexuality: 'to ensure the survival of the race, [whites] have to have sex – but having sex, and sexual desire, are not very white: the means of reproducing whiteness are not themselves pure white'.[17] Spirit, therefore, in both its meanings as spirituality and 'enterprise', is opposed to desire, which deals in materiality and bodies. Bodies are there for the imperial subject to tame and control but the discourses which sustain its power are constantly traversed by ideas of embodiment, reproduction and desire. As Dyer says later on: 'Whiteness as an ideal can never be attained, not only because white skin can never be hue white, but because ideally white is absence: to be really, absolutely white is to be nothing.'[18]

Deborah Kerr, as one of Hollywood's prime embodiments of white spirituality in the 1950s, carries these theoretical contradictions in her persona at a time in which the imperial project is moving on to a new phase and, simultaneously, a time in which Victorian images of submissive femininity, a crucial component of the imperial project, are being replaced by a different type of female submissiveness, one which is more literally embodied and openly sexualised. Apparently presenting the counterpart of such 'fleshy' stars as Marilyn Monroe, Ava Gardner or, in Britain, Diana Dors, the complexity of the meanings surrounding Deborah Kerr is closely linked with the initial power of her spirituality, her moral fortitude and her imperial righteousness but also their frequent surrender, whether real or metaphorical, to various forms of carnality and desire. This ambivalence sets her not so much as representative of a period but of a moment of change: neither a modern Lillian Gish nor Ava Gardner (with whom she appeared in two films: *The Hucksters* and *The Night of the Iguana*, 1964), Kerr symbolises the movement from spirituality to desire, from translucence to embodiment, while simultaneously representing the historical shift from a traditional form of imperialism based on the power of the (white) spirit over the colonised body of the native to one based on the power of the image, the conquest of the spirit by the fascination of the material. In this sense, Kerr also moved from representing an idea of Englishness fraught with contradictions to being co-opted not only literally by Hollywood but also as part of filmic discourses of US imperial power.

While the specific US dimension of her star image would obviously not become apparent until she moved to Hollywood, the rest of the meanings that constitued this image were articulated, for the first time, in *Black Narcissus*. The first time she appears in this film, in the first of many magnificent close-ups, the extreme whiteness and translucence that Dyer singles out as constitutive of classical filmic discourses of white supremacy mark her, almost literally, as 'beautiful absence', as 'touched by the light from above'. As Sister Clodagh she represents both pure spirituality – the nun whose body has been surrendered to the service of God – and the enterprising spirit of colonialism – the person in charge of a small religious community in the Indian mountains whose mission is to 'civilise' the natives. However, Sister Clodagh fails miserably in both tasks. For all her translucence and whiteness, the character has to learn to acknowledge the strength of her desire, the unsolvable complications of embodiment.

The film is, from the outset, equally concerned with the mechanisms of colonial power, with the complexities of repressed female desire and with the interactions and links between the two. In the first scene, the Mother Superior announces to Sister Clodagh that she does not consider her apt for the job because she is too proud and ambitious while the nuns' main concerns should be humility, renunciation and a spirit of service to others. This brief reference to the nuns' mission goes to the heart of colonial discourse: the white person's destiny as leader of nations is disguised as a grave responsibility and a vocation of service, which justify their right to power, ownership and oppression of the colonised. In the Mother Superior's formulation, it is the young nun's difficulties in hiding her ambition under a mask of service, rather than the unfair exercise of power, that may eventually thwart her mission. This warning, of course, comes as an anticipation of Clodagh's final failure to keep the convent open and bring civilisation to the natives, whom Mr Dean (David Farrar), the British agent, describes as noble savages and 'children'. Mr Dean voices the text's general view that the nuns' failure is due to the fact that they are women. Anne McClintock points out that colonial women held an ambiguous position in the imperial project, both colonisers and colonised, privileged and oppressed, complicit with male colonial power and subjected to it.[19] A great deal of the power of Black Narcissus lies precisely in its exploration of the predicament of a woman in a colonial situation. The religious order is an ideal narrative mechanism to explain this position: as the person in charge of the mission, Sister Clodagh holds a similar power to that of male characters in other imperial narratives; but, as the narrative develops, it becomes increasingly clear that Clodagh's femaleness is a insurmountable impediment to her mission. In her analysis of the film, E. Ann Kaplan suggests that, at a historical moment of visible decline of British rule in India, the film uses white women as surrogates for men in order to show the end of imperialism and blame it on women.[20] Kaplan uses Mulvey's theory of the cinematic gaze in order to describe what happens when women, usually objects of the oppressive male gaze, become the subjects of the imperialist gaze. Her answer is that the outcome of this irregularity is the destabilising of imperial discourse and the eventual end of the empire. In a similar vein, Dyer concludes his account of the television series The Jewel in the Crown (1984) with the following words: 'Women take the blame, and provide the spectacle of moral suffering, for the loss of empire.'[21] In Black Narcissus, the white nuns' inability to keep the convent open symbolically marks India's imminent independence and, quite fantastically, blames it on women, or, to be more precise, on the feminisation of empire. Deborah Kerr becomes the primary signifier of this beleaguered or defeated imperial femininity.

If we are to believe the Mother Superior's initial words and Mr Dean's frequent accusations, it is Clodagh's excessive pride and ambition that bring about the various disasters that ensue, but the narrative never really bears out their assessment of the nun. It is not her failure to serve others but the increasing visibility of the nuns' desires, their unstoppable surrender to the exotic lure of Mopu – the convent is set up in an old palace where the Raja used to keep his women and is called 'the house of women' – that brings about the end of the mission. The idea of grafting the new convent on the old house of sexual pleasure is both shocking and significant of the stereotypical patriarchal association of the female with sexuality: both ends of the spectrum, the virgin and the prostitute, the woman who is all spirit and the one who is all carnality, are part of the same sexual continuum. To use Michel Foucault's famous phrase, both female stereotypes are 'thoroughly saturated with sexuality'.[22] In this way, although threatening to overturn a few taboos, the nuns' gradual abandon to their desires and the sensuality of their bodies is made culturally understandable to the spectator. At the same time, a further discursive collapse is produced in the course of the film: that between the coloniser and the colonised, between the imperial self and the exotic other. Here, the gender of the nuns is also crucial since, as McClintock argues, in colonial discourse the Orient was consistently feminised, considered, in Jules Michelet's definition, as 'the womb of the world', and variously conceptualised as mother, evil seducer, licentious aberration or life-giver.[23] In *Black Narcissus* the nuns are, through the weakness 'inherent' in their femininity, gradually 'polluted' by the sensuality of the exotic: the openly sexualised ghosts of the palace, the mountain wind constantly blowing and bringing back memories of the past as well as scenarios of suffering and masochism or the young general (Sabu) with his gaudy clothes and cheap perfume. Perhaps the most obvious metaphoric indication of the film's collapsing of white femininity and exoticism is the casting of Jean Simmons as a young Indian woman, defined solely in terms of her untrammelled sexuality. Even Mr Dean, the representative of traditional (and traditionally unproblematic) male colonial power, seems to have fallen prey to the attraction of the Orient: his decadence, his passivity, his role as object of the nuns' desire, even his external appearance and his visual objectification, all point to the loss of empire through the feminisation of male imperial power. Victorian femininity and colonial power are, therefore, finally defeated by the association of female desire and the exotic.

Sister Clodagh's failure as civilising force is, therefore, less due to her excess of ambition than to her excess of sexual desire. The film's conceit of both suppressing and obviously representing the emotional and sexual turmoil under the cool, severe exterior of the nun became the missing ingredient of the Deborah Kerr persona before she went to Hollywood. The way in which the film articulates this conceit relates to classical theories of film melodrama: the displacement of forbidden desires, of unutterable truths, on to the mise en scène, the music or the actors' performances. Famous for Jack Cardiff's colour photography, the film anticipates the 1950s Hollywood melodramas of Douglas Sirk, Vincente Minnelli and Nicholas Ray both in its use of Technicolor and its hysterical displacement of repressed meaning on to the surface of the text.[24] But *Black Narcissus* is a film marked by excess even in the nature and the number of its displacements. Not only do the mise en scène, the music and the performing body of Deborah Kerr become signifiers of the character's repressed or irrepressible sexuality; the flashbacks, which re-enact the events in Clodagh's youth that led to her 'vocation', also become the space of her desire, both in the narrative incidents they relate – how she was engaged and in love and her fiancé left her to seek fortune in America – and in the fantastic nature of their articulation: the music, the frame movements, the frantic rhythm of the editing, especially in the flashback of the fox hunt, all contribute to the presentation of the past as repressed and transformed into 'pure', inchoate desire in the present. But the most important 'melodramatic' displacement is provided by the character of Sister Ruth (Kathleen Byron).

Sister Ruth's feverish desire for Mr Dean signifies literally the return of the repressed. As various commentators have pointed out, Ruth is not only Clodagh's rival in the film but also her double, the embodiment of those desires which the protagonist nominally represses. Kathleen Byron is initially made up to look strikingly like Deborah Kerr and the growing difference between them in visual terms signals not only the younger nun's psychological deterioration but also the articulation of Clodagh's increasingly obvious unspeakable feelings. As Michael Walker suggests, 'Sister Ruth represents the "full-blooded" enactment of the forces resurfacing, despite and against these attempts at repression, from Sister Clodagh's unconscious. She is the monster from the Id.'[25] Other times in the film, Sister Ruth, who is often found jealously eavesdropping on the conversations between Clodagh and Mr Dean, appears as the child in the Oedipal triangle, a fantastic daughter of the protagonist who, in fiercely defending her own desire, reaffirms the existence of Clodagh's towards the metaphoric father. In one of the final scenes of the film, Clodagh comes as close as she can to confessing her feelings to Mr Dean and, although this is one of melodrama's unutterable truths, both the actors' expressions and the deep red colours of the mise en scène make those meanings explicit. Ruth's presence as the Freudian child of the primal scene serves to sanction, even more definitively, the erotic nature of the relation between the other two.[26] After having, for long hours, looked as if into a mirror at the woman who has dared transgress the rules and expressed her sexuality, and then metaphorically killed that part of herself with her unwitting participation in Sister Ruth's death, a defeated Sister Clodagh says goodbye to a resigned Mr Dean in a final scene in which, once again, the two lovers seem ready to confess their feelings for one another and are prevented, literally, only by the ending of the film.

At the end of what Geoffrey Andrews describes as 'the most genuinely erotic film ever made in Britain',[27] Clodagh seems to have come to terms with her humanity (that is, her sexuality) and leaves Mopu aware both of the inflexible reality of social norms but also of the power of her inner instincts, an awareness that may have brought about the failure of her mission but has turned her into a more complex, less repressed human being. Symbolically, Kerr is leaving Britain for Hollywood the defeated colonial subject, embodying, to use Dyer's words, the spectacle of colonial suffering, the stubborn adherence to an old-fashioned idea of social decorum and, simultaneously, the acceptance of the fires within. In one of the best articulations of this doubleness in Kerr's persona, David Denby affirms: 'Deborah Kerr was a restrained performer, but what she held in was as vivid as what she let come to the surface.'[28] When gentleness, class and restraint gave way to passion and sexual anger in the famous beach scene of *From Here to Eternity* (Zinnemann, 1953), there was nothing new about Kerr's sexuality that had not already been part of her characters' personalities in earlier films, but, since *Black Narcissus*, it was those films in which the passion became almost visible but remained just under the surface that best captured the power of the Kerr persona. In films such as *The King and I* (Walter Lang, 1956), *Heaven Knows Mr Allison* (Huston, 1957) or even *The Innocents* there always comes a moment in which Kerr is ready to surrender to the force of her own desire and she is interrupted by some external event which prevents full expression. These moments are, in my view, the most impressive in the films and the most characteristic of her image.

If her femininity and sexuality had proved incompatible with her position as representative of colonial power in *Black Narcissus*, *Quo Vadis* (LeRoy, 1951) provides an interesting variation which is also significant of her mediating role in the shift from traditional European colonialism to US cultural colonialism. Kerr plays Lygia, the Christian slave (although adopted by a family of Roman patricians) whose love redeems Marcus Vinicius, the pagan Roman captain played by Robert Taylor. By the time she stars in this film, Bruce Babington and Peter William Evans can say that she, and the other actresses playing leading female roles in Biblical epics of the *Quo Vadis* plot type, represent 'a complex oxymoron of sexuality and purity', and their Englishness is a mixture of aristocratic aloofness and sexual fervour.[29] This 'Biblical' oxymoron is a different version of Dyer's description of white sexuality as 'conundrum',[30] discussed above, but becomes perfectly understandable in the construction of the star persona of Deborah Kerr: 'Not only beauty but spirit, as well', says Marcus when he first sees her, and, although this is the Victorian spirit of enterprise that Richards and Dyer refer to, it represents also the Christian spirituality that she problematically embodies, the whiteness that men such as Marcus search after, the light that will illuminate them and save them from darkness.[31] For Babington and Evans, the sexualised ingredient of the oxymoron serves to lead the male away from pagan promiscuity 'to the higher sexuality of romantic Christian monogamy',[32] but, as usual in the Biblical epic, the narrative resolution which demands a return to Christian simplicity is consistently overpowered by the exuberant spectacle of the genre, one which attracts spectators both through its multiplicity of desire and through its frequent use of sadomasochistic scenarios, in which Kerr often appears as victim. Although the strength of her spirit tames and converts Marcus to the 'superior morality' of Christianity, this is accomplished at the expense of her constant submission to his superior strength and power as conqueror. In this power struggle, Kerr's Englishness – her spirituality and moral fortitude and her capacity for sexual fervour – is conquered by the superior power, represented by Robert Taylor's Rome (read USA), and used as a tempering device to reinforce its authority over the colonized world (read everywhere Hollywood can reach).

In *The King and I*, one of her most popular films of the 1950s, Kerr plays the part of Anna, the English governess who is hired by the King of Siam (Yul Brynner) to teach his sixty-seven children and help him modernise the country. Apparently a traditional colonial narrative, in which the benign colonial power supervises the progress of the country towards civilisation while constantly lurking and waiting for an excuse to fall on it, the film introduces, almost inadvertently, a new morality, superior to both the primitive ruthlessness of the savage and the decadent and openly intrusive discourse of traditional colonialism. This new morality is mainly articulated through the references to Abraham Lincoln's fight for freedom and to the 'subversive' narrative of *Uncle Tom's Cabin*. At the end of the film, as the king dies, his son, the new king, explains, in a broad American English accent, the main principles by which he will govern, principles of freedom and democracy that, in a blatant breach of historical accuracy, identify Siam as a mythical product of the neocolonial spread of US ideology. An earlier scene underlines Kerr's participation in this Americanisation of the concepts of imperialism and freedom. In the musical number 'Getting to Know You', she apparently sets out, as the song's title indicates, to find out about the children's culture but ends up teaching them English customs, an apt metaphor of the inconsistency of the colonial discourse. As in the final scene, the children repeat Anna's teachings in an unaccounted-for American accent, a detail which, unimportant as it is in the context of the film's musical fantasy, may serve as a concluding metaphor of Deborah Kerr's Englishness in Hollywood: the old power, as represented in its very precariousness by a neo-Victorian femininity adapted to postwar gender realities, is not only replaced but incorporated by the new one in order to assert its superior values over the rest of the world.

Just before Kerr's Hollywood career got under way, when she was making *The Hucksters*, W. H. Mooring prophetically wondered 'whether she will become "an international screen personality" or will remain a "British film star"'.[33] At one level, she continued to play English characters, in both British and US films, and even when the characters were nominally not British (*From Here to Eternity*, *Tea and Sympathy* (Minnelli, 1956), *An Affair to Remember* (McCarey, 1957) and others), the basic ingredients of her persona, as discussed here, remained firmly in place. Yet her success as a Hollywood star, who held her own against the other most marketable female stars of the 1950s, such as Monroe, Doris Day or Audrey Hepburn, would indicate not only that her Englishness did not constitute an obstacle for her but, rather, it became a fundamental reason of her success. Given Hollywood's truly imperial ambitions of universality, the internationality hoped for by Mooring can be unproblematically translated as 'Americanness'. In other words, no actor can be successful 'universally' unless she or he is American, and, on the other hand, international means US, in what amounts to a candid acknowledgement of the nature of the USA's 'postcolonial' imperialism. In what is perhaps one of the deepest insights in her filmic career on this issue, the Cary Grant character who plays her English aristocratic husband in *The Grass Is Greener* (Donen), accuses Robert Mitchum, playing a wealthy American character who has an affair with Kerr and threatens to steal her away from her husband, of being an Anglophile, by which he means that, as a representative of the new empire, he is in the habit of taking what he desires, in this case Grant's English wife. Although, as befits a traditional romantic comedy, Grant finally recovers the love of Kerr, who remains in England when Mitchum leaves their mansion (accompanied by Jean Simmons), his statement neatly summarises the extent to which, in remaining quintessentially English, Deborah Kerr had become truly Americanised.

Notes

1 K. Doeckal, 'Deborah Kerr', *Films in Review*, 34.1 (1978), 4.
2 E. Braun, 'A Code of Behavior', *Films and Filming*, 16.7 (1970), 24.
3 Throughout this chapter, I will be using the terms 'English' and 'Englishness' instead of 'British' and 'Britishness' when I refer to discursive constructions in order to convey the content of those constructions rather than to naturalise the ideology they evoke. For an account of the historical success of this ideology see Jef-

frey Richards, *Films and British National Identity* (Manchester University Press, Manchester, 1997), pp. 1–28.

4 David Shipman, *The Great Movie Stars: The International Years* (Macdonald, London, [1972] 1989), p. 306.

5 J. Bulnes, 'Deborah Kerr: Toutes les femmes en une', *Ciné-Revue*, 66.18 (1986), 42.

6 P. Evans, *Daily Express*, 2 December 1965.

7 W. H. Mooring, 'Deborah Kerr', *Picture Goer*, 16:684 (1947), 37.

8 Doekal, 'Deborah Kerr', p. 4.

9 Richards, *Films and British National Identity*, p. 92.

10 Ibid., p. 96.

11 Ibid., p. 113.

12 Her part in her previous film, *I See a Dark Stranger* (1945), as a vivacious, determined supporter of the Irish nationalist cause, proves the extent to which her persona was far from fixed at the time.

13 R. Dyer, *White* (Routledge, London and New York, 1997).

14 Ibid., p. 16.

15 Ibid., p. 23.

16 Ibid., p. 121.

17 Ibid., p. 26.

18 Ibid., p. 78.

19 A. McClintock, *Imperial Leather: Race, Gender and Sexuality in the Colonial Contest* (Routledge, London and New York, 1995), p. 6.

20 E. A. Kaplan, *Looking for the Other: Feminism, Film and the Imperial Gaze* (Routledge, London and New York, 1997), p. 81.

21 Dyer, *White*, p. 206.

22 M. Foucault, *The History of Sexuality*, vol. 1 (Penguin, Harmondsworth, [1976] 1990), p. 104.

23 McClintock, *Imperial Leather*, p. 124.

24 G. Nowell-Smith, 'Minnelli and Melodrama', in C. Gledhill, ed., *Home Is Where the Heart Is: Studies in Melodrama and the Woman's Film* (BFI, London, [1977/8] 1987), pp. 70–4.

25 M. Walker, '*Black Narcissus*', *Framework*, 9 (1978), 11.

26 The uncanny double, the useful embodiment of the desires that she, the 'MGM lady', will conventionally have to repress, will return in many of the most remarkable films of her career: the two Ava Gardner characters in *The Hucksters* and *The Night of the Iguana*, Empress Poppea (Patricia Laffan) to her Lygia in *Quo Vadis* (1951), Rita Moreno in *The King and I* (1956), Jean Simmons (again) in *The Grass Is Greener* (1960) or her dead predecessor as a governess in *The Innocents* (1961).

27 G. Andrews, 'Staying On', *Time Out*, 776 (1985), 12.

28 D. Denby, 'Fire and Ice', *Première* (US), 7.5 (1994), 43.

29 B. Babington and P. W. Evans, *Biblical Epics: Sacred Narrative in the Hollywood Cinema* (Manchester University Press, Manchester, 1993), pp. 188–9.

30 Dyer, *White*, p. 26.

31 Ibid., pp. 74, 134.

32 Babington and Evans, *Biblical Epics*, p. 188.

33 Mooring, 'Deborah Kerr', 6.

Trevor, not Leslie, Howard

10

The scene is an undertaker's basement in the East End of London just after the Second World War. Black-marketeer Narcy and his gang are standing round a coffin filled with nylon stockings, planning their next heist. They need to brief their new accomplice, Clem Morgan. He's different from these cockney archetypes – unmistakably officer class. His accent, jacket and upright bearing tell us as much. Yet he's not stiff or inhibited and he has a rude physicality about him. When he sees his girl, he strides up to her and engulfs her in the kind of violent hug that Boris Karloff's monster gives his victims. Then it's back to work.

Trevor Howard is playing Clem. The film is Alberto Cavalcanti's *They Made Me a Fugitive* (1947), 'an astoundingly sordid' affair in the opinion of one critic[1] and part of the notorious 1940s British 'spiv cycle'[2] It was made only a year or so after *Brief Encounter* (Lean, 1945), but Clem doesn't seem anything like Howard's self-effacing doctor, the one who famously plucks the splinter out of Celia Johnson's eye. Clem is aggressive and boisterous; he drinks, smokes (with the cigarette hanging from his bottom lip) and freely admits that he craves both employment and excitement.

Orthodoxy has it that Trevor Howard was one of those actors who never changed much from film to film. He had the permanently craggy looks of someone used to the midday sun and a voice with a rasping edge seemingly steeped in officer's mess gin. His old producer Sir Anthony Havelock-Allan, now in his nineties, insists that Howard's genius lay in this consistency. He was, Sir Anthony claims, the perfect 'ordinary Englishman ... a professional of no particular class at all – efficient, kind, understanding and very good at his job'.

Howard, Sir Anthony implies, didn't have much of a range. 'Essentially, what he played always was an extremely nice, genuine, distinctly English man – a man who couldn't be anything else but English ... he always played exactly what he was – I don't remember a part in which he

Trevor Howard. 'The more he aged, the more depth was in his face.'

had to be profoundly different to the way he was in real life.' Even his 'whiskey priest' in *Ryan's Daughter* (Lean, 1970) was not, Havelock-Allan insists, such a radical departure.[3] Father Collins was dependable, honest, the kind of man you could trust. Likewise his gruff, hirsute miner with a grudge against the world ('I'm not loved 'ere 'cause I'm low – so I act low') in Jack Cardiff's *Sons and Lovers* (1960). Scrape away the coal dust, forget the distemper and the character emerges as yet another of the actor's doughty underdogs.

To portray Howard as a reliable middle-class English everyman is surely to demean him. At a time when the other nations of Britain are finding some form of devolution, of self-redefinition, the English are noted to be lagging behind, and part of what holds them back is the internationally popular image of the classic middle-class Englishman and Englishwoman of county and colony, an image bound to the now dead legacy of empire. Given the status of *Brief Encounter* as a touchstone of departed Englishness, Howard might seem a natural fit for this tweed shroud. But he is arguably a more complex, modern figure than this allows. Take three of his best-known roles in the 1940s: as Clem in Cavalcanti's murky, austerity-era spiv thriller; as the tousle-haired doctor Alec, enjoying illicit trysts in rowing boats and cinemas with Laura (Celia Johnson) in *Brief Encounter*, and as Major Calloway in *The Third Man* (Reed, 1949). Each of these characters is completely different in the way he walks, dresses and speaks. Calloway is the professional military policeman in his duffel-coat and army beret being driven around corrupt, rubble-strewn postwar Vienna by his faithful sergeant. He has a thin, cruel face. He's cold and sarcastic though he harbours more human sympathy than he'd ever admit. As the plot unfurls and we learn about Harry Lime's part in peddling adulterated penicillin to the kids in the hospitals, we may conclude that Calloway is a good man. That doesn't make him any less disappointed or cynical. Howard's Alec, by contrast, is so courteous, romantic and politely spoken that you half suspect it is Leslie, rather than Trevor, Howard in the role.

In the summer of 1998, a very curious set of documents about Howard was released to the public. File MEPO/3/1954 is kept in the Public Record Office in Kew. Nestling near the top of the dossier is a letter written by a Detective-Sergeant William Mogford to his Chief Inspector. The subject is Howard's war record. 'On the 2nd October, 1943', Mogford notes, he (Howard) had to relinquish his commission on the grounds of ill-health as he was suffering from psychopathic personality and considered unfit for military service.'

The story of Mogford's investigation of Howard itself sounds like something out of a British B-thriller of the 1940s. A handsome young actor beginning to make a name in films is suspected of puffing up his war record for publicity reasons. His alleged crime, taken very seriously, is posing 'as a person entitled to the Military Cross decoration'. A dogged Scotland Yard detective is sent to investigate. The case of Trevor Wallace Howard-Smith is baffling. As far as Mogford is concerned, Howard is as much a Walter Mitty figure as a glamorous, 'apparently successful' movie star. There is talk of charging him under Section 156A of the Army Act, 1881.

Mogford's report was commissioned after Vincent Evans, Assistant-Director of Public Prosecutions, noticed a string of newspaper features and reviews referring to Trevor Howard MC. These are clipped into Howard's file alongside Sgt Mogford's letters and reports. 'Two years ago he was winning the M.C. with the Red Devils, risking a life which it is now clear the British cinema needs very much', runs one such piece to which Evans seems to have taken particular objection.

You can imagine the movie. Howard would not play himself but Mogford, the jaded but fair-minded police officer. Some handsome young British contract actor, Dermot Walsh, perhaps, or David Farrar, might be cast as the neurotic star. What starts as a routine investigation into 'a self-made hero' (to borrow the English title of Jacques Audiard's film of wartime imposturing in France) turns into a complex character study as we learn more about the actor's past. Not even the diligent Mogford can determine where the stories about Howard's wartime heroics originate. One journalist interviewed by Mogford claims that he heard about the MC from 'members of the theatrical profession'.

Howard denied that he was to blame. He suspected he was being con-fused with two other men of the same name who served in the same air-borne division and that the myth was perpetuated by studio publicists. 'It was just a load of crap for the sake of building up my image as some kind of hero', he later told his biographer Michael Munn. 'Obviously it was good copy for the papers, but there was never a grain of truth in it'.[4]

Another theory has it that his mother was responsible and that he didn't have the heart to tell her that he had a lousy war. In the end Mogford cautions him and Howard apologizes, but stories about the actor with the MC keep appearing. And the publicists have sound reasons for perpetuating the lie. The idea of Howard as a neurotic ex-soldier harbouring a guilty secret does not exactly fit his screen image. We've seen him in *Cockleshell Heroes* (Ferrer, 1955) and *The Battle of Britain* (Hamilton, 1969). We know his mettle. Like John Mills, he is one of those British actors who sometimes seems most comfortable in uniform. In real life, he may have hated being in the armed forces, but he had an instinctive understanding of how soldiers thought and behaved. As his biographer Vivienne Knight notes: 'Ironically, his later portrayals of British officers were not only beautifully played but the truth in them was perfectly observed. The true beauty of those wasted years was that they could, and should, have been put to very good use.'[5]

When Mogford talks about Howard as a 'psychopathic personality' (by which he presumably means an individual without any sense of moral responsibility who is capable of performing violent or anti-social acts), he is describing the exact opposite of Howard's best-known characters. The one exception, though, is Clem Morgan. There is nothing anodyne about him. He boasts about his time as a POW and how he escaped by killing a Nazi guard. After his betrayal by Narcy (who frames him for the killing of a policeman and steals his girlfriend), he is remorseless in his bid for revenge. Seen as a fugitive on the run from prison, he looks as unkempt and wild-eyed as Stevenson's Ben Gunn. Here Howard is cast in a darker light than in any of his earlier roles and yet Clem's essential decency is never in doubt. 'I may be a crook but not that sort of a crook,' he protests when Narcy tries to rope him in to dealing in 'sherbert'. Even the police officer who catches up with Clem realises that, beneath his bitterness and cynicism, he's really a 'gentleman'. The critics seemed to be of much the same mind about the actor. 'Mr Howard always suggests a likable sort of a chap even when playing an unskilful thug', wrote the *News Chronicle*.[6] Narcy, by contrast, was beyond redemption. His sadism, flashy clothes and sneering voice (pitched somewhere between the Artful Dodger and Jimmy Cagney) underline the fact. 'He's not a respectable crook,' we're told by one of his victims, 'he's just cheap, rotten, after-the-war trash.'

In January 2000, British Home Secretary Jack Straw, speaking in a Radio 4 series about what it means to be British, observed that the English are 'potentially very aggressive, very violent'. If Howard really was, as Havelock-Allan proclaims, the quintessential Englishman, perhaps we shouldn't be too surprised by the potential for brutality his characters sometimes showed. He seldom played out-and-out villains. The conflicts he faced were more likely to be internal: between duty and desire. In *Brief Encounter*, Alec acknowledges that he is not free to love Laura (Celia Johnson). She is a married woman and he has his career as a doctor to attend to. The same tension exists in *The Heart of the Matter* (O'Ferrall, 1953), adapted from Graham Greene's novel. Howard plays Harry Scobie, deputy-commissioner of police in wartime Sierra Leone. Scobie is the typical Greene anti-hero: disillusioned but idealistic, keen to do good (or at least not to harm anyone) but morally weak. He is stuck in an unhappy marriage. His wife (Elizabeth Allan) doesn't understand either his sense of duty or his affection for the physically harsh, badly paid life of the middle-ranking colonial officer. When he borrows money from a local crook and then falls in love with a young, widowed bride (Maria Schell), his life comes apart. The melancholic intensity with which Howard plays Scobie is almost painful to watch. 'Do you seriously believe in hell?', Schell asks him. 'Yes, I do', he says in his quiet, forlorn voice, smoking his pipe. His Catholic religion tells him that if he commits suicide, hell is where he'll go, but, given his predicament, killing himself still seems like the logical course of action.

As the producer Ian Dalrymple noted of Howard's performance, 'Howard is unique among British actors in his ability to present a man of action in the round – to suggest even the most straightforward of characters are victims of stress and bewilderment'.[7] With his upright bearing, Scobie may look the archetypal repressed English hero – not a type who can express emotions in an extravagant, physical way. However, Howard brilliantly exploits the limitation – his energy is focused inward. He's tense, awkward, and his eyes never lose their forlorn quality. Just occasionally, he lets himself go. Early on, for no apparent reason, he suddenly yells at his wife: 'You've got no conception of what peace means!' Later, when he kisses Schell, he pounces on her in the same predatory way he did with the girlfriend in *They Made Me a Fugitive*.

Howard's career blossomed at about the same time that the great Method actors – Brando, Dean, Clift – emerged, and it's intriguing to compare his career with theirs. He was never a leading man in the way they were. (He had been acting for ten years before he landed the lead role in *Brief Encounter*.) Nor was he ever likely to steep himself in the theories of Stanislavsky or Stella Adler. He took a commonsense approach to acting and was very censorious of actors who did not. He gave up a promising stage career to work in movies. When playing Captain Bligh to Brando's Fletcher Christian in *Mutiny on the Bounty* (Milestone, 1962), he grew exasperated with the US star's behaviour on set. Brando used to stuff his ears with cotton wool so he couldn't hear Howard's lines. 'He [Brando] may be the biggest bloody star in Christendom', Howard told one journalist, 'but the man can't act.'[8]

Much has been written about the chequered production history of *Mutiny*: how directors were sacked and how Brando continually held up shooting. Perhaps Brando deliberately goaded the older actor. Brando is louche and relaxed as Fletcher Christian. The more cavalierly he behaves, the more Howard's Captain Bligh seethes. If the two actors loathed each other, their best performances nevertheless had something in common. In Jeff Young's book *Kazan on Kazan*, Elia Kazan reflects on Brando's ability 'to project the inner struggle of conscience', and to show self-doubt, schism and pain.[9] That's exactly the skill at which Howard also excelled.

Trevor Wallace Howard-Smith was born in September 1913. That, in itself, is worth noting. Whether because he was vain about his age, forgetful or the victim of incompetent publicists, it used to be assumed that he had been born in 1916. (The truth came out only at his memorial service.)

The accounts of his childhood given in the press and by his two biographers, Michael Munn and Vivienne Knight, suggest he had a conventional middle-class upbringing. His father, Arthur Howard-Smith, worked in Colombo for Lloyds of London. Although Trevor spent some time in Ceylon (Sri Lanka) with his father, he was based for most of his youth in Bristol, where he attended Clifton College. Here, he excelled at cricket more than anything else. His other pet obsession was jazz. It was, or so Vivienne Knight claims, his admiration for the powerful but understated acting of Gerald du Maurier (whom he saw several times on stage at Bristol) which prompted him to become an actor. He won a scholarship to RADA in 1933, something which didn't surprise him in the slightest. 'They never refused men. There were five men to twenty five girls'.[10]

Howard was typical of his generation in believing cinema to be a very second-rate medium in comparison to theatre. Just as John Gielgud grumbled that making movies required getting up at an unearthly hour in the morning[11] and Jack Hawkins saw cinema as 'a means of paying one's income tax',[12] Howard, at first, looked down on the movies from a very great height. No sooner had he left RADA than he was talent-spotted by Paramount in one of his first professional engagements, in the comedy *Aren't We All* at the Royal Court Theatre. He turned the Hollywood studio down. 'I was offered a five year contract,' he recalled, 'but I was rather a snob about it, as we all were at RADA. We didn't think that serious actors did films and I wanted to be a serious actor. Making films was the last thing on my mind.'[13] He was steeped in Shakespeare, which, he said, gave him 'grounding and confidence', and taught him how to move. His ambition was to become a classical actor.

It was drawing-room comedy which put Howard off the stage. His big break was winning a part as one of the juvenile leads (opposite Rex Harrison) in the 1936 West End production of Terrence Rattigan's *French Without Tears*. The play ran for two years, long enough to convince the young actor of the tedium of repeating the same role night after night. By the time he had escaped Rattigan, the war had started and there was a four-year hiatus in his career. However, Havelock-Allan and David Lean had seen him in *French Without Tears*. They noticed him again in small roles in *The Way Ahead* (Reed, 1944) and *The Way to the Stars* (Asquith, 1945). When they were looking to cast the doctor in *Brief Encounter* Howard was already in his thirties when he won the part. In other words, he was no fresh-faced juvenile. In her book on the actor, Vivienne Knight claims that the reason the film failed in Italy was that local audiences considered Howard 'brutto', meaning, among other things, ugly. His career as a male lead lasted barely half a dozen years, and even in those years he rarely carried a film on his own. In *The Third Man* he already seems middle-aged and careworn. In *I See a Dark Stranger* (Launder, 1944), he is the foil to Deborah Kerr's high-spirited IRA-supporting colleen, but it is her film, not his. He was never given roles comparable to, say, David Niven's dashing squadron-leader in *A Matter of Life and Death* (Powell and Pressburger, 1946), or Rex Harrison's dashing British agent in *Night Train to Munich* (Reed, 1940). It's telling that his one great Shakespearian stage role was not as Antony or Coriolanus but as the soured, bullying husband in a 1947 production of *The Taming of the Shrew*. Critics were already drawing attention to his sardonic, world-weary qualities. 'These quizzical gifts carry him through Petruchio with absolute, even priggish conviction', wrote Kenneth Tynan. 'In spite of its astonishing laziness, this is a brilliant performance with charm and phlegm in equal measure.'[14]

The image of Howard that emerges from contemporaries' accounts and newspaper reports is of a stereotypical hell-raiser in the vein of Hollywood stars such as Bogart, Mitchum and Tracy. 'One of the greatest actors in the world', John Huston remarked of him. 'He has much in common with the late Humphrey Bogart, you know, although Howard is the greater virtuoso.'[15] There are countless stories about his antics: how he was arrested during the shooting of *The Third Man* for impersonating an officer and conducting the hotel orchestra, how he became so obsessed with cricket that he demanded his film contracts allowed him time off to watch Test matches, his boozing sessions, his driving scrapes and his unerring ability to turn up to work on time, whatever he had been doing the night before. One journalist who played cricket with him noted, 'Trevor Howard is a sort of throwback to robust Regency or Restoration days. He carries the air of a buccaneer and goes through life, as he himself says, bellowing.'[16] Another pointed out how much he resented being typecast as the gallant English everyman. 'He has the sandpaper raw masculinity of a Bogart and the force of a Tracy', the journalist wrote. 'Why has this never properly been recognized?' 'Because,' said Howard, 'I once made a film called *Brief Encounter* which did me a lot of harm. I was playing a part but to some extent I became identified with that role and was thought of as a kindly, suburban Englishman, with far more scruples where women are concerned than any him hero can afford to have.' 'The real Trevor Howard is, of course, completely unlike this. He is a roisterous character whose small talk is more Rabelaisian than suburban.'[17]

Marion Hansel, who directed Howard in one of his last films, *Dust* (1985), offers a familiar description of the actor as a consummate professional on set, and a flamboyant drunkard off it. 'I wouldn't dare to cast someone that is on drugs because I don't know how to handle that,' she says now, 'but somebody who is an alcoholic – I can handle that.' The first evening, when Howard arrived in the remote Spanish hotel where the crew was staying, he was so inebriated that he didn't recognise Hansel and seemed to think she was one of the production assistants. The next morning, he roared with laughter, and told Hansel that he had been testing her out. 'I wanted to know what you were like. I have two solutions: either I work with you or I work against you, but apparently you're good so I'll work with you.'

In the film, which Hansel adapted from J. M. Coetzee's novel *In the Heart of the Country*, Howard plays a patriarchal Afrikaaner sheep farmer who treats his devoted daughter (Jane Birkin) with contempt and seduces the young black wife of one of his farm hands. The daughter, intensely jealous but also appalled by the way he blunders into the young wife's life, reacts by killing him. Hansel recalls that Howard took his costume very seriously. He'd done research on how South African farmers looked and dressed, and gave his hair a blondish-reddish rinse to make him look more like a Boer. He wasn't much interested, though, in discussing the psychology of the character. 'He did exactly what I asked him to do. He followed my storyboard exactly as I designed it. He never asked whether it was a close-up. Looking at the lens, he knew how close he was. I never had to tell him and he never asked.'[18]

One critic wrote of him in *Dust* as looking like 'a mangy, grand old lion'.[19] It's a description which Hansel recognises: 'the more he aged, the more depth was in his face'. In the latter part of his career, Howard's grizzled features and natural air of authority made him ideal casting as establishment types gone to seed. From his blustering Lord Cardigan in Tony Richardson's *The Charge of the Light Brigade* (1968) to his role as the drunken, raddled Jack Soames in Michael Radford's *White Mischief* (1987), his last film, this was how he was used.

Perhaps because he was so prolific (his filmography, including television movies, stretches to well over a hundred titles) and appeared in so many forgettable movies, he was taken for granted. He became just another of that tribe of dependable, unsung British character actors. 'British actors pay a price for their versatility,' US critic Andrew Sarris noted in his obituary of Howard, 'they seldom become big stars, and worse still, they tend to gravitate ever more to gargoyles and grotesques even when they are vibrantly young enough to fire up the historic repertory.'[20] Howard was a victim of his professionalism. He was so efficient at playing officers and police inspectors or, in his later years, crusty colonial types that he was rarely offered roles which taxed him. Directors began to take him for granted. Film-maker and cinematographer Jack Cardiff, who worked with him half a dozen times, recalls that 'I'd always look for a part for Trevor if I directed because he was one actor I could rely on to be on time, remember his lines and give a first-rate performance without me having to explain it all to him'.

He existed in a sort of purgatory. He wasn't exactly a character actor but nor was he a fully blown star. Having worked with Cubby Broccoli on *Cockleshell Heroes* he was briefly in the frame to play James Bond. 'I couldn't see Eton behind that wonderful craggy face of his', Broccoli wrote in his autobiography,[21] seemingly oblivious to the fact that (according to the Ian Fleming novels) Bond was supposed to have been educated at the Scottish public school, Fettes, not Eton. Whatever the case, Howard was surely too old for 007 by the early 1960s.

He was working on a different level to the 'chaps' in their slacks and tweed jackets – the Kenneth Mores and Ian Carmichaels – who were his contemporaries in postwar British movies. He had a saturnine quality and a physical presence that they did not. He worked better with – and seemed more interested in – women than they ever did. Whether Celia Johnson in *Brief Encounter*, Deborah Kerr in *I See a Dark Stranger*, Schell in *The Heart of the Matter* or Sally Gray in *They Made Me a Fugitive*, there was always a sensual spark and an erotic quality (albeit often understated) to his characters' relationships. Elsa Martinelli, who played the half-caste ingénue to his cynical sea captain in *The Key* (Reed, 1958), at first suggested that the idea of her falling in love with such a crusty old figure was 'highly implausible', but soon became smitten by him.

However buttoned up and stern his endless parade of authority figures, Howard was able to covey their vulnerability, anger, yearning – and their perversity. His last screen role, in *White Mischief*, was hardly one of his most rewarding. He was, yet again, the ex-pat, but when Jack Soames sidles off into a back room so he can peep at the beautiful Diana (Greta Scacchi) in the bath, a character who seems well-meaning and harmless takes on a vaguely sinister and pathetic air. As Sgt Mogford had discovered way back in the 1940s, Howard was never quite the upright, one-dimensional English gentleman he appeared.

Notes

1 *News Chronicle*, 27 June 1947.
2 See Peter Wollen's piece on the 'spiv cycle' of the 1940s, *Sight and Sound*, April 1998.

3 Havelock-Allan interviewed by the author, January 2000.

4 Michael Munn, *Trevor Howard: The Man and His Films* (Robson, London, 1989), p. 36.

5 Vivienne Knight, *Trevor Howard: A Gentleman and a Player* (Muller, Blond & White, London,1986), p. 45.

6 News Chronicle, 26 June 1947.

7 BFI microfiche *The Heart of the Matter.*

8 BFI microfiche *Mutiny on the Bounty* (1962). The cotton wool incident is also discussed in Munn, p. 82, where it is suggested that Howard was so unhappy with Brando's behaviour that he took to smoking opium.

9 Jeff Young, *Kazan on Kazan* (Faber, London, 1999), p. 127.

10 Knight, *Trevor Howard,* p. 27.

11 John Gielgud, *An Actor and His Time* (Penguin, London, 1981), p. 53.

12 Quoted in Jeffrey Richards, *The Age of the Dream Palace* (Routledge, London, 1984), p. 169.

13 Munn, *Trevor Howard,* p. 22.

14 Quoted in Knight, *Trevor Howard,* p. 72.

15 BFI microfiche Trevor Howard.

16 *News of the World,* 21 July 1957.

17 *Evening Standard,* 21 January 1957.

18 Hansel interviewed by the author, January 2000.

19 *Village Voice,* 4 November 1986.

20 *Village Voice,* 2 February 1988.

21 Cubby Broccoli, *When the Snow Melts* (Macmillan, London, 1988) p. 165.

NEIL SINYARD

Sir Alec Guinness:
the self-effacing star

11

> We've never really produced stars – someone like Guinness is more a char-
> acter actor. (Daniel Angel)[1]

> If I had been freed from my self-imposed straitjacket three decades ago, I
> might – who knows? – I might have taken off and been a sort of star. Not
> that I had any ambition to be a film star; I saw a few actors cease to be real
> people when they succeeded and some of those who failed became
> ingrained with bitterness. And some of the good ones who made it to the
> top didn't know how to cope with their success and reached for the bottle.
> Updike's *In the Beauty of the Lilies* gives a full-length devastating portrait of
> a Hollywoodized human being. No thank you. (Alec Guinness)[2]

I once nearly bumped into Alec Guinness. I had been interviewing Fred
Zinnemann in his Mayfair offices in the early 1980s in connection with
a book project and, coming out afterwards into Mount Street, I almost col-
lided with a bespectacled, elderly gentleman dressed immaculately in a
dark coat and black hat. My immediate response was that I had suddenly
encountered George Smiley, Secret Service Controller of John le Carré's
Tinker, Tailor, Soldier, Spy, which had been recently dramatised for the
BBC: it was only a split second later that I recognised the actor. Significant that I should register the character first and then the performer. On
sensing my recognition, Sir Alec's immediate response was to look suddenly apprehensive and to scuttle away. It was as if a cover had been
blown.

Of all Britain's theatrical and cinematic knights, Sir Alec Guinness has
surely been the least flamboyant, the most reticent. Think only of the
titles of his volumes of autobiography. *Blessings in Disguise* (1985) is particularly eloquent. On the face of it, it seems a gracious acknowledgement
of the life-gifts his acting career secured for him. However, as with much
else in Guinness, there is the hint of a subtler sub-text: that disguise is the
real blessing that acting bestows. Similarly with *My Name Escapes Me: The
Diary of a Retiring Actor,* his journal published in 1996. Note the key

words: <u>Disguise, Escape, Retiring – the core of Guinness's acting persona is in that formulation</u>. His first biographer, Kenneth Tynan, referred to him as unrecognised and unrecognisable, and wrote that 'were he to commit a murder, I have no doubt that the number of false arrests following the circulation of his description would break all records'.[3] Alexander Mackendrick, who directed Guinness in two of his greatest screen performances in *The Man in the White Suit* (1951) and *The Ladykillers* (1955), said he found him a complete enigma, to the point of wondering whether, when the actor removed his makeup, there was anything behind the mask.

In a recent re-evaluation of the definitions of the star in cinema, Christine Geraghty divided the star actor into three categories: star-as-celebrity, star-as-professional and star-as-performer.[4] The first category is defined by the way the personality, whether it be Greta Garbo or Tom Hanks, subsumes the role. Garbo does not become Camille, Anna Karenina, Queen Christina: rather, they all become different facets of the performing personality we know as Garbo. As one of the earliest theorists on stardom, Edgar Morin, wrote: 'Actor and role mutually determine each other.' In Morin's famous formulation, Gary Cooper does not so much play a multitude of roles as assimilate all these roles to his single, singular persona: in other words, he *garycooperises* them.[5] Guinness, however, was the complete antithesis of this, fitting much more into the star-as-performer category where the actor does not so much dominate the role as disappear into it. This was noted as early as 1951 by *Picturegoer* magazine in its edition of 11 August, just after its readers had voted Guinness actor of the year for his performance of Disraeli in *The Mudlark* (Negulesco, 1950). 'There are not many actors who become stars without forcing their own personalities on to the public', wrote John K. Newnham in that issue, in his article 'The Man You Never See'. He went on, 'That is one of the reasons why Alec Guinness is different.'

There are other qualities that made Guinness 'different'. Whereas stardom commonly connotes prominence and presence, Guinness's persona tended to the opposite: something furtive and elusive. He was happiest, he said, playing parts that were completely unlike himself. Guinness compensated for a shortage of glamour with a surplus of imagination. One danger of this is a variation of not seeing the wood for the trees: you cannot see the character past the ingenuity of the disguise. Just as Paul Muni's facial disappearance behind whiskers and spectacles as Louis Pasteur and Emile Zola seemed to dissipate the energy that was exciting about his acting in earlier films such as *Scarface* (Hawks, 1932) and *I Am a Fugitive from a Chain Gang* (LeRoy, 1932), so Guinness sometimes seemed trapped in a role where characterisation had difficulty in emerging from under the makeup. One example of this would be his heavily criticised performance as the Hindu Professor Godbole in David Lean's *A Passage to India* (1984), the kind of casting that now looks racially patronising. Another is his role as a Japanese businessman who becomes involved with a Jewish widow (Rosalind Russell) in Mervyn LeRoy's *A Majority of One* (1961). Given the film's theme of the possibility of East–West integration, the casting seems incongruous, to say the least: Penelope Gilliat simply remarked on the implausibility of Guinness's makeup, which, she wrote, caused him to look as if he had ravioli stuck to his eyelids.[6] Not for nothing, one feels – as if he has learnt from experience – did Guinness quote the Dr Johnson maxim in his journal: 'Almost all absurdity of conduct arises from the imitation of those we cannot resemble.'[7]

Allan Hunter has neatly expressed the other danger of Guinness's acting strategy: 'There is a thin line between his finely honed individual method and a bleakness of expressing too little.'[8] As an example of the latter, one might cite his performance as the vacuum-cleaner salesman-cum-spy in Carol Reed's *Our Man in Havana* (1960), which is a cipher at the centre of the film. 'We don't want any of your character acting. Play it straight. Don't act', Reed is supposed to have told him,[9] and the result is a performance of such wan restraint as to be virtually invisible. At the same time, there is something engagingly modest about this self-effacement. He must be one of the few great actors to be more often criticised for underacting rather than overacting.

There is a striking passage in *Blessings in Disguise* when Guinness quotes with approval his friend Alan Bennett's dislike of what he calls 'Great Acting'. Guinness goes on to gloss the phrase: 'the self-importance, the authoritative central stage position, the meaningless pregnant pause, the beautiful gesture which is quite out of character, the vocal pyrotechnics, the suppression of fellow actors into dummies who just feed, and the jealousy of areas where the light is brightest, and above all the whiff of "You have come to see me act, not to watch a play"'.[10] It is a convincing castigation of self-serving display. Still it is fair to say that some roles require big guns and forceful projection that Guinness seemed both technically and temperamentally unwilling or unable to provide. Indisputably amongst the outstanding actors of his time, he nevertheless always seemed to fall short in the great Shakespearian roles. Hamlet eluded him; he himself described his 1939 Romeo as the worst ever to disgrace a stage;[11] and his 1966 Macbeth was the subject of such vehement critical hostility that the director William Gaskill threatened to ban the press from all future productions at the Royal Court. Two sample reviews catch the flavour of the occasion: B. A. Young's comment in *The*

Financial Times that 'it must have taken a great deal of work to persuade Alec Guinness to give a performance so totally colourless'; and Hugh Leonard's in *Plays and Players* that 'it says much for Sir Alec's gift of anonymity that, although he is standing and speaking in full view of the audience, with only the witches and Banquo present, it is two or three minutes before we even notice him'. (Leonard was to suggest that Guinness would be better off playing the title role of *The Invisible Man* than Macbeth.)[12] He was always more of a Prufrock than a Hamlet, more of a Fool than a Lear: indeed, his portrayal of the Fool in the 1946 Old Vic production of *King Lear* is said to have quite upstaged Olivier's monarch.[13] In *My Name Escapes Me*, Guinness mentioned that he had been making notes on the small parts in Shakespeare that he was planning to work up into a talk; and one has an insight here into him as actor as miniaturist rather than master of the grand gesture, an actor who favoured understatement to bombast, irony to naked emotion, and an actor who served the text rather than the other way round.

So what made a star of Alec Guinness, and what kind of stardom is it? At the preview of Robert Hamer's classic Ealing comedy *Kind Hearts and Coronets* (1949), producer Michael Balcon ventured the opinion that Guinness had the range of a Chaplin and would be a big star. An executive bluntly told him that 'you must be out of your bloody mind'.[14] One can understand both responses. Guinness's impersonation of eight members of the D'Ascoyne family is an undoubted tour-de-force. It was the first indication of one distinctive quality that was to make him exceptional: namely, his range, which has enabled him on screen to play roles as diverse as Freud and Hitler; Marcus Aurelius and Charles I; Father Brown and Obi-wan Kenobi from *Star Wars* (1977); and, in David Lean's films alone, an Arab, a Russian, a Hindu, an uptight English colonel and two Dickensian characters about as far removed from each other as it is possible to imagine (the gentle Herbert Pocket in *Great Expectations* and the villainous Fagin in *Oliver Twist*). It is this virtuoso versatility rather than power of personality that has attracted American admiration, I suspect, because, by and large, it is not the kind of acting Americans are very good at (the best of their screen actors seem to stamp their personality on their roles) and it is also a style of acting quite unlike the prototype of the Method (that is, whereas an American actor would work from the inside out to get a handle on the role, Guinness builds his characterisations from the outside in). On the other hand, the executive's bafflement with Balcon ('you must be out of your bloody mind') seems not entirely misplaced. Guinness's performance now seems quaint and slightly freakish – the great acting in *Coronets* comes from Dennis Price – and the comparison with Chaplin somewhat grandiose. He never had Chaplin's slapstick agility, nor Chaplin's pathos: not that one feels he would have wanted it. The clue to the distinctive nature of Guinness's stardom comes not from *Coronets* but from his roles in the following decade, and it is a stardom that creeps up unawares.

Philip Kemp has an interesting phrase for Guinness: he calls him Ealing's 'accidental' star.[15] Ealing, after all, was not in the business of creating stars: it was dedicated to fostering team spirit. Stardom appears to have startled Guinness himself, much in the way that celebrity catches out Sidney Stratton in *The Man in the White Suit*. In both cases, they rise to sudden eminence not so much through personal charisma as through quirky inventiveness – something that was previously completely unsuspected in them. Guinness could surprise you and often brought an air of deep secrecy to the roles he played. This made him perfect casting for the Head of the British Secret Service, of course, but, in another sense, it is a quality that has been connected by Michael Redgrave to Guinness's extraordinary flair in comedy ('He had ... that most valuable asset for comedy: the appearance of possessing an impenetrable secret').[16] Here it is worth remembering that, until the mid-1950s, Guinness's predominant screen association was with comedy; that the most priceless quality of his memoirs is the dry wit; and that the modern films he particularly extolled are more notable for humour than their histrionics. Indeed, the actor with whom he has often been compared in his screen career is Stan Laurel,[17] a comparison made as early as 1937 in a review by J. G. Bergel in *The Evening News* of his performance as Sir Andrew Aguecheek in an Old Vic production of *Twelfth Night* ('Mr Guinness reminded me powerfully of Stan Laurel ... He sustains throughout a character of well-intentioned, almost agreeable silliness which is beautifully controlled').[18] Certainly some roles as hapless innocent bring Laurel to mind, and even some poses and gestures; the slightly dopey smile, the whimsical scratching of the head.

Yet if there was an air of Laurel about him, he was a very solipsistic Stan: there was no Hardy in sight.[19] Nor was he harmless. The introductory title to the Laurel and Hardy short *The Hoosegow* (Parrott, 1929) reads: 'Neither Mr Laurel nor Mr Hardy had any thoughts of doing wrong. As a matter of fact, they had no thoughts of any kind.' By contrast, there is a lot going on beneath the surface of Guinness's smiling simpletons: he did have thoughts, and sometimes they were thoughts of doing something wrong, or mischievous, or subversive. Guinness's most memorable screen roles occur often when that 'impenetrable secret' to which Michael Redgrave referred is discovered to reveal something startling. Guinness played these ostensibly ordinary, even dull, men who have a hitherto undisclosed obsession that, on exposure, makes them suddenly appear unusual and intriguing – like the inventor Sidney Stratton in *White Suit*, or the timid clerk in *The Lavender Hill Mob* (Crichton, 1951), who privately dreams of, and then executes, a bullion robbery.

There is usually something deeply hidden in Guinness's characters, that only surfaces reluctantly. It means that, when he does explode on screen (as in his gloriously unzipped display in *Tunes of Glory*), the effect is all the more electrifying. More typical, though, is the Guinness character who reveals the core of his being by stealth, as it were, as in *The Bridge on the River Kwai* (1957), when his Colonel Nicholson makes his most self-revealing speech with his back almost entirely to the camera. There might be an essential Englishness at work here, where the most powerful feelings are held under restraint, and the intensity felt is in inverse proportion to what is visually disclosed. In his article 'Feeling English' (*Sight and Sound*, March 1994), Richard Dyer observed that 'some of the great emotional moments in British cinema occur when the performance allows the pressure of feeling to be felt beneath a flatness of expression'. They also occur when understated emotion is matched by a director's visual discretion. Nicholson's awkward, covert English way of expressing his deepest feelings in *Kwai* is complemented by Lean's eloquently oblique, indirect framing.

Of Guinness's clandestine obsessives, Colonel Nicholson is the most fascinating and the most extreme. It is well known that Guinness had enormous misgivings about the part, wondering how he could get audiences to take the man seriously. That fine critic Gordon Gow, more alive than most to the film's satire, felt that Guinness gave a 'fine but possibly too straight performance'.[20] But 'straightness' is of the essence with Nicholson. It is in how he moves – that exaggeratedly erect military posture, which he even tries to retain when staggering out of the hole after torture. It is also in how he thinks, doing everything by the rules, even describing thoughts of escape as 'an infringement of the law', even though his Japanese captor reminds him: 'This is war! This is not a game of cricket!' This straightness hardens into an *idée fixe* of a bridge that will be his personal monument to British morale and courage in time of adversity, a fixed perspective that makes him oblivious to the counter-argument that his zeal in constructing the bridge could be construed as collaboration with the enemy. Guinness's performance walks a tightrope between tragedy and farce, being dignified and authoritative enough to make the men's loyalty to their colonel seem perfectly credible, and yet also a hilariously deadpan study of delusion. His interplay with James Donald's Dr Clipton has always been one of the highlights of the film for me; it now looks like a forerunner of the Bird–Fortune double-act, with Guinness playing the establishment straight man to Donald's rational sceptic, finally dismissing the latter's eminently sensible disquiet with a damning put-down that reverberates with unconscious irony: 'You're a fine doctor, Clipton, but you've a lot to learn about the Army.'

Much of the enigma of Guinness's stardom comes out in his six films for David Lean, on three of which, he said, 'we got on swimmingly and on three we had our differences'[21] – which is itself a mysterious sort of partnership. Aside from *Kwai*, the films on which they had their differences were *Dr Zhivago* (1965) and *A Passage to India*. In the former, the problem was that Guinness's role was little more than a framing device for the narrative, as he questions Tonya (Rita Tushingham) to discover whether she is the love-child of the union between Lara and his half-brother Zhivago. Yet his delivery of the film's very last line, 'Ah ... then it's a gift' (when he discovers that she can play the balalaika like an artist), is enormously moving in the slight lilt and lift he gives to the phrase, as if half-sensing its resonance (it has been said much earlier to the young Zhivago by his grandfather) and that he has come to the end of his search. *Passage* seems to have been an unhappy production, and his performance came in for heavy criticism for reasons indicated earlier. Even here, though, it is hard to imagine any actor giving more gravity and aura to Godbole's strange 'salutation' to Mrs Moore (Peggy Ashcroft) as she leaves India for the last time, a gesture that seems both homage and omen.

The happy experiences were on *Lawrence of Arabia* (1962), where Guinness clearly relished the political shrewdness that Robert Bolt's writing brings to the part of Prince Feisal, and the two Dickens adaptations, *Great Expectations* (1946) and *Oliver Twist* (1948). In *Expectations*, he managed to establish Herbert Pocket's essential goodness within thirty seconds of his first appearance, not simply by the food he thoughtfully bought for his new companion in lodgings, but through the open delight of the face, the warmth of the voice, and the way he bounds up the stairs in greeting: it is one of the most eloquent and effective entrances in movies. In *Oliver Twist*, his Fagin is a remarkable feat of impersonation, the appearance clearly modelled on the Cruickshank drawings (Olivier would say that you could always rely on Guinness to have done his homework). At the same time, one can understand postwar sensitivities being ruffled by a portrait teetering on caricature of a Jewish villain: it is not surprising that some found it anti-Semitic and that seven minutes were cut before it was to be shown in America in 1951. The cuts made it seem more anti-Semitic, Lean thought, because they eliminated the humour. Guinness made Fagin amusing and therefore not entirely unsympathetic. In striking contrast to the workhouse authorities, Fagin does at least offer Oliver food willingly when he arrives; and, when demonstrating the art of picking pockets, he achieves the remarkable feat of making Oliver laugh

– a sound so unusual in his young life that it startles the boy himself. Near the end of the film, when he is cornered by a mob baying for his blood, Guinness gives a real anguish to Fagin's cry, 'What right have you to butcher me?', a moment that alone would acquit the film from the charge of anti-Semitism: on the contrary, it seems to summon up a post-Holocaust horror at the fury of Fascism.

Although he has arguably faltered in the major Shakespearian roles, Guinness was always supreme in Dickens. Whereas one might say that Olivier had majesty but lacked the common touch, with Guinness it seems more the other way round. Indeed, one of his best Dickensian performances is of a character who feigns a fragile majesty against incongruous surroundings: namely, William Dorrit, the father of the Marshalsea debtors' prison in Christine Edzard's *Little Dorrit* (1987). In one of the rare negative notices of the film, thinking it tepid and melancholy rather than containing an authentic Dickensian radicalism, the great Marxist historian Raphael Samuel thought Guinness too regal for the role: 'a figure of dignity rather than pathos ... he looks positively majestic and serene ... even his breakdown is played as a kind of triumph'.[22] Yet the character has to be invested with some dignity to explain the respect he inspires in the prison; and I sense not an inappropriate majesty in the performance but a vulnerable hauteur and insecure pomposity (particularly in a weariness of the voice) that will disintegrate in a breakdown scene a good deal more traumatic than triumphant. His performances in the two Lean films and *Little Dorrit* made Guinness the screen's most distinguished Dickensian, so that when he crops up in the jungle as the half-caste illiterate Mr Todd towards the end of *A Handful of Dust* (Sturridge, 1988), preventing the hero from leaving because at last he has found someone who can read Dickens to him, the casting seems almost like an in-joke. 'We will not have any Dickens today', he pronounces in his final statement to an aghast James Wilby, 'but tomorrow, and the day after that, and the day after that ... Let's read *Little Dorrit* again. There are passages in that book I can never hear without the temptation to weep.'[23]

Usually a model of restraint, Guinness gave two screen performances where he really let rip. One is as the criminal mastermind Professor Marcus in *The Ladykillers*, a lithe, lugubrious display of comic malevolence that is worthy of Alistair Sim, from whom indeed it seems derived, particularly the Sim of Launder and Gilliat's *London Belongs to Me* (1948). The other is as Colonel Jock Sinclair in Ronald Neame's *Tunes of Glory* (1960), who becomes locked in conflict with his new commanding officer, Colonel Barrow (John Mills). Guinness always thought that his key to a character came from how he looked and the way he walked. In the case of Sinclair's appearance, the key seems almost to lie in the colour red: the ruddy complexion, the spiky ginger-red hair, that seem indicators of a volcanic temperament always on the verge of erupting. The walk is purposeful, direct, but sometimes veers into a parody of militarism, bordering on insolence. In the film's comic moments, when Sinclair is nudging his cronies into insubordination, the performance is sharp and sly: as he often did, Guinness made the humour more pointed by a use of droll mimicry of his companions, mocking their sophistication and polish and, by implication, highlighting his own class-free, salt-of-the earth masculinity. Hauled up for possible court-martial after striking an NCO for fraternising with his daughter, Sinclair is at first maudlin and self-pitying, but then becomes brazen and defiant. Guinness catches this renewed resilience simply in the lengthening stride of the man towards the officers' mess and in the gesture of clapping his hands and then rubbing them together with relish, as if scenting and welcoming the forthcoming fray. In the aftermath of Colonel Barrow's suicide, Sinclair orders a full-scale military funeral that seems part guilt at driving the man to his death: any qualms one might have about the motivation here are swept aside by Guinness's command of the final scene. His delivery of the final lines, as he is left with just Gordon Jackson and Dennis Price in attendance, is quiet, spaced, self-communing: on set, it reduced Jackson to tears. Like Macbeth, Sinclair is a soldier who has 'murdered' his leader and is now haunted by ghosts, but Guinness seemed more at ease with the modest scale of the emotions in this context: an actor who preferred to confide rather than declaim.

In Peter Glenville's otherwise rather dull film of Graham Greene's *The Comedians* (1967), there is one superb scene between Guinness and Richard Burton where the two flawed characters, Jones and Brown, sit upon the ground and tell sad stories about the death of their illusions. Guinness has typically played a character whose façade bears no relation to the secret reality; his shy, whispered revelation of self, which also lets slip an unexpected innocence, is magical acting. It prompted Burton, in a subsequent diary entry, to propose a distinction between actors he had known whose voices offstage are the same as onstage and those (here he lists Guinness, Olivier, Paul Scofield) whose voices are quite different. 'I wonder what it means', he wrote. 'Does it mean that Olivier, Guinness and Scofield are basically and essentially character actors while the rest of us mentioned above are simply extensions of ourselves? Well, the more I act and the more I think about it (which is not very often) the less I know of the heart of its mystery.'[24]

The heart of Guinness's mystery is particularly hard to penetrate. Part of it lies with the voice, and, because he was a fine writer himself, the intelligence he brought to fine writing.[25] In *Blessings in Disguise*, he reveals that he learnt from the great actress Martita Hunt (an unforgettable Miss Havisham in Lean's *Great Expectations*) a particular way of speaking lines. 'Unless there is a reason to the contrary,' he writes, 'she taught me that, in speaking, the verb which is the driving force of a sentence, should have first importance, then the noun, and that the adjectives and adverbs would take care of themselves and that personal pronouns should never be emphasised except in special circumstances.'[26] In Guinness's delivery, lines have a cadence of their own and are never garbled. In *The Fall of the Roman Empire*, for example, when a soldier pledges to bring the Emperor his enemy's head, Guinness as Marcus Aurelius replies: 'Please don't bring me his head, I wouldn't know what to do with it'- the character's gentle wisdom is distilled in Guinness's wry delivery. When George Smiley takes command at the end of *Tinker, Tailor, Soldier, Spy*, he says: 'There will have to be some redeployment for those of you who wish to remain in the service.' Guinness times the line with the rhythmic finesse of a master musician, inserting a threatening caesura after 'redeployment', allowing the pause to become impregnated with the heavy sense of Smiley's rebuke.

Back in an issue of *Harper's Bazaar* in April 1952, when trying to summarize Guinness's quality, Kenneth Tynan recalled Charles Lamb's tribute to a well-loved actor: 'He is not one, but legion. Not so much a comedian, as a company.' In a similar way, Guinness's stardom comes not from singularity but from many-sidedness; but a many-sidedness that never degenerates into caricature. Other qualities come into play: modesty, irony, self-control and understatement. Tynan's conclusion was that 'there will always be those who smile, finding him quaint, and these will be his enemies; while, on the other side, a much quieter throng, there will be those who stare, finding him unique'.[27] Fifty years on, those words still seem apposite.

A final word about Guinness and *Star Wars* (1977), the film that almost brought him the celebrity he so studiously avoided and whose popularity sometimes, so he said, made him long to be Ernest Thesiger. In his memoir, *A Positively Final Appearance* (1999), he records a cautionary anecdote about meeting a sweet-faced 12-year-old in San Francisco who, to his mother's evident approval, tells him he has seen *Star Wars* over a hundred times. Fearing for the boy's sanity, Guinness asks him to promise never to see the film again. 'He burst into tears', Guinness relates. 'His mother drew herself up to an immense height. "What a *dreadful* thing to say to a child!" she barked and dragged the poor kid away.'[28] Maybe a dreadful thing to say to a child, but what a terribly eccentric and English thing to say about one's most famous film: please promise never to see it again. Guinness's career was a triumph of anti-stardom, a war against the blandishments of the star, and a war which, on his own terms, and with characteristic civility ('No thank you'), he won.

Notes

1 Quoted in Brian McFarlane's *An Autobiography of British Cinema* (Methuen, London, 1997), p. 23.
2 Alec Guinness, *My Name Escapes Me: The Diary of a Retiring Actor* (Hamish Hamilton, London, 1996), p.155.
3 Quoted in Allan Hunter's *Alec Guinness on Screen* (Polygon Books, Edinburgh, 1982), p. 5.
4 'Re-examining Stardom: Questions of Texts, Bodies and Performance', in Christine Gledhill and Linda Williams, eds, *Reinventing Film Studies* (Arnold, London, 2000), pp. 183–201.
5 Edgar Morin, *The Stars* (Vista Books, London, 1960), p. 38.
6 Guinness, *My Name Escapes Me*, p. 103.
7 Quoted in Alec Guinness's *Blessings in Disguise* (Hamish Hamilton, London, 1985), p. 82.
8 Hunter, *Alec Guinness on Screen*, p.5.
9 Guinness, *Blessings in Disguise*, p. 206.
10 Ibid., p. 172.
11 Alec Guinness, *A Positively Final Appearance* (Hamish Hamilton, London, 1999), p. 18.
12 Quoted in Robert Tanitch's *Guinness* (Harrap Books, London, 1989), p. 118.
13 My former English teacher J. Large – who was also fondly recalled by Tom Courtenay in a piece for the *Guardian* ('My Inspiration', *Guardian Education*, 28 March 2000, p. 5) – told me that this performance, for him, became ever after the model for how the part should be played. 'He never took his eyes off Lear', he told me.
14 Michael Balcon, *A Lifetime of Films* (Hutchinson, London, 1969), p. 162.
15 Philip Kemp, *Lethal Innocence: The Cinema of Alexander Mackendrick* (Methuen, London, 1991), p. 15.
16 Michael Redgrave, *In My Mind's Eye: An Autobiography* (Weidenfeld & Nicolson, London, 1983), p. 97.
17 See, for example, Pauline Kael in *Kiss Kiss, Bang Bang* (Bantam, New York, 1969), p. 341; and Philip Kemp's discussion of Guinness's performance in *The Man in the White Suit* in *Lethal Innocence*, p. 51.
18 Tanitch, *Guinness*, p. 24.
19 Solipsism was the quality Bette Davis tartly singled out when she described their unhappy working relationship on *The Scapegoat* (1959): 'This is an actor who plays by himself, unto himself. In this particular picture, he plays a dual role, so at least he was able to play with himself.' Quoted in David Shipman's *Movie Talk* (Bloomsbury, London, 1988), p. 91, though perhaps Davis is not the most reliable of guides in the assessment of acting egos.
20 Gordon Gow, *Hollywood in the Fifties* (Zwemmer, London, 1971), p. 81.
21 Guinness, *Blessings in Disguise*, p. 216.
22 *Guardian*, 19 February 1988.
23 Dickens crops up in one of Guinness's cryptic asides about awards in *My Name Escapes Me*, p. 16: 'I wouldn't mind betting Dickens would fail to win the Booker Prize (too readable and too funny).'

24 Quoted in Melvyn Bragg's *Rich: The Life of Richard Burton* (Hodder & Stoughton, London, 1988), p. 455.

25 It is worth remembering that, as well as volumes of memoirs, Guinness has written stage adaptations of *Great Expectations* and *The Brothers Karamazov* and was nominated for an Oscar for his screenplay for Ronald Neame's *The Horse's Mouth* (1958), adapted from the novel by Joyce Cary.

26 Guinness, *Blessings in Disguise*, p. 55.

27 Kenneth Tynan, *Profiles* (Nick Hern Books, London, 1989), p. 40.

28 Guinness, *A Positively Final Appearance*, p. 11.

CHARLES BARR

'Madness, madness!': the brief stardom of James Donald

12

If this were a collection of essays about least favourite British actors, then my contribution would be on Derek Elphinstone, whose performances are as stolid and uncharismatic as his name. At the start of *The Four Feathers* (Zoltan Korda, 1939), he is the officer who is thrilled to be posted abroad in place of the defecting John Clements. At the start of *The Red Shoes* (Powell and Pressburger, 1948), he is Lord Oldham, who seems to be some kind of boyfriend of Moira Shearer. On both occasions, his function is to disappear without trace from the film and the memory as soon as the story proper gets started. In between these two films, *In Which We Serve* (Coward/Lean, 1942) gives him a more substantial role, that of Number One, the First Officer on HMS *Torrin*. Never can an actor have had so many lines, and occupied centre screen for so long, and made so little impression. He is there all the time, on the bridge and on deck and at the dinner table, looking determined, and giving a lot of orders. His big moment comes as the survivors, clinging to the raft, watch the *Torrin* sinking, and he speaks its epitaph, reading back to the Captain, with a rather creepy sincerity, his formula for what he wanted it to be: 'a very happy and a very efficient ship, sir'. Appropriately, he dies at the precise moment that the ship finally disappears beneath the waves. His function has been to embody in the purest form the ideology of the ship, emblem of the nation at war, and to do so without distracting attention from the more interesting figures around him: Coward himself as the Captain, Celia Johnson as his wife, and the various present and future stars who support them, all of whose characters are given some kind of personal story, quirk or anxiety. Not so Number One.

Actor fits role so perfectly that it seems irrational to be hostile to him, *qua* actor, but it is hard not to resent those who so thoroughly embody the dull and the oppressive; or, conversely, to be drawn to actors who incisively embody qualities which we find attractive, or with which we can empathise. Is this too obvious to be stated?

The role of the ship's doctor is at the other extreme: minimal screen time, maximum impact. He is in the wardroom with some other officers when Number One comes downstairs, uttering the quintessentially Elphinstonian line, 'It's a stinking awful night'. The doctor is chafing at idleness, and sinks back in his chair, speaking half to the others, half to himself: 'Years of expensive medical training, resulting in complete inactivity. The doctor wishes he was dead.' Later, as the ship goes into action, the film cuts briefly and startlingly away from this action to a shot of the doctor on his own, playing a game of Patience, surrounded by his instruments, waiting to be used. He is glimpsed, in the scenes that follow, doing his job wholeheartedly, a part of the team, but the card-game shot, and the complaint spoken in languid close-up, have established him vividly as a man of ironic detachment, possessing what Denis Healey always said politicians ought to possess, a 'hinterland': a life and a perspective beyond the immediate task.

This doctor is played by James Donald, a stage actor in his first credited screen role. Little has been written about him, and the obituaries in 1993 concentrated on his stage work and on his own hinterland activity as a Wiltshire wine-grower. But he made over thirty films between *In Which We Serve* and 1978. He is best known, probably, for his role in another Lean film, *Bridge on the River Kwai* (1957), as another doctor/officer, again shrewdly cast for his ability to express a sardonic detachment; it is he who looks down on the wrecked bridge and the dead bodies and speaks the (in)famous last words: 'Madness, madness.' Around this time, Donald played some other high-profile second-order roles: Vincent van Gogh's brother in Minnelli's *Lust for Life* (1956), and leading parts in two of the half-hour dramas that Hitchcock directed for his own television series, *Poison* (1958) and *The Crystal Trench* (1959). Before that, he had his brief period of stardom, in Britain in the early 1950s, billed first or second, and getting or keeping the girl, in several features, of which two stand out: *White Corridors* (Jackson, 1951) and *The Net* (Asquith, 1953).

The intelligent, potentially subversive, detachment glimpsed in *In Which We Serve* remains the basis of his appeal. He was one of three actors whom Michael Powell tested, and asked David O.Selznick to choose between, for the role of the minister who marries Jennifer Jones in *Gone to Earth* (1950). As Powell recalled it in *Million-Dollar Movie* (1992):

> I had had my eye on James Donald for some time. He was lean, all intelligence, knobbly, with a gift for making enemies ... He was secretive and detached and rude, and I liked him. No doubt there were points of resemblance between us. I thought that his secretiveness and his humour would give a double dimension to the film.[1]

James Donald. Michael Powell recalled that, 'He was lean, all intelligence, knobbly, with a gift for making enemies.'

Though his test was 'a beautifully paced performance: brittle, thoughtful, a Darcy out of *Pride and Prejudice*', it made both Selznick and Jones uneasy. In Powell's view, 'it was James's intelligence that lost him the part'.

Secretiveness, detachment, rudeness, humour, intelligence: this is a wonderfully exact description of Donald's distinctive persona, and offers a key both to his attractiveness and to his marginalisation. British cinema, especially in the 1950s, the decade of his prime (he was born in 1917), had difficulty in coping with those qualities perceived by Powell, and indeed, as he suggests, shared by him; Powell's own career notoriously went into steep decline in this decade.

Those qualities were, however, invaluable to *The Way Ahead* (Reed, 1944), whose project is to show army conscripts of varied backgrounds and temperaments shaking down into an efficient unit. In such films, the stronger the centrifugal forces of individual resistance, the more telling the eventual achievement of unity. *The Way Ahead* has a variety of moaners, played by efficient character actors such as Stanley Holloway, Raymond Huntley and John Laurie, but they are one-dimensional compared with Donald.

A prologue set in March 1939 establishes the future conscripts in their respective civilian jobs. Donald is a rent-collector, Evan Lloyd; in a scene that comes just two minutes into the film, we see him speaking to a tenant on the doorstep of her terraced house:

> – It's the war, Mrs Williams – that's the trouble, you see. It may start at any moment. We'd like to do lots of repairs, but our hands are tied.
>
> – They're not tied when it comes to taking the rent.
>
> – If times were normal, Mrs Williams, we'd be giving you a bath with a geyser, and new paint, and everything of the best.
>
> – I don't want any geyser. I want the guttering put right. Drip drip drip, all over the upstairs, it nearly drives you mad.
>
> – We can't all be thinking of ourselves in times like these, Mrs Williams; and with the summer coming on, it won't be bothering you so much, will it?

The scene as written could be played in many different ways. Reed chooses to take it in a single static shot, looking over the woman's shoulder at the man in close-shot at the right of frame, against the process background of a street: the whole emphasis is thrown on to actor and dialogue. The scene might very well have been conceived, originally, for the Raymond Huntley character: it's easy to imagine it being played, without the need to change a word, by that rightly cherished character actor, giving the lines a slow, ingratiating, supercilious reading. Donald reads them rapidly, almost throwing them away: he is sardonic, ironic, rather than supercilious, the irony operating at the expense not just of the woman but of himself and of the job that he is doing.

Part of the freshness of this introductory scene comes from the fact that Donald's is, in contrast to Huntley and company, an unfamiliar face, young and handsome. But the platoon has another abrasive young recruit of the same age in Stainer, played by Jimmy Hanley. The Hanley/Donald opposition is comparable with the Hanley/Bogarde one in Ealing's *The Blue Lamp* (Dearden, 1949): two juveniles, one of them much more dangerous and interesting than the other.[2] Stainer is immediately established as truculent, Lloyd as shrewd and watchful. Six weeks later, Stainer is still boasting to the others about the bold protests against authority that he plans to make, and Lloyd is stung into a response: 'You make me sick. You keep on talking, and you never do a damn thing.' If Stainer won't get round to making a complaint about their treatment direct to Captain Perry (David Niven), then Lloyd will complain himself, and does so. And it's Lloyd who takes action when they're in the middle of a field exercise, deciding that 'this is too silly for words', and prompting them to break cover, and thus to be captured, eliminated from the exercise and sent home early. Alone among the conscripts, he translates insubordinate thoughts into a strategy.

Of course this strategy is destined to fail, just as the deviant Bogarde character must be captured at the end of *The Blue Lamp*. In the film's central scene, Captain Perry 'dresses down' the platoon for opting out of the exercise and thus betraying the traditions of a regiment that fought Napoleon. Lloyd is the only one who can still articulate a response after the Captain's exit – 'All that talk, you'd think we'd lost the war' – but he will duly come round and become a loyal part of the unit. This has been foreseen by the Sergeant, in dialogue with Captain Perry: 'All soldiers like a bit of a grumble don't they sir? ... He hasn't got the hang of things yet, but he's got the knack of handling men all right. He's a bit of a nuisance at the moment, but later he'll make an NCO.'

This is the Prince Hal syndrome: Henry V is a more effective king for having been a rebel in youth. We don't see much of Lloyd as a leader – the film ends at the moment when the platoon goes into serious action – nor do we really want to: the impact of his nonconformist stage, his nonconformist *self*, has been too strong. Donald was a sufficiently skilled and handsome actor for British cinema to want to go on using him, and it would do so in a variety of ways, but only rarely did it take advantage of those creatively abrasive qualities which Powell recognised, and which make those two minor roles in *In Which We Serve* and *The Way Ahead* so memorable.

One line of development from them leads to *The Bridge on the River Kwai* (1957), of which more later, which does make intelligent use of him, at least until its final moments. The other line leads to *White Corridors* (1951) and *The Net* (1953), which provide easily his most fulfilling parts. Contrast his much less appropriate casting in two other main roles of this period. In Group Three's *Brandy for the Parson* (Eldridge, 1951) he is a romantic lead who works in the City, messes about in boats and drifts passively into some mild smuggling. Encased in a blazer with silver buttons, he looks out of place from start to finish. If the correct word for this film, with its echoes of *Whisky Galore*, is, as for so much of this company's output, 'sub-Ealing', *Cage of Gold* (Dearden, 1950) is Ealing proper.[3] Donald plays an idealistic doctor, which sounds promising, but his idealism is simply a matter of dogged loyalty: to his aged father's practice within the new National Health Service, which he leaves Harley Street to take over, and to the woman (Jean Simmons) to whom he is devoted, marrying her and taking on her child when she is deserted by the caddish David Farrar. His role is essentially passive, and the only medical work we see him doing is a routine bandaging.

In *White Corridors* he is again a doctor, Neil Marriner, but in addition to hospital duties he runs a medical research project. In *The Net* he is a research Professor, John Heathley, who has developed a supersonic plane. The two films are in many ways very different. *White Corridors*, directed by ex-documentarist Pat Jackson, is the last great product of the celebrated 1940s 'marriage' between fiction and documentary, putting over a public service message about the functioning of the new National Health Service. *The Net*, directed by Anthony Asquith, is a much more conventional melodrama. But they have powerful elements in common, centred very precisely on the two James Donald characters.

Marriner is developing a new serum to combat infections that resist penicillin. We first see him at the institutional breakfast table, hidden behind the issue of *The Lancet* that carries his latest findings. He evidently has an understanding, amounting almost to an engagement, with a colleague, Dr Sophie Dean, but he soon excuses himself: 'I've got an experiment cooking in the labs.' Heathley, in the first scene of *The Net*, is seen to be obsessed with his plane, the M7, and determined to get it into the air for tests as soon as possible. He returns to his house, where his wife Lydia is hosting a party for his colleagues, but soon excuses himself and heads back to the office: 'I'm sorry, dear, I have a job to do.'

These may sound like tired stereotypes – absent-minded professor, middle-class Englishman's evasion of intimacy – but these early scenes set up themes and conflicts that are worked through in unusually searching ways. The women are major British stars of the time – Googie

Withers as Sophie, Phyllis Calvert as Lydia – and both convey, with some inwardness, their feelings of love and of irritation towards their man, and the temptation of alternative possibilities: Sophie has the offer of a job in London which would take her away from the provincial hospital where the film is set, while Lydia is flattered by the attentions of one of her husband's colleagues. On the other side of the equation, both doctor and professor convey a commitment to their research which is visionary in its intensity. I know of no actor in British cinema, or indeed beyond it, who has expressed this visionary quality as believably, strongly and sanely as Donald does in these two roles – in one film quietly, in the other more articulately and combatively.

Marriner's researches are clearly going to do good by curing the sick. A boy brought into the hospital dies from a penicillin-resistant infection; if the new serum had been fully developed and tested, it might have cured him. And Heathley shares with Lydia his vision of what the supersonic plane may be able to achieve:

> I suppose I've always had the feeling that in this world everyone lives just around the corner and just out of sight of everyone else. But M7 can change that. It could make this *all one place* [he handles a model of the globe that is part of their living-room furniture]. I may be simple-minded, but I believe that when that happens we may learn to trust each other. And M7 could help us to do it, at least the physical part. She flies so high you can see the shape of the world ... and now I'm on the track of something else. Something that can take us right out into space.

The rhetoric may be dated, but, thanks to Donald's performance, the professor persuades both Lydia and us that he passionately believes in it, with head and heart alike.

Writing about *The Wings of the Dove*, Robin Wood reflects that effective screen acting

> cannot be adequately described in words. Even several pages of frame enlargements from a single scene would not offer more than an approximation, as the essence of acting is movement – the movement of the lips or of an eyebrow, the flicker of an expression that changes constantly – rather than a frozen moment. One can only offer some crude approximation of the effect, and then say 'Look for yourself'.[4]

As Heathley, Donald has a scene where he is on the telephone to Sir Charles, the man with ultimate responsibility for the research unit; a young colleague, Brian, is at his side. The Director of the unit, Carrington, who consistently overruled Heathley's wish to take M7 up himself on a test flight, has just died; Heathley sees an opening for achieving his own ends, and tells Sir Charles that 'I shall go ahead with the schedule as planned'. To the question 'Had you and Carrington agreed on the method of control for these flying tests?', he answers that 'The director and I were almost in agreement about that' – and gets away with it. Apart from a cut-away to Sir Charles, the scene is taken in a static close-shot of Brian and Heathley. Donald pauses before the word 'almost' and directs a rapid ironic flick of the eyes towards Brian, who (not really approving) remains inexpressive. Having put the phone down, he confirms with quiet satis-faction that 'We start phase two first thing on Thursday morning. Good night, Brian.' As he exits purposefully from the left of frame, the set of his mouth and a tiny, private, punching of the air with his right fist are beau-tifully judged signifiers of his mood and his vision.

'Look for yourself', then, if you get the chance, at this scene from an almost forgotten British film of the early 1950s; and look, too, at the scene, in that other film in the same category, where Donald as Marriner shows the members of the Management Committee around his labora-tory. We know that this PR effort grates on him, but Sophie has per-suaded him to be adult and pragmatic about it. So, patiently, he shows the committee round and answers their questions, conveying simultaneously an ironic amusement at their flashes of ignorance and a transparent com-mitment to the value of his research, which impresses them and earns the extra resources he needs. Again, the balance between public performance and private subtext is beautifully judged.

These two films deserve rescuing from obscurity for, if nothing else, the vivid way they express particular kinds of early 1950s idealism. On the one hand, a social vision that looks back to the experience of the Second World War and the reforms of the 1945 Labour government, exemplified in the NHS; on the other, a pursuit of new technology and new frontiers in the spirit of the 1951 Festival of Britain and the New Elizabethan Age. And both are deceptively artful narrative structures in the 'classical' tradi-tion. They tell a public story (hospital, aircraft unit) and a personal story, which are interconnected, and which move, in comparable fashion, to a joint resolution.

In treating the dying boy, Marriner accidentally infects himself, and then insists to Sophie that the untested serum must, in defiance af all the rules, be used on him – if not to cure him, then at least to gain more knowledge of its effects. Heathley, forbidden by bureaucracy to take the plane up a second time after narrowly surviving a first flight, likewise takes the law into his own hands in a thrillingly transgressive dawn break-in. Marriner is injected by Sophie, and the serum saves him. Heathley is unconscious at the controls, apparently doomed, when Lydia speaks to him on the intercom, and her voice revives and inspires him, and guides him home. In the crisis, the man demonstrates his need and his trust; the woman enters into, and shares, the ordeal and the vision. The climactic transgression, too, is in each case refreshingly vindicated by its success in pushing back the frontiers of knowledge.

The director of *White Corridors*, Pat Jackson, told me that he found James Donald 'cold', echoing a perception of his awkwardness expressed by both Powell and David Lean.[5] 'He was cold. I had to take him to 17 takes in the lab scene with Googie. "What's the matter?", he kept asking me. "You're supposed to be in love with the woman. Until you show a little warmth I shall go on retaking". 17th take showed a suspicion of affection.'[6] All I can say is that this tension seems in the end to have worked to the advantage of this complex and touching film. Marriner, the character, has difficulty in showing his emotions, and is aware of it – he tells a new nurse (Petula Clark) that in hospital work 'you've got to hide your feelings, grow a crust' – but manages to do so in a variety of understated or oblique ways; just as Heathley in *The Net* is able to express in a letter, read by Lydia to the accompaniment of his voice-over, the emotions he finds difficulty in expressing face to face. According to the actor Ian Richardson, 'English acting tends to be understated and depends heavily on nuance and irony'.[7] 'Ironic' is, along with 'sardonic', an adjective I have applied repeatedly to James Donald, and he certainly belongs, like Richardson himself, to the stage and screen tradition that is here evoked. But I hope to have established that this understatement need not be a negative, bloodless quality. Perhaps it is no surprise that this actor is such an attractive figure to a middle-class male British academic who has no problem identifying with the inhibitions and the ironic style, and in entering, in fantasy, into the pursuit of research achievements that actually have some kind of spectacular meaning.

There are few if any such romantic visionaries in the years that follow. British cinema is taken over by a set of male stars whom Geoff Macnab, echoing Andy Medhurst, has characterised by the noun 'chaps' and the adjective 'tweedy'.[8] James Donald was never a chap, nor can one imagine him jostling among the tweedy Kenneth Mores and Richard Todds of the mid-1950s either on the screen or in the promotional literature of Pinewood and *Picturegoer*. He goes back into the theatre and into secondary film roles, the most visible of which is in *The Bridge on the River Kwai*.

Set in 1943 but made in 1957, *Kwai* takes a more critical perspective on the conduct of the war than films of the time such as *In Which We Serve* or *The Way Ahead* were able to, or wanted to. James Donald has fifth billing behind three big current stars (William Holden, Jack Hawkins, Alec Guinness) and one from the silent period (Sessue Hayakawa, playing the commandant of the prison camp). His role as the army doctor,

Clipton, is crucial: he is the one person in the camp with the intelligence, and the will, to challenge the British commander, Colonel Nicholson, and to question his project – that of taking over command of the construction of the railway bridge, and completing it more efficiently than the Japanese could ever have managed. Nicholson, though, rebuffs him: 'You're a fine doctor, Clipton, but you've a lot to learn about the Army.' The doctor is left, then, to do his own job, and to keep his own counsel, while the work goes ahead, and while Holden and Hawkins prepare their expedition through the jungle to blow up the bridge on the day of its opening to traffic. On the day of completion he again makes his point firmly as the two men walk to the bridge:

– If you don't mind, sir, I'll watch the ceremony from up on the hill ... I'd rather not be a part of it.

– As you please, but honestly, Clipton, sometimes I don't understand you at all.

– As you once said, I've got a lot to learn about the Army.

With this typical Donald combination of plain speaking and irony, he goes off up the hill and sits on a tree stump, with a close enough view to be able to smile wryly to himself – typical Donald expression – at Nicholson's action in fussily clearing a leaf or two off the bridge's railway track.

Now comes the film's spectacular climax. The fall of the river level overnight has exposed part of the mechanism put in place to blow up the bridge. Nicholson spots this, and calls the Japanese commander to help forestall any threat to the construction in which both of them have invested so much. Holden and company watch incredulously, then intervene. After a succession of shootings and stabbings, the dying Nicholson falls on to the detonator, the bridge blows up and the train plunges into the river.

Back to Donald, who takes in the scene, says 'Madness!', and starts to move. Back to him again a few shots later, and he repeats 'Madness, madness!'. As he moves towards the river and the bodies, the camera sweeps up and away, leaving him in long-shot.

So, he gets the last words of the film, spoken in close-up, and everyone remembers them. But how crudely the film here manipulates him, and wastes him.

Nearly ten minutes have passed since we saw the doctor sit down to watch, so what has he been doing meanwhile? If he was attentive enough to register Nicholson's action in tidying up the track, then surely he was attentive enough to have become interested in the much more dramatic action that follows, and to have at least suspected what was going on. An alternative scenario would have him watch carefully, start to cotton on, run to Nicholson and argue with him – and perhaps then be accused of treason, even handed over to Japanese custody. Or he could, instead, have been shown in the odd cutaway, rooted to the spot in horror, embodiment of the ineffectuality of the well-meaning liberal. As it is, the shunting of this intelligent observer out of the action for so long is the most shameless of dramatic cop-outs. The final threefold repetition of 'Madness!' is as crude as the Malcolm Arnold score that now surges back to usher in the closing credits. He simply doesn't need to *say* 'madness' once, let alone three times: he can speak much more forcefully through eyes, eyebrows, the set of the mouth. The master of the sardonic smile/grimace, who can use it to express such subtle variations of meaning, is, at this climax, made to speak the clumsy words as though he were some bystanding extra – or Derek Elphinstone.

Kwai and its ending nevertheless represent, along with his self-effacing performance as Theo van Gogh the previous year, the nearest approach James Donald made to international stardom. But among his subsequent character roles, most of them on predictable professional lines – sardonic doctors and padres and teachers – comes the only film other than *Brandy for the Parson* in which he gets top billing: *Quatermass and the Pit* (Roy Ward Baker, 1967).

He does not, despite the billing, play Professor Quatermass, but a Dr Roney, who runs a scientific research institute, and is called in when excavations in London encounter a mysterious obstacle – a metallic object which others take to be a German bomb from the Second World War, but which turns out to be something much older and more menacing. Roney is visionary, bold, and transgressive, ready from the start to challenge the establishment instinct for unimaginative reassurance. He doesn't conceal his contempt for Breen (Julian Glover), the rationalist soldier put in charge, remarking that 'he's a type I loathe on sight'. As Glover's men go in to deal with the object, he remarks bitterly, half to himself, as he eats some chocolate, 'That's right, tear it all up!'. At 50, Donald's face has become gaunter, but he has lost none of his ability to put across intellectual energy and sardonic humour, and gives full value to the salutary abrasiveness of his role as a defender, once again, of the principle of scientific enquiry. The one disappointment is that this function is shared with Quatermass himself, played by the competent but less incisive Andrew Keir; having carried the opening scenes and set up the terms of the conflict, Roney yields centre stage to the Professor, and is offscreen for much of the middle part of the film. But he comes back from his laboratory in time to take charge again, and to combat the satanic monster which now hovers over London – solving the problem first scientifically (expose it to iron), and then by direct action as he climbs to the top of a huge crane and steers it into the monster, destroying both it and himself.

It's a peculiarly satisfying reprise, translated into the excessive terms of the horror film, of his two major parts in the naturalist dramas of the early 1950s: testing his own serum in *White Corridors*, flying his own experimental plane in *The Net*. In his last significant film part, James Donald, by his intelligence and his boldness, saves the world.

Notes

1 Michael Powell, *A Life in Movies* (Heinemann, London, 1992), p. 64.
2 See Andy Medhurst's essay 'Dirk Bogarde' in Charles Barr, ed., *All Our Yesterdays: 90 Years of British Cinema* (BFI, London, 1986).
3 For more on *Cage of Gold*, see Charles Barr, *Ealing Studios* (3rd edition, Cameron & Hollis, Moffat, 1999), pp. 10–11 and 150–2.
4 Robin Wood, *The Wings of the Dove* (BFI Modern Classics series, London, 1999), p. 79.
5 Kevin Brownlow, *David Lean* (Faber and Faber, London, 1996), p. 365.
6 Pat Jackson, letter to the author, 12 April 2000.
7 Carole Zucker, interview with Ian Richardson, in Peter Kramer and Allan Lovell, eds, *Screen Acting* (Routledge, London, 1999), p. 164.
8 Geoffrey Macnab, *Searching for Stars* (Cassell, London, 2000), e.g. pp. 121, 183.

PAM COOK

The trouble with sex: Diana Dors and the blonde bombshell phenomenon

13

Diana Dors has a unique status in British popular culture. Other screen actresses of her generation, such as Joan Collins, achieved long-term national and international recognition for their sassy, earthy humour and transgressive sexuality, skilfully trading on their camp appeal to maintain public interest. Like Dors, other female film stars of the 1950s and 1960s acquired enduring popularity by developing second careers as television personalities (Barbara Windsor, for example). Diana Dors's star persona shares many features with such images, which encapsulate conflicting cultural and social values surrounding class, gender and sexuality. Yet the Dors image moved beyond the level of representation to become symbolic, a public monument. During her life, and since her death, this monumental quality, her public display of aspects of British culture that are usually swept under the carpet, has inspired profound ambivalence in the media while endearing her to audiences across class and gender. She died in May 1984 after a struggle with cancer which, like the rest of her life, received much publicity that focused on her ability to survive the slings and arrows of outrageous fortune. Since then, she has been the subject of two television documentaries and a recent two-part biopic, testifying to the fact that her image continues to have cultural currency, despite the disdain with which she is generally treated by the arts establishment.[1]

There is no doubt that Diana Dors's tumultuous and often scandalous private life contributed to this ambivalent response. While the tabloid media fed greedily on her self-publicising exploits and her sexual misadventures, manifesting a grudging admiration for her success in manipulating the publicity machine in her own interests, they also kept a sardonic distance intended to undermine her talent as an actress. Any recognition of her performance skills was generally framed by a sense of surprise that a self-confessed sex symbol should manifest any acting ability at all.[2] The 'sex symbol' label both helped and hindered Dors's career. She was very conscious of it, and maintained it to the end of her life: the platinum blonde helmet and careful makeup, the voluptuous body encased in tight clothing, mementoes of her heyday as a 1950s glamour icon, remained her trademarks, even when in the 1960s and 1970s, as a television personality and character actress, she developed the nubile vamp persona into a mature female sexuality. She was often referred to as Britain's only real sex symbol, the national answer to Italy's Gina Lollobrigida, France's Brigitte Bardot, Sweden's Anita Ekberg and America's Lana Turner or Marilyn Monroe. The press celebrated her as an export with international value, a key to the British industry's success in the US market. Yet it was precisely the commercial value of her sexuality, and the bravado with which she put it on display, that the media found so troublesome. In an era of rampant consumerism, the British obsession with 'quality' and distrust of the excesses of trashy popular culture associated with 'Americanisation' came to the fore. In the postwar expansionist economy, Diana Dors was a shiny, newly minted coin. Like all new currency, she was treated with suspicion.

In what remains the only academic article to take Diana Dors seriously,[3] Christine Geraghty[4] points to the performance element in the female sex symbol's construction of her identity. Stylised body language, gesture and stance combined with exaggerated physical attributes such as a tightly corseted, statuesque figure, fashionable designer clothes, sleek blonde hairstyle and full, sensual lips separated out Diana Dors from the other female members of the cast, irrespective of the roles they were playing, and the demands of character and narrative. The self-conscious performance of sexuality, while it does not have the direct address to camera characteristic of pin-up photography, nevertheless does recognise the existence of the camera and the presence of the viewer. This extratextual quality is what lends Diana Dors an iconic dimension, connecting her persona to cultural discourses around gender, sexuality and modernity in which she becomes a key figure, both idolised and despised, literally embodying the aspirations and anxieties of a society in transition.

Diana Dors was by no means Britain's only sex symbol. The 1950s gave birth to a host of exotic, glamorous blonde starlets – Sabrina, Belinda Lee, Shirley Eaton, Sandra Dorne *et al.* – who offered similar exhibitions of excessive sexuality modelled on the likes of Jayne Mansfield and Lana Turner. Although outside the scope of this chapter, they merit serious attention as members of the British contingent of the postwar blonde bombshell phenomenon, of which Dors was by far the most visible representative. She is also the only one who has been given a place in the blonde bombshell international pantheon, along with Marilyn Monroe and Brigitte Bardot.[5] It is interesting that she is perceived to merit this status despite the fact that, although she acted in several international productions, she never achieved international stardom on a level with Bardot, Monroe and others. This suggests that her extratextual persona, the Diana Dors who constructed herself through publicity machines as an image that both embodied and challenged national boundaries, was more powerful and influential than her onscreen performances. This makes Diana Dors something of an anomaly in traditional star study, which generally perceives the extratextual star persona as a secondary, or subsidiary element that feeds into the primary, onscreen image. Richard Dyer (1979) cites Brigitte Bardot as an example of a star whose films are less important than her offscreen persona, but Diana Dors would also fit this category.

The sex symbol is usually defined in terms of her excessive sexuality, which is seen as a manifestation of, and commentary on, shifting social relations of class, gender and sexuality. She is a transgressive figure who is driven by sexual desire and materialism to challenge traditional social boundaries, and is often demonised or criminalised as an instrument of consumerism, even if she is celebrated for her independence. Rather like the *femme fatale* of the 1940s, the post-Second-World-War sex symbol represented an ambivalent cultural response to the increasing sexual and economic emancipation of women and its perceived threat to the family. The combination of sexual transgression, mercenary motives and hedonistic lifestyle that defined the postwar, post-Kinsey sex symbol was

Diana Dors in flagrant pose. 'During the 1950s she was emblematic of conflicting forces of social change in a way no other British star was able to achieve.'

an international phenomenon that could be found in many other female stars of the period, from continental Europe as well as Britain and the USA, all of whom shared certain key features even though their star personas emerged from different national contexts.

Gina Lollobrigida, Sophia Loren and Brigitte Bardot, among others, belonged to a new breed of international film star whose buxom sexuality was the embodiment of contradictory impulses. It was maternal, even though it was divorced from reproduction, at least in its onscreen manifestation. It was an adult sexuality, even when it was represented as precocious. This was most apparent in the case of Brigitte Bardot and Marilyn Monroe, both of whom projected a childlike sexual naiveté embodied in a voluptuous physique with large breasts and hips which were far from infantile. When it came to the 1950s blonde bombshell in particular, her statuesque figure, always displayed to full advantage by revealing clothing and boned underwear, was often combined with facial characteristics which were remarkably uniform: round face, small, upturned nose and full, sensual, pouting lips. Indeed, the similarity in terms of physiognomy between Jayne Mansfield and Brigitte Bardot was remarkable.[6] If there is always an element of performance and masquerade about the sex symbol, then the blonde bombshell took this to extremes until she became a parody of herself, an image that commented on prevailing images of female sexuality, a simulacrum rather than the real thing. This is nowhere more obvious than in the bleached blonde hair itself, quite consciously faked with the help of a bottle of peroxide. In her book about official attempts in Britain to manage representations of femininity during the Second World War, Antonia Lant[7] points to the significance of hair in redefining sexuality. Women were encouraged to keep their hair short or tie it back for war work, while the restrictions on cosmetics militated against the use of hair dye. Glamour, associated with erotic display and sexual excess, was perceived as dangerous and against the national interest. The female body was also brought into line: uniforms and utility clothing flattened the breasts to produce a more unisex body shape that effaced the signs of sexual difference. The postwar blonde bombshell, then, with her abundant curves, explicitly seems to mark the return of the repressed.

The 1950s blonde bombshells clearly belonged to an international 'group', defined by certain physical and performance codes. This lent them an almost mythic dimension. Although, because of national and cultural differences, they may not have been exactly interchangeable, they were all on some level versions of an 'earth mother' archetype with strong Dionysian overtones.[8] That this powerful, Dionysian figure, celebrating a primeval fertility associated with eroticised, active female sexuality, should emerge at this point challenges those accounts of the postwar period which stress the predominance of discourses of domesticated female sexuality centred on the home and family. The blonde bombshell, in her most extreme form, was a harbinger of the death of the patriarchal family (Bardot in *Et Dieu ... créa la femme* (Vadim), Malone in *Written on the Wind* (Sirk), both 1956), even when she was punished and/or recuperated by the social order. The circulation of such images, with their emphasis on voracious sexual appetite and materialist cravings, suggests an ambivalent response to the increased power of women as mothers and consumers, which was acknowledged to be central to the growth of the postwar economy. Female fertility and cupidity were essential to this economy; however, they could not be allowed to develop into a destabilising concupiscence.

The blonde bombshell's dangerous sexuality was also informed by debates around the relaxation of censorship and the increased visibility of pornography in the postwar period. In Britain, the X certificate was introduced in 1951 'in an attempt to stem the decline in cinema audiences by moving into sensational and previously forbidden areas of sex and violence, under pressure on the one hand from the influx of "Continental" sex films and European art cinema, and on the other from competition for audiences from television'.[9] The mid-1950s witnessed a series of moral panics in response to films such as *Baby Doll* (Kazan, 1956) and *Et Dieu ... créa la femme*, which were controversial in their own countries for their graphic representation of adult sexual material (the opening shots of *Et Dieu ...* show Bardot sunbathing naked). Their notoriety followed them to Britain, where they figured in media discourses around censorship and sexuality, some of which were condemnatory, while others used them to argue for the greater liberalism of British society in relation to Europe and the USA.[10] Both Marilyn Monroe and Jayne Mansfield contributed to the climate of sexual liberation by posing nude for promotional purposes, while legend has it that the young Diana Dors also obliged publicity photographers by taking off her clothes when offered an additional fee.[11] The blonde bombshell, then, played a significant role in the process of redefining cultural attitudes in the shifts towards modernity that took place during the 1950s, shifts which often focused on the regulation and deregulation of sexuality, and which had an international dimension as well as a national one. Thus, although the blonde bombshell's sexuality was closely tied to consumerism, it also figured prominently in wider cultural debates about morality and social reform, the penal system, censorship and decriminalisation.

In the British context, Diana Dors's persona intersected with these cultural developments from an early stage in her career. In 1948, when she was an up-and-coming 17-year-old starlet, while Rank's studio promotion emphasised her promise as a dramatic actress and her status as a star graduate of the London Academy of Music and Dramatic Art, the media focused on the challenge that she represented to outmoded, puritanical attitudes towards sex. Press coverage of the Gainsborough production *Here Come the Huggetts* (Annakin, 1948) told the story of a scene in which Dors appeared in scanty underwear that had to be reshot for the USA because it contravened the American censorship code.[12] Dors's response to the situation was reported as highly critical of the hypocrisy of the censorship ruling. Although her first minor film roles varied widely from comedies such as *Holiday Camp* (Annakin, 1947) to prestige literary adaptations such as Cineguild's *Oliver Twist* (Lean, 1948), there was a theme of social rebellion running through her parts in films such as *Dancing with Crime* (Carstairs, 1947) and *Good Time Girl* (MacDonald, 1948), which dealt with the state's attitude towards young offenders. Even in an apparently lighthearted family comedy such as *Here Come the Huggetts*, there was more than a hint of sexual subversion in her performance as the flighty young niece who created havoc in the Huggett household. This double thread of sex comedy and social problem melodrama ran through Diana Dors's films until the late 1950s, when her cinema career began to decline. Many of her roles engaged with contemporary social issues – sometimes indirectly, but more often than not quite explicitly. Press coverage focused on her physical attributes, excessive sexuality and talent for publicizing herself, but it also connected these features to her participation in changing social attitudes, though generally adopting a condescending tone. In 1954 there was intense media interest in the obscenity trial featuring *Diana Dors in 3-D*, a book of photographs of Dors sold together with red and green 3-D spectacles, which had been confiscated along with a number of 'dubious' publications from a shop in Halifax. The report in the *Manchester Guardian*[13] was deadpan: the publishers on trial stressed the quality of their books and the artistic reputation of the two men responsible for inventing the 3-D process used in the book. The bench found that although some of the books were close to obscenity, *Diana Dors in 3-D* was not obscene. It is difficult not to see this incident as a camp precursor of the *Lady Chatterley's Lover* obscenity trial in 1960. However, the particular combination of sexual transgression, spectacularization, technology and moral panic surrounding *Diana Dors in 3-D* was characteristic of the 1950s blonde bombshell and the scandal caused by the vision of modern femininity she projected.

The year 1954 was also the one in which Dors caused a media sensation by parading in a gondola at the Venice Film Festival in a mink bikini, an incident which has become as legendary as Marilyn Monroe's famous billowing skirt in *The Seven Year Itch* (Wilder, 1955). Although 1954 was a turning point in her career, she had been tabloid headline material for some time. Following her first major role as a saloon girl in *Diamond City* (MacDonald, 1949), her contract with Rank ended as the British film industry entered another of its periodic crises. A series of minor legal scandals featuring Dors and her first husband Dennis Hamilton kept her in the public eye, and between 1950 and 1953 she appeared in a number of films that developed her nubile vamp persona: *Dance Hall* (Crichton, 1950), and *Lady Godiva Rides Again* (Launder, 1951) among them. During this period, the publicity surrounding Dors emphasized her acquisition of the kind of wealth and luxury more characteristic of Hollywood than a Britain tentatively emerging from postwar austerity. In common with many Hollywood stars in the late 1940s and 1950s, who set up their own production companies in the wake of the end of the contract system tying them to the studios, Dors and Hamilton formed their own company, Diador Ltd, though its role as an independent production company never materialised. According to Dors herself, the wealth, power and sexual gossip associated with her image at this time were more apparent than real, and masked some real financial and personal problems.[14] Nevertheless, the publicity spell woven by Hamilton was seminal in enabling Dors to make the transition from starlet to full-blown icon. While spectacular stunts such as the 1954 mink bikini escapade, or press stories featuring Dors dripping jewels, furs and powder-blue Cadillacs, were part of that transition, they were not the whole story.

A 1955 article in *Picture Post* which sets out to examine 'the Dors myth' is one of the more searching and illuminating pieces devoted to the star. The writer begins by focusing on the platinum blonde hairstyle, immaculate makeup and vamp persona, but is won over by the directness and intelligence of the replies from Dors and ends the piece with a sympathetic analysis that takes a swipe at the snobbery of the establishment and the quality press. Dors is described as 'daring, desirable, uncompromising, non-conformist ... the personality the public want to see'. Later in the article she is compared favourably with Hollywood stars: 'Unlike some of her more famous Hollywood contemporaries, Diana Dors is no hypocrite.' When questioned about the notorious *Diana Dors in 3-D* obscenity trial, she is quoted as responding with characteristic, if disingenuous, candour: 'I don't know what all the fuss was about. Some of the old stills the Rank Organisation did of me were no less revealing. If that man in Halifax hadn't drawn attention to the 3-D stuff nobody would have bothered.'[15] The sympathy expressed in this piece for the straight-talking Dors and her challenge to the stuffy British establishment is the key to her popular appeal and to the qualities that made her national icon. It is also a symptomatic response to the social changes affecting the country in its transition to modernity, in which the idea of a liberal, civilised Britain was crucial, and social freedoms were intimately linked to the notion of freedom of choice central to an expansionist consumer economy. In Dors's phrase, 'that man in Halifax', there is a pre-echo of the 'man on the Clapham omnibus', the symbol of respectability that figured centrally in the debates around social reform and regulation after the Wolfenden Report of 1957 that continued until the late 1960s.

In his article 'Reformism and the Legislation of Consent',[16] Stuart Hall outlines the profoundly reformist nature of British society in the 1950s and 1960s, when active steps were taken by government to restructure sexual and social conduct. During the 1950s, a series of key acts dealing with the limitation of the death penalty (1957), prostitution (1959) and obscenity (1959) inaugurated a process of change in cultural attitudes towards permissiveness which sparked intense debate.[17] The reformist debates were characterised by a tension between liberalisation on one hand and fears about the undesirable effects of unregulated sexuality on the other. Post-Wolfenden moves to decriminalise prostitution, homosexuality and pornography, and to transfer them from the public arena to the private sphere of mutual consent, were to some extent complicit with moral panics about the erosion of traditional moral values, which were concerned about the increasing visibility of pornography and prostitution. According to Hall, the privatisation of sexual behaviour was tied in to private, domestic consumption centred on middle-class married women and the home, which was opposed to the conspicuous public consumption indulged in by the working classes, prostitutes and social climbers.

As we have seen, the international blonde bombshell phenomenon testifies to the fact that such concerns around the deregulation of sexuality were not confined to Britain. However, Hall's attempt to map a continuity between the 1950s and 1960s, and between the reformist character of the Conservative and Labour governments responsible for the legislation, reveals a dynamic between the impulse to reform and the inclination for constraint that seems to be a peculiarly British vision of social change.[18] It also provides a frame of reference for the Dors icon: on one hand unashamedly putting libido and conspicuous consumption on display ('spend, spend, spend'), on the other tightly encasing her voluptuous body in constricting whalebone and figure-hugging evening dresses. The bondage implications are not far from the surface, and certainly the Dors image was consciously imbued with sexual and commodity fetishism. But these pornographic associations need to be placed in context. Diana Dors had a voice, which was determinedly pro-sex. Her outspoken stand against hypocrisy and petit-bourgeois morality also placed her with a progressive strand in British society that wished to eradicate puritanism and narrow-minded intolerance. During the 1950s, she was emblematic of conflicting forces of social change in a way no other British star was able to achieve.

Between 1954 and 1956 Diana Dors appeared in a handful of films that played a crucial part in the development of her career. In 1954 she performed with Glynis Johns in *The Weak and the Wicked* (Thompson), a social melodrama about women in prison scripted by Joan Henry. The film was liberal in its approach to the theme of penal reform. Dors played a young woman led astray by her boyfriend who abuses the freedom of the open prison system by running away, betraying the trust placed in her by fellow inmate Johns and the prison governor. She has a change of heart, and returns to serve out her sentence, thus vindicating the humane message underlying the liberalisation process. Most of the prison inmates are presented as misguided or their criminal actions justified in some way: they are victims rather than hardened offenders, and the implication is that they may not belong in prison at all. In Carol Reed's more upmarket colour adaptation of Wolf Mankowitz's book set in the Jewish community in the East End of London, *A Kid for Two Farthings* (1955), Dors's role was that of a mercenary blonde who uses her sexuality to push her wrestler fiancé into a fight he does not want to take so that he can buy her an expensive engagement ring. Dors's physical appearance in this film was very different. The puppy fat had given way to an hour-glass figure displayed in pencil skirt and tight, powder-blue sweater (powder-blue was the colour of the Cadillac Dors and Hamilton purchased in 1955),[19] and the hair was bleached platinum blonde in the sleek, shoulder-length style that had become her trademark. The dialogue points up these changes, with other characters making fun of the hairstyle as a poor imitation of Marilyn Monroe, until Dors is driven to say that she wishes she had never done it. Needless to say, there was no turning back: the blonde bombshell persona was by this time firmly in place, even down to the pin-up iconography implied by the exaggerated uplift and the vampish body language. *A Kid for Two Farthings* encapsulates a key aspect of the Dors version of the blonde bombshell: the hedonist driven by commodity fetishism who is redeemed when she realises the error of her ways.

Value for Money (Annakin, 1955), in which she played a sexy London showgirl who sets her sights on John Gregson's naive northern factory owner, and *An Alligator Named Daisy* (Thompson, 1955), in which she starred as the wealthy daughter of an aristocratic family engaged to impoverished musician Donald Sinden, were both comedies in which Dors's characters were forced to reassess their consumer-oriented priorities and to recognise the power of love, though in both cases this conversion was achieved with a degree of pragmatic cynicism. Both played on her offscreen persona, making a feature of the trappings of glamour and wealth that defined her star image. Dors's appearance in both these films was as star attraction rather than as an actress playing a character. With the acquisition of star status came the power to turn down the offer of a lucrative contract from Rank and to choose her own scripts.[20] The choice, made with international stardom and Hollywood in mind, was to film *Yield to the Night* for Associated British, with a script by John Cresswell and Joan Henry, based on the latter's novel, and direction by J. Lee Thompson.

Yield to the Night, perhaps more than any other film in which she appeared, was a Dors star vehicle. It exploited current debates around capital punishment inspired by the case of Ruth Ellis, who was hanged for the murder of her lover amid great controversy which focused on the barbarity of the death penalty and the sadistic manner in which condemned prisoners were treated. The film belongs with the social problem melodrama strand of Dors's career, and was promoted by the studio, and by Dors herself in interviews,[21] as the breakthrough into serious dramatic acting that she had been waiting for. She was deglamorised for the role of the condemned murderess confined to a prison cell, dressed in shabby overalls with the platinum mane dulled and dark roots showing. However, a judicious use of flashbacks allowed the glossy glamour to be glimpsed from time to time, and the film played on the pin-up image as much as that of the serious actress. As a bid for critical recognition, *Yield to the Night* was not entirely successful. The blonde bombshell image was so firmly established that the British press were not sure what to make of this new departure, and found it difficult to take Dors's performance seriously, even when they recognised the value of the film's contribution to the capital punishment debate.[22] Nevertheless, *Yield to the Night* took the Cannes Film Festival by storm, and Dors was much in evidence, posing with furs and Cadillac, waving to photographers and acknowledging the cameras at every opportunity, in true pin-up style. This was the high point of her career.

Despite the success of *Yield to the Night*, it did not lead to offers of more serious acting roles. Instead, Dors accepted the offer of a three-picture deal from RKO and went to Hollywood. There she made a comedy with George Gobel, *I Married a Woman* (Kanter, 1956), a thriller with Victor Mature, *The Long Haul* (Hughes, 1957) and a *film noir*ish melodrama starring Rod Steiger, *The Unholy Wife* (Farrow, 1957), none of which made a lasting impression. Her encounter with Hollywood was not a happy one, either personally or professionally. The US press were hostile, perceiving her as an unwelcome challenge to Marilyn Monroe, and her extramarital affair with co-star Rod Steiger was not received sympathetically by the studio. Dors returned to Britain, but by the end of the 1950s the power of the blonde bombshell image was waning. Her cinema career went into decline, despite the fact that she appeared in more than thirty films between 1960 and 1984, some of them, such as *Deep End* (Skolimowski, 1970) and *Steaming* (Losey, 1984), well received by critics. Like Jayne Mansfield, she performed in cabaret, reinventing herself as a personality by trading on the image of the star she had once been.[23] As a television performer, she recycled her blonde bombshell persona, developing its camp potential and ensuring that, even after the star had faded, the icon would continue to shine.

With thanks to Esther Ronay and Jenny Hammerton.

Notes

1 A documentary produced by Harlech Television, screened on Channel 4 in May 1990, is a routine investigation of the seamier side of Dors's life. More recently Dors was the subject of an hour-long BBC2 Arena arts programme transmitted in December 1999, part of a series called *Blondes* which included Jayne Mansfield and Anita Ekberg. The two-part biopic, called *The Blonde Bombshell*, was screened on ITV in 1999.

2 See the press reviews of *Yield to the Night*: *Sunday Times* (6 May 1956); *The Times* (18 June 1956); *Financial Times* (18 June 1956); *Evening Standard* (14 June 1956); *Sunday Despatch* (17 June 1956); *Sunday Express* (17 June 1956); *Daily Mail* (15 June 1956), held on microfiche in the British Film Institute Library.

3 See, however, the sections on Diana Dors in G. Macnab, *Searching for Stars* (Cassell, London, 2000).

4 C. Geraghty, 'Diana Dors', in C. Barr, ed., *All Our Yesterdays: 90 Years of British Cinema* (BFI Publishing, London, 1986).

5 The Internet site http://www.bombshells.com/gallery/dors (7 July 1999) features colour publicity glamour photographs of Diana Dors. They appear to date from the 1950s, possibly originating from Rank.

6 The final shot of Jayne Mansfield in the BBC2 Arena documentary about her cited above is evidence of this remarkable resemblance.

7 A. Lant, *Blackout: Reinventing Women for Wartime British Cinema* (Princeton University Press, Princeton, 1991), p. 105.

8 This is particularly marked in Anita Ekberg's orgiastic dance in *La dolce vita* (1960) and is underlined by Marcello Mastroianni's awed question: 'Who are you – an Earth Goddess?' The 1950s blonde bombshell often indulged in such dances of hedonistic display – see, for example, Brigitte Bardot in *Et Dieu ... créa la femme* (1956) or Dorothy Malone in *Written on the Wind* (1956).

9 P. Cook, '*Mandy*, Daughter of Transition', in Barr, *All Our Yesterdays*, p. 355.

10 See press discussion of *Baby Doll*: *News Chronicle* (17 December 1956); *Daily Mail* (19 December 1956); *Daily Mirror* (20 December 1956); *Daily Express* (20 December 1956); and *Daily Telegraph* (22 December 1956). Also press discussion of *Et Dieu ... créa la femme*: *Daily Sketch* (25 February 1957); *News Chronicle* (15 March 1957); *Observer* (17 March 1957); *Daily Mail* (3 April 1958); and *Daily Mirror* (4 September 1958).

11 The *Playboy* calendar featuring a nude photograph of Marilyn Monroe is well documented. The BBC2 *Arena* documentary on Jayne Mansfield claims that she agreed to be photographed in the nude to save her failing career. ITV's biopic *The Blonde Bombshell*, partly based on Diana Dors's own accounts, has her taking off her clothes for photographers.

12 *Star*, 31 March 1948. This piece identifies Diana Dors specifically as blonde, though at this point her hair was fair rather than platinum.

13 *Manchester Guardian*, 5 October 1954.

14 See, for example, the account given by Diana Dors in the BBC Radio programme *Desert Island Discs*, broadcast on 17 November 1981. I am grateful to Esther Ronay for making the transcript of this interview available to me.

15 *Picture Post*, 22 January 1955.

16 S. Hall, 'Reformism and the Legislation of Consent', in National Deviancy Conference, ed., *Permissiveness and Control: The Fate of 60s Legislation* (Macmillan, Basingstoke, 1980).

17 Ibid., pp. 1–26.

18 See P. Cook, '*Mandy*, Daughter of Transition', in Barr, *All Our Yesterdays*.

19 Dors was quoted in the press as saying, 'Blue is a wonderful colour for blondes; even our lawnmower is blue'. *Time*, 10 October 1955.

20 *Picture Post*, 22 January 1955.

21 See press release for *Yield to the Night*, held on microfiche in the British Film Institute library. Diana Dors gave several interviews to the papers to promote the film – see, for example, the *Daily Mail* (3 November 1955) and made a television appearance on ITV's cinema programme *Film Fanfare* in 1956, when she was interviewed on her way to the Cannes Film Festival and stressed how important the film was to her. *Film Fanfare* is held in the Pathé archive. I am grateful to Jenny Hammerton for making the *Yield to the Night* material available to me.

22 See the press reception of *Yield to the Night*, cited above.

23 The Diana Dors episode of the BBC2 *Arena* series *Blondes* includes archive footage of Mansfield and Dors meeting one another on the northern club circuit in Britain.

'The Angry Young Man is tired': Albert Finney and 1960s British cinema

14

Without doubt, Albert Finney remains one of British cinema's most distinctive stars, an immediately recognisable national icon. Despite a long international stage and screen career as an actor, director and producer, he is none the less most likely to be remembered as the young 'working-class hero' of British New Wave cinema. Since so much critical attention has focused on his landmark performance as Arthur Seaton, the truculent young factory worker of *Saturday Night and Sunday Morning* (Karel Reisz, 1960), it is little wonder that Finney's first major screen role should continue to dominate critical accounts of his star image. What is perhaps more surprising is just how neatly perceptions of the actor have dovetailed with those of his screen incarnation as Seaton, to a degree that the one has virtually become synonymous with the other.

One need only cast a cursory glance across typical descriptions of Finney's star image to appreciate how distinctions between the star and the character have often been blurred. David Quinlan summarises Finney as 'beefy, scowling, tow-haired',[1] while Alexander Walker expands on the theme: 'With his wary eye, cocky banter, short neck and jutting chin, Finney possessed the naturalistic vitality of a working-class environment.'[2] Such descriptions hardly conjure up an image of an orthodox glamorous screen idol (though Finney was successfully promoted as a pin-up in the early years of his career). What they do suggest is the extent to which explanations of Finney's appeal rely on highlighting physical characteristics that invoke and celebrate clichés about working-class masculinity (resilience, belligerence, exuberance, even loutishness) – characteristics more appropriately ascribed to Seaton the fictional 'working-class hero', than Finney the versatile movie star.

In an article entitled 'Albert Finney – Working-class Hero', Christine Geraghty offers a thoughtful exploration of Finney's iconic status. Analysing *Saturday Night and Sunday Morning* across a range of formal, thematic and performative levels, Geraghty maps the composite construction of the star and the character. She argues that Finney's sexual charisma physically dominates the mise-en-scène: through the use of framing techniques, camera angles and voice-overs, the film's formal devices invite the 'audience's engagement with and contemplation of Finney as a star whose image has so clearly been constructed around sexual presence'.[3] Geraghty concludes that, whatever narrative containment and retribution is eventually meted out to Seaton, Finney's sexual power and star charisma are not simultaneously subdued. After Seaton has thrown a stone at a new housing development where he will almost certainly live once he is married, the final shot of the film shows Seaton leading his future bride down the hill. It is a closure that seems to signal the hero's recuperation and resignation: his rebellion is finally no more than an impotent gesture. But for Geraghty, as Arthur Seaton walks down the hill towards conformity, 'Albert Finney, the star, stays up there throwing his stones'.[4] Thus she argues that, by the closing scene of *Saturday Night and Sunday Morning*, there is a certain distance between the star, who remains visually (and therefore sexually) powerful and the character, who has been curtailed by conventional narrative events that demand that he should pay the penalty for his earlier sexual and social transgressions.

To argue that a star's presence is so forcefully inscribed that its meaning can exceed the ideological constraints of the narrative is certainly a useful starting point to begin to explain the extraordinarily powerful and enduring icon of Finney as a 'working-class hero'. However, the full impact and cultural resonance of Finney's star status, as it was constructed and fixed in the role of Seaton, needs to be mapped beyond the textual operations of the film itself. Thus, I want to respond to and build upon Geraghty's discussion, to provide a contextual as well textual explanation of Finney's star identity. In doing so, I will assess Finney's specific appeal as a working-class icon within the broader historical milieu of a national culture undergoing profound social, economic and moral shifts during the late 1950s and early 1960s. How are prevailing discourses about class and gender expressed through Finney's star image and what might his iconic status tell us about British cinema of the period? In addition to considering the wider cultural resonance of Finney's formative role as Seaton, I also want to trace the development of Finney's star image after *Saturday Night and Sunday Morning*; in effect, to ask how long Finney stayed 'up there throwing his stones'. Here I am particularly interested in the five films Finney made between 1963 and 1967. By any standards, they constitute an odd assortment of roles: an eighteenth-century 'Jack-the-lad' in *Tom Jones* (Tony Richardson, 1963); a Russian soldier in *The Victors* (Carl Foreman, 1963); a psychotic killer in *Night Must Fall* (Karel Reisz, 1964); a disillusioned husband in *Two for the*

Road (Stanley Donen, 1967); and a jaded writer alienated from his northern working-class roots in Finney's own directorial debut, *Charlie Bubbles* (1967). I intend to focus primarily on Finney's roles in *Night Must Fall* and *Charlie Bubbles*: the former because it explicitly constitutes an attempt to undermine, even destroy, the glamour of his role as Seaton; the latter because it returns to the terrain of *Saturday Night and Sunday Morning*, as if at once both to acknowledge the power of Finney's star status as a 'working-class hero' and to finally lay it to rest.

The impact of Finney's performance as Arthur Seaton can be measured in numerous features and reviews produced to coincide with the general release of *Saturday Night and Sunday Morning*, but nowhere was it more explicitly expressed than in the *ABC Film Review*: 'Suddenly the name Finney is big film news. Suddenly Finney is the talk of the town, the talk of nation'.[5] Thus Finney was heralded as a new British sensation, a new breed of actor for a new decade: here at last was a British movie star

Albert Finney. 'This beautiful boy.' A publicity still in which it seems possible to read both elements of the sexualised working-class hero and the actor's ironic separation from role.

distinct from those that had gone before, quite distinct from his American or, worse, Americanised contemporaries. Finney was welcomed as a fresh, youthful and, most importantly, *authentic* new star who could render a credible depiction of British provincial working-class masculinity, not least because he hailed from precisely those roots himself.

To understand how and why Finney was so swiftly acclaimed as the first of a new breed of actor one needs to compare his emerging star identity with the pantheon of popular male stars who had dominated British cinema during the previous decade. The 1950s have generally been remembered as an era of cultural conservatism and consensus in which, as Andrew Spicer identifies, actors such as John Mills, Jack Hawkins, Stanley Baker, Kenneth More and Dirk Bogarde were among the most successful and marketable stars.[6] Mainstream British cinema heavily promoted its male stars (indeed, generally far more so than its female stars), and many of the most commercially successful films of the 1950s were designed to be vehicles to showcase their talents.

In this version of British cinema history, it is little wonder that Finney's sudden stardom in 1960 should feel like a welcome novelty. This 'beefy, scowling, tow-haired' young star with his authentic working-class accent and unapologetic brashness must have seemed a vivid contrast to the debonair, restrained and generally mature middle-class actors who were the established fixtures of the previous decade. But to draw an absolute distinction between the dominant trends of the 1950s and the emerging trends of the 1960s, between Finney and his predecessors, is to oversimplify the complex and far more piecemeal developments in cultural discourses about masculinity and they way they were cinematically represented. Although films centring on middle-class male characters were certainly a staple of British cinema during the 1950s, those films by no means uniformly celebrated or reaffirmed traditional ideals of masculinity. On the contrary, the decade is littered with films that seem to have set out to deflate male egos or poke fun at the often pompous, irresponsible, incompetent or naive behaviour of their male protagonists, for example *Genevieve* (Henry Cornelius, 1953), *Raising a Riot* (Wendy Toye, 1955) and the *Doctor* films (all directed by Ralph Thomas). In many such films, male protagonists are subjected to processes of transformation whereby they must learn sensitivity and humility. Despite being remembered as a decade of conservatism, then, British cinema of the 1950s was dominated by representations neither of machismo nor of male self-assurance. By the late 1950s, More and Bogarde were confirmed as the most popular British actors. As Spicer also points out, More offered a 'modernisation of the debonair gentleman, a combination of tradition and the contemporary', while Bogarde shrugged off his earlier stereotyping as a delinquent in favour of a 'star image of the passive and sensitive male – a soft, expressive masculinity'.[7] It is also clear that neither the stars nor the films that had held sway in the 1950s ceased to possess currency in the new decade. Although *Saturday Night and Sunday Morning* was a critical triumph, its commercial success was dwarfed by another box-office sensation in 1960, another film about a young man's rite of passage from sexual and social irresponsibility to conformity – *Doctor in Love*.

The impact of *Saturday Night and Sunday Morning* and the simultaneous confirmation of Finney as a major new star is probably better understood, then, less as a distinct watershed between stasis and change, and more as a new configuration of an ongoing process in which the terms of masculinity were being slowly interrogated and transformed in postwar British cinema and culture at large. Nonetheless, Finney's specific appeal as a 'working-class hero' constitutes one of the more dramatic and self-consciously articulated shifts in this process, and *Saturday Night and Sunday Morning's* apparent repudiation of older star types needs to be considered carefully.

From the moment the film begins, Arthur Seaton is characterised as tough, abrasive, self-centred and hedonistic. In the interior monologue that precedes the opening credits, Seaton declares that 'all [he's] out for is a good time: all the rest is propaganda'. This maxim is immediately put into practice as Seaton energetically throws himself into a night's entertainment, beating a drunken sailor (Colin Blakely) in a drinking competition and opportunistically spending the night with his married lover, Brenda (Rachel Roberts), while her unsuspecting husband is away. As Seaton guzzles and staggers his way through the night, all the exuberance and arrogance that were to galvanise Finney's image as a 'working-class hero' are displayed to the full; just as Seaton positively relishes offending those around him, so Finney's performance of aggressive self-confidence and high-spirited vulgarity can be read as a surly riposte to the urbane refinement that had characterised so many representations of masculinity in mainstream British cinema.

Seaton's singleminded pursuit of a good time echoes many of the anxieties about postwar working-class culture voiced by the New Left during the late 1950s. While he drinks, a live band blasts out the then popular song, 'What do you want if you don't want money?', as if to underscore Seaton's rejection of any prospect of social and economic mobility – that his world is more or less bereft of ambition or direction. In some quite specific ways, Seaton shares many of the characteristics that Richard Hoggart attributed to an emerging postwar youth culture in his celebrated study of British working-class life, *The Uses of Literacy* (1957). Like

Hoggart's 'Juke-Box Boys' who enjoy an 'unvaried diet of sensation without commitment',[8] whose lives have 'no aim, no ambition, no protection, no belief',[9] Seaton is emphatically signalled as apolitical: his only aim is to earn enough money to gratify his appetite for a good time. Hoggart's description of these working-class youths is undoubtedly rhetorically embellished to fit his overarching polemic that a once vital and indigenous working-class culture was becoming dissipated by the onslaught of mass consumerism as the economic benefits of postwar prosperity filtered down to an increasingly affluent working class. Even so, given the significant impact that the publication of *The Uses of Literacy* had upon cultural discourses of the time, it seems reasonable to assume that, for many, Finney's performance as Seaton must have seemed remarkably reminiscent of Hoggart's 'hedonistic but passive barbarian'[10] whose 'job is to be done by day, and after that the rest is amusement, is pleasure'.[11]

Finney's Seaton thus brought many of Hoggart's criticisms of postwar working-class culture to life on the screen. Yet his iconic appeal found further resonance because, somewhat paradoxically, it also embodied precisely the version of traditional working-class culture valorised by Hoggart in *The Uses of Literacy*. If, as Walker suggests, Finney possessed 'naturalistic vitality', then the star clearly constituted an antidote to the pallid apathy with which Hoggart characterised contemporary working-class youth culture. Likewise, Seaton's disdain for the trappings of consumerism (the pristine new home that his girlfriend Doreen (Shirley-Ann Field) aspires to own, the family television set that so absorbs his father's attention) rescues him from being subsumed into the 'shiny barbarism'[12] of consumer culture and endows him with the dignity and vigour that Hoggart ascribes to traditional working-class life.

The Uses of Literacy is underpinned by two anxieties: that working-class culture was becoming both Americanised and feminised in postwar Britain. If, as I am suggesting, it makes sense to understand Finney's iconic status as a 'working-class hero' in the context of the New Left's agenda, then it is essentially these dual anxieties that the construction of his star image in *Saturday Night and Sunday Morning* sought to redress. In some obvious ways, Finney's iconic status reads as a cinematic reassertion of British national identity. As has often been noted, New Wave cinema's preference for working-class, provincial realism constituted an intentional, politicised attempt to reassert an indigenous British national cinema. With his performance as Seaton, Finney was established as the most potent icon of New Wave cinema and thus his popular image was powerfully charged with their prescriptions for a national cinema – and, by extension, a national identity – that could differentiate itself from Hollywood and what was perceived as the rising tide of Americanism. In

HOLLYWOOD   V.   BRITAIN
Bond   Poluer

the immediate wake of *Saturday Night and Sunday Morning*'s success, this aspect of his star image was further reinforced by the fact that, although Finney was offered various lucrative Hollywood contracts, he refused to surrender the relative creative freedom that his collaboration with Wood-fall afforded. For many, then, his ability to resist the allure of Hollywood provided an inspiring example of how British cinema itself could retain its integrity and defy Hollywood's domination.

The ways in which Finney's iconic status can be read as a response to the perceived threat of feminisation are rather more complex. Most critical accounts of the film highlight the ambivalent representation of its female characters. I would argue, however, that there has been a tendency to overstate the misogyny of the film. After all, Brenda may ultimately pay dearly for her infidelity, but in a positive sense she too is 'out for a good time' and shows little sign of guilt about pursuing her own sexual desires beyond the constraints of a dull and passionless marriage. Likewise, Doreen may aspire to precisely the kind of monotonous marital respectability from which Brenda is eager to escape, but her self-confidence and pragmatic insight into Seaton's flaws hardly mark her out as a passive or naive bystander. Nonetheless, it is clear that both women are problematically signalled as the means by which Seaton's final entrapment will be secured; their primary function to ensure that the hero's freedom from responsibility and domesticity will only be temporary. Thus Seaton has to face the consequences of his earlier actions and succumbs to the inevitability of marriage. In doing so, he seems symbolically to re-enact Hoggart's narrative of a once virile and 'muscular' working-class culture being steadily emasculated.

But of course, if we accept Geraghty's argument, *Saturday Night and Sunday Morning* offers the possibility of a second-level of closure in which Finney, the star, continues to be signified as physically and sexually powerful. Unlike Seaton, who has undergone a rite of passage (albeit ambivalently), Finney's star image remains fixed in the spectacle of his performance of Seaton's earlier sexual power. In this way, one might argue that the separation between star and character that occurs in the final moments of the film facilitates a confrontation with the perceived threat of emasculation, while simultaneously sustaining the fantasy of the continued virility and machismo of working-class masculinity.

Finney's Seaton certainly signalled a paradigm shift towards representations of working-class masculinity that, prior to the New Wave, were virtually absent from mainstream British cinema. However, it would be too simplistic to assume that, by virtue of its novelty, this shift was necessarily politically progressive. When one remembers the 'soft', 'expressive' and 'passive' masculinity that actors such as Bogarde represented, it seems more logical to argue that Finney's performance as Seaton reasserted a version of masculinity – tough, belligerent and active – that was becoming increasingly untenable in populist, mainstream representations of middle-class men. Displaced from discourses of middle-class masculinity, Seaton's (and Finney's) working-class identity provided an alternative means of articulating, even romanticising, a machismo which was increasingly deemed unacceptable in middle-class representations.

After the resounding success of *Saturday Night and Sunday Morning*, Finney appears, quite intentionally, to have set out to disrupt and diversify his star image. Had two planned film projects come to fruition (one to play Australian folk hero, Ned Kelly, the other to repeat his stage success as Billy Liar), his image as a rebellious 'working-class hero' might well have been further set in aspic. But both projects foundered and it was to be almost three years before Finney returned to star in Woodfall's adaptation of Henry Fielding's novel *Tom Jones*. On the face of it, this bawdy comedy was no reprise of the gritty realism of his role as Seaton. Yet, even the journey to another century and another genre could not completely disguise some striking similarities between Jones and Seaton. The lugubrious contemporary mise-en-scène and northern working-class accents might have disappeared, but Seaton's appetite for life's pleasures, the penchant for womanising and drinking, were once again reincarnated in Finney's performance as Tom Jones. What is more, because *Tom Jones* had no pretensions to social realism, the film was not obliged to reprove or censure its hero's sexual transgressions. Indeed, it is possible to see *Tom Jones* as providing an opportunity to relive and celebrate the spectacle of Finney's roguish charisma in a diegetic space less fettered by the imperative to deliver a topical, socially responsible punitive closure.

Night Must Fall represents a very different mutation of Finney's star image. An adaptation of Emlyn Williams's dark thriller, it provided another opportunity for Finney, as both star and co-producer, to collaborate with director Karel Reisz. Finney plays Danny, a Welsh working-class waiter, who inveigles his way into the Bramsons' middle-class home where his pregnant girlfriend, Dora (Sheila Hancock), works as a housekeeper. The film begins with a disturbing sequence which cuts between Olivia Bramson (Susan Hampshire) as she sits pensively in the serene setting of a garden swathed in early morning mist, and Danny in a wood, wielding an axe and then disposing of what appears to be a female corpse in a nearby lake. The sequence is disorienting for a number of reasons. Coming at the very beginning of the film, the relationship between the two contrasting scenes is unmotivated and unexplained. But the primary reason why this sequence has such power to disorient is that it presents an image of Finney that both specularises his physical presence (engaged in strenuous activity, he is stripped to the waist) while, at the same time, undercutting our pleasurable expectations of Finney's star image through a disturbing spectacle of violence. Throughout the subsequent narrative, the film's formal devices continue to foreclose the possibility of specular pleasure; while they offer the sorts of lingering close-ups of Finney's face and torso that in *Saturday Night and Sunday Morning* and *Tom Jones* showcased his sexual presence, here Finney's contorted facial expressions and some darkly surreal lighting suggests menace rather than sexual charisma.

In the scenes that follow, however, a more recognisable version of Finney's popular image is re-established. Danny finishes his shift at the smart hotel and sets out on his scooter to keep an appointment with Mrs Bramson (Mona Washbourne). He speeds through the country lanes, exuberantly riding his scooter, his legs splayed over the side while he laughs at his own ability to disrupt the tranquillity of rural middle England. Within the context of the narrative, the scene functions to establish Danny's lack of intimidation at the prospect of being grilled by the authoritarian Mrs Bramson: just as he gleefully disrupts the peace of the country lanes, his presence will overturn the ordered and repressed Bramson family home. But the scene works also to recall Finney's rebellious and ebullient star image, suggesting that the disturbing narrative that follows is in some way a response to and revision of popular perceptions of Finney's established celebrity.

In choosing to adapt *Night Must Fall*, the intention was to update Williams's play to become less of a gothic melodrama and more of a topical exploration of class conflict. Thus, when Danny invades the Bramsons' affluent home, he transgresses class boundaries. He ingratiates himself into the affections of both mother and daughter (initiating a perverse Oedipal relationship with Mrs Bramson, whom he calls 'Ma', and embarking on a sadistic sexual relationship with Olivia) until he finally colonises the home. But Danny's invasion and the crimes he commits are also acts of misogyny. He dominates both of the Bramson women by performing the version of masculinity each craves (the indulged and indulgent boy, the sexually aggressive lover). Moreover, the only motivation provided for his first murder is that his victim was promiscuous, while Mrs Bramson finally meets the same fate because she refuses to continue to participate in Danny's infantile Oedipal fantasies. Thus, while his previous incarnations as Seaton and Jones never overtly confront their character's problematic attitudes towards women, Danny's perverse behaviour is explicitly signalled as misogynous.

By the final scene, Olivia, having discovered her mother's mutilated corpse, remains to confront Danny. Once he no longer intimidates Olivia,

Danny is reduced to a cowering, infantalised figure, huddled on the bathroom floor like a cornered animal. The film ends to the sound of Danny's deranged rant, and his final, inappropriately juvenile words, 'I can handle myself in a punch-up', seem to recall Seaton's none too convincing bravado after he is 'bested' by the soldiers. Spoken by Danny, the words are a confirmation of his impotence and childishness. That they so closely echo Seaton's defiant bragging after a humiliating beating adds a certain retrospective irony and dubiousness to the swaggering machismo of Seaton's – and Finney's – 'working-class hero'.

Night Must Fall was neither a commercial nor a critical success. Karel Reisz describes the anger with which the film was greeted at a preview when a group of 'MGM wives' descended upon him demanding to know 'what have you done to this beautiful boy? It really rubbed people up the wrong way.'[13] Walker suggests that few were ready to witness this disturbing mutation of Finney's star image:

> Finney's popular image of virile charm and natural candour as regards the normal man's appetites had been well and truly (and profitably) fixed by *Saturday Night and Sunday Morning* and, even more, by *Tom Jones*. And the image was so absolutely denied by his character in *Night Must Fall* that many of those with reservations about the film's success now hated it with an almost militant antipathy.[14]

This explanation of the film's hostile reception is convincing enough, though I would argue that it is was not so much that the film 'so absolutely denies' Finney's popular image, rather that it intentionally warps and exploits it. Perhaps one reason why the film had such power to offend was that it provided enough reminders of Finney's popular image to push the terms of his iconic appeal to perverse extremes.

After the hostilities unleashed by *Night Must Fall*, Finney's popular appeal seems to have waned somewhat in the mid-1960s. He increasingly focused his attention on the theatre, appearing in and directing a string of successful productions in Britain and America. In 1967, however, he returned first to appear alongside Audrey Hepburn in *Two for the Road*, then to direct and star in *Charlie Bubbles*, a film that would ambivalently recall his performance in *Saturday Night and Sunday Morning*.

That *Charlie Bubbles* so explicitly reworks Finney's original iconic status as a 'working-class hero' was certainly not lost on the critics of the day. One reviewer proclaimed: 'The Angry Young Man is tired: the rough-and-tumble hero of *Saturday Night and Sunday Morning*, the angry young man lashing out blows on every side, has become a blasé, bored and, chiefly, terribly tired young man.'[15] From the opening credits of *Charlie Bubbles*, parallels between the two films are set up through their respective differences as well as their similarities. In place of the bicycle ride through the factory gates seething with life and the back-to-back Nottingham streets that accompany the opening credits in *Saturday Night and Sunday Morning*, *Charlie Bubbles* introduces its hero as he drives his conspicuously luxurious Rolls-Royce along half-deserted London streets dominated by impersonal architecture. Just as Seaton 'bests' the sailor played by Colin Blakely in a drinking competition, Bubbles embarks on a drinking spree with Smokey (played, of course, by Blakely), only this time it is Blakely's character who urges them to drink up while Bubbles looks bemused and exhausted.

The absence of an interior monologue at the beginning of *Charlie Bubbles* also sets up a further comparison with *Saturday Night and Sunday Morning*: unlike Arthur Seaton, Charlie Bubbles has no individualist maxim for life, no rhetorical defence against a society from which he has become alienated. This is essentially Charlie's predicament and the film goes to some lengths to establish his estrangement from the world. Charlie is a highly successful writer who hails from northern working-class roots. He enjoys a kind of clichéd celebrity as 'the working-class boy made good', but his fame and wealth have not brought him happiness, only complacency and boredom. He has lost his appetite for everything. Whereas Seaton sarcastically remonstrates with his father for staring blankly at the television screen, Charlie prefers to experience life by voyeuristically watching the inhabitants of his house through a closed-circuit monitoring system installed in his office. Likewise, while Seaton 'wolfed up life like hot dinners',[16] his world revolving around his appetites – particularly sexual – Charlie is apathetic and virtually impotent. When his secretary seduces him, he responds with indifference, preferring sleep to sex.

After an angry phone call from his ex-wife, reminding him of his forgotten promise to visit their son, Charlie leaves London and drives through the night to arrive in Manchester early the next morning. The camera lingers on the road signs that point the way north, suggesting that Charlie's journey to see his son is also a kind of pilgrimage back to his own roots and the possibility of rekindling his lost appetite for life. However, his journey brings no such redemption: he is as out of place in the north as in London. He meets people whom he knew as a younger man and, in what can only be read as a self-consciously ironic touch, they hail him as a 'working-class hero', but he is unable to respond to their enthusiasm and remains totally estranged from his environment.

Ultimately, *Charlie Bubbles* offers no life-affirming epiphany as he returns to his northern roots, no transformative rite of passage at the end of the narrative. In fact, there is no palpable sense of closure at all. After spending the night alone in his ex-wife's bed, he walks out into the morning sunshine where he spots a hot-air balloon in the distance and walks purposefully towards it. In a surreal closure which refuses to comment explicitly on the hero's motivation, Charlie hurls sandbags over the side until the balloon ascends and Charlie floats away. Thus, the film leaves us with little more than a metaphor as closure, though perhaps one conclusion can be drawn: the 'working-class hero' has stopped throwing his stones.

There are a number of ways in which *Charlie Bubbles* might be read as an autobiographical film, and many have commented that, like Bubbles, Finney was never entirely comfortable with the fame that his roles in *Saturday Night and Sunday Morning* and *Tom Jones* brought him.[7] While I think it would be too heavy-handed simply to read *Charlie Bubbles* in this way, it is certainly viable to understand the film as a self-conscious attempt to explore the nature of stardom and offer a critique of Finney's popular image as a 'working-class hero'. Retrospectively, it seems that *Charlie Bubbles* marks the point at which Finney's potential to embody the star image fixed for him during the early 1960s finally came to an end. Only three years later, Finney was starring in a musical production of *Scrooge* (Ronald Neame, 1970): heavily made-up to portray Dickens's miser, not a trace of the sexy, ebullient 'working-class hero' seemed to remain. Yet the currency of his original iconic status as a 'working-class hero' persists in the acclaim and critical attention that his performance as Seaton still receives. Perhaps the primary reasons why this version of Finney's star image has stood the test of time is that it still has the power both to articulate a nostalgia for a virile, unreconstructed version of masculinity and a utopian desire to produce a defiantly independent British national cinema, both of which became increasingly untenable as the 1960s wore on.

Notes

1 D. Quinlan, *The Illustrated Directory of Film Actors* (Batsford, London, 1985), p. 168.
2 Alexander Walker, *Hollywood England: The British Film Industry in the Sixties* (Michael Joseph, London, 1974), p. 83.
3 Christine Geraghty, 'Albert Finney – Working-class Hero', in P. Kirkham and J. Thumin, eds, *Me Jane: Masculinity, Movies and Women* (Lawrence and Wishart, London, 1995), p. 65.
4 Ibid., p. 71.
5 E. Hardie, 'Suddenly – It's Finney', *ABC Film Review*, 11, 2, February 1961, p. 5.
6 A. Spicer, 'Male Stars, Masculinity and British Cinema, 1945–1960', in R. Murphy, ed., *The British Cinema Book* (BFI, London, 1987), pp. 144–53.
7 Ibid., p. 150.

8   R. Hoggart, *The Uses of Literacy* (Penguin, London, 1957), p. 246.
9   Ibid., p. 249.
10 Ibid., p. 250.
11 Ibid., p. 249.
12 Ibid., p. 28.
13 Karel Reisz quoted by Q. Falk, *Albert Finney in Character* (Robson Books, London, 1992), p. 73.
14 Walker, *Hollywood England*, p. 149.
15 K. Vanková, 'The Angry Young Man is Tired', *Young Cinema and Theatre* (1969), n.3, p. 5.
16 Walker, *Hollywood England*, p. 84.
17 See, for example, Walker, *Hollywood England*; Falk, *Albert Finney in Character*.

Song, narrative and the mother's voice: a deepish reading of Julie Andrews

> My sole consolation when I went upstairs to bed for the night was that Mama would come in and kiss me after I was in bed (Proust, *Swann's Way*)

In *Mary Poppins* (Stevenson, 1964) after their first day of adventures with their new nanny, Jane and Michael are safely in bed, but refusing to sleep. As Mary Poppins, Julie Andrews, who has already overcome their reluctance to take medicine by turning it into cordial, manages their obstinacy in a double motion of maternal discipline and indulgence, first by suggesting she might summon a policeman, and second by disarmingly agreeing with their rebellion. Then she sings a lullaby.

> Stay awake, don't rest your head
> Don't lie down upon your bed
> While the moon is in the skies
> Stay awake, don't close your eyes.

The 'practically perfect' surrogate mother's tact triumphs. Without opposing the children, she lulls them into a sleep of perfect security in which, however, lessons in reality have been inculcated, as they often are in fairy tales.

The scene is paradigmatic for acting out in its most basic form – surrogate mother addressing rebellious, puzzled, frightened or mistaken children – a situation both reassuring and educational in which a compendium of idealised maternal traits are exhibited, a scene constantly reactivated in different forms over more than thirty years of Julie Andrews's films. So fundamental is it that in its multiple restagings the star's deepest meanings are unlocked. Some of these restagings mirror the 'Stay Awake' scenario, like 'Favourite Things' in *The Sound of Music* (Wise, 1965), with its night address to children frightened by a storm. Some transpose it, like the opening of *Darling Lili* (Edwards, 1970), sung not in a bedroom but from stage darkness, to assuage the fears of an adult audience, Lili's spotlit face irresistibly recalling the night visiting mother.

Others echo the ur-scene's accents of maternal comfort, and sometimes correction, as in the television movie *Our Sons* (1991) in which Andrews brings Ann Margret to accept her dying homosexual son. Or personal relationships may be structured like a child–mother bond, as Samantha's with George (Dudley Moore) in *10* (Edwards, 1979), this particular case emphasising the ambivalences, even hostilities within the pairing. Even where romantic relationships evade such categorisation, a pronounced residue of the teacherly ethical, the solicitously maternal, is usually present, for example as Julie Sparrow argues with Sverdlov (Omar Sharif) over his materialism in *The Tamarind Seed* (Edwards, 1974), or for much of *Torn Curtain* (Hitchcock, 1966), where the apparently defecting Michael Armstrong (Paul Newman) is followed and then upbraided by (the hints are inescapable) a maternally concerned Sarah Sherman. Such examples suggest how deep-seated the maternal motif is in Andrews, to the extent that exceptional roles resisting this reading – such as Gertrude Lawrence in *Star!* (Wise, 1968), and Sally Miles in *S.O.B.* (Edwards, 1981) – are explicable only as parodies or assaults upon the good mother of which she is the cinematic embodiment, a late secularised version of that

Julie Andrews circa *The Sound of Music* with first child Emma Kate – the Madonna with Child motif blatant rather than displaced as in her films.

figure who, as Julia Kristeva says of Piero della Francesca's painting of the Holy Mother in 'Stabat Mater', 'reduces social anguish and gratifies a male being ... [and] also satisfies a woman so that a commonality of the sexes is set up, beyond and in spite of their glaring incompatibility and permanent warfare'.[1]

In *The Uses of Enchantment* Bruno Bettelheim demonstrates in many fairy tales the dual presence of good and bad mothers, the latter often the wicked stepmother, seeing them as embodiments of what is argued in Freudian (especially Kleinian) psychoanalysis, the infant's splitting of the mother into wholly good and bad projections in order to deal with ambivalent situations in which the all giving mother also appears harshly ungiving. Eventually the child is able to restore the good mother within a more mature understanding, realising that her discipline, which appeared harsh and terrible, was a form of love.[2] As the good mother restored, Julie Andrews is both all-giving and disciplining. Perhaps because her Mary Poppins is sweeter than the abrupt figure of B. H. Travers's books,[3] the second term is often overlooked, but her maternality, as Jane and Michael experience it, contains both. Interestingly, Andrews's films usually eschew any simple good-mother/bad-mother conflict (it is only vestigially present in a few films, such as *Mary Poppins*, *The Sound of Music* and *Our Sons*, and burlesqued by Beatrice Lillie in *Thoroughly Modern Millie* (Hill, 1967)), thus placing the whole complex of maternal meanings on the star.

That lullaby scene is also paradigmatic because Andrews sings in it. Pre-eminently a musical star, despite the fact that the genre's 1970s decline led her to films where singing was restricted or even non-existent, at her highest intensity of meaning her singing comes into play, as memory even when absent, forming a continuum across both the characteristics of her singing and speaking voice, and what it says or sings, as well as her typical modes of address (teacherly, gentle, solicitous, candid, occasionally commanding).

Tracing this theme, one proviso must be made. A star is, as we have learned to say, a text characterised by a 'structured polysemy ... a finite multiplicity of meanings'.[4] That is, Julie Andrews is not a closed text only readable in one way. But, despite the different parts she plays (psychoanalyst in *The Man who Loved Women* (Edwards, 1983), half-German, half-English spy in *Darling Lili* etc.), drawing out different aspects of the persona, there is always a pronounced sense in which Julie Andrews is always Julie Andrews. This sameness, composed of her unchanging Home Counties RP, only slightly overlaid by American influences, that didactic habit of emphasising a single word in a cluster of words – 'the sky was so *blue* today and everything was so *green* and fragrant I just *had* to be part of it' – accompanied by a characteristic slight emphatic forward motion, redolent of concern, towards the addressee, and a pleasant, healthy attractiveness that nevertheless is not too disturbingly erotic, generates the patterns that underlie other meanings, just as the combination of sexiness and innocence inflects everything else in the star text Marilyn Monroe.

Julie Andrews's impersonations or personifications of the restored mother fall into five categories. First, the biological mother with her own child or children. This obvious manifestation is relatively rare, found only in *Hawaii* (Hill, 1966), *Star!* (in a dark version), *10*, *That's Life* (Edwards, 1986) and *Our Sons*, with the children as adults in the last two. Second, nanny, governess or stepmother to children not her own. Though this is the case in only three films, one of them, *Little Miss Marker* (Hall, 1980), very minor, significance enormously outweighs frequency, for Mary Poppins and Maria are much her most famous parts, establishing an image which later films complicate or subvert, but never escape. Third, metaphorical rather than literal mother–child relationships – much the largest of the categories – ranging from ones that structure whole narratives to fragmentary allusions. Fourth, instances where the mother suffers attack, parody, denigration. Fifth, a rare, inverted category, where the mother role reverses to that of the daughter – thus letting Andrews fulfil the triad of female functions, mother–wife–daughter (Kristeva in 'Stabat Mater' again).[5] Some instances are (parts of) Jerusha's relationship with the Queen in *Hawaii*, Stephanie's with the Italian maid in *Duet for One* (Konchalovsky, 1986), (parts of) *The Americanization of Emily* (Hiller, 1964) and the beginning of *The Sound of Music*.

The low-keyed infrequency of Andrews as biological mother, and the overriding force of Mary Poppins and Maria, argue that surrogacy, not literal motherhood, is what audiences desire of this star. Is this because the close bond with her own child inhibits the audience's approach to her maternity? Is it because the more indirect role connects with a richer vein of fantasy for the viewer, those daydreams of substituting different parents for the real ones that Freud writes about in 'Family Romances'?[6] What is indubitable is how vestigial the biological children are in *Hawaii* and *10*. Where they are adults, in *Our Sons* and *That's Life*, the same problems do not seem to apply.

The cover of Andrews's second song album, 'The Lass with the Delicate Air' (1958) presages the simultaneous foregrounding and displacement of the maternal imago typical of Andrews's screen appearances to come.[7] On it the youthful vocalist sits cradling a floral basket in such a way there might well be an infant, hidden from view, in her arms. The album has several tracks, particularly 'London Pride' and 'Oh, the Days of the Kerry Dancing', where her voice's youthfulness combines paradoxically with the narrator position of a much older parental figure instructing younger listeners. If the textual utterer of these songs is allusively the mother, that of 'Matelot' (on *Julie Andrews Sings*, 1958),[8] is veiledly but unambiguously her. Jean Louis Dominic Pierre Bouchard becomes a sailor and journeys from place to place, and woman to woman, never finding absolute love, always followed by one voice singing his 'true love song'. 'Matelot' is ambiguously capable of both heterosexual and homosexual interpretations. If heterosexual, the hero passes from woman to woman unaware he is seeking his lost first love through them; if homosexual, then that iconic figure of homosexuality, the sailor, moves from man to man (screened in the lyrics as women), but ultimately seeking through them the same lost maternal plenitude. Coward's auteurial rendition foregrounds gay connotations, the mother's words being filtered through his brittle delivery that cultivates and deflects sentiment equally.[9] But Andrews's becomes the mother's unfiltered utterance (or projection of the son's desire for it), unironically embracing, perhaps even, if we credit psychoanalytic musical theory, pulling the hearer back past the mother's lullaby to the 'sonorous envelope' of the womb.[10] While it may be potential in all female singers to awaken such memories, not all female singing stars, any more than all actresses, signify the maternal, such latencies being triggered only by the narratives or the lyrics, and most importantly the appearance, persona and vocal characteristics of the star. If, even after this catalogue of examples, the reader is sceptical, she or he should turn to *Darling Lili* and consider the presentation of the maternal in two numbers, 'The Girl in No Man's Land' sung to a group of wounded soldiers ('the angel who at break of day, / comes round to kiss their cares away'), and 'I'll Give You Three Guesses Who Loves You', where it is so blatant that the lyrics explicitly, but implausibly, deny it.

Variations

Jane's view. Male structures? Female audiences

The argument that Julie Andrews invokes memories of the lost mother crosses both sexes. Yet many of the films are romantically structured as if their primary appeal is to male fantasies of the loss and regaining of the mother. Though I recognise this fantasy in my own ('male being') fascination with Julie Andrews, as a general statement it needs refining, since Andrews's fans are predominantly female. There are, however, many females in the narratives with whom Andrews's characters bond, thus providing points of identification in relation for female spectators, to (as distinct from with) the mother. These include Jane in *Mary Poppins*, Liesl in *The Sound of Music*, the Queen in *Hawaii*, Ann Margret in *Our Sons*, and both Gillian's daughters in *That's Life*. This is not to deny male Oedipal fantasies – *The Man who Loved Women* and *That's Life* are particularly powerfully structured in that way – but to suggest the presence of elements that equally satisfy female viewers, particularly around the male lover who is also the son. It can be speculated that the female spectator enjoys, first, identifications with Andrews as mother or surrogate mother or protagonist; second, identifications with female characters in a daughter-like relationship to her (probably the most potent of all the identifications); and, third, cross-gendered identification with the male who has access to the body of the mother. There is one instance in the narratives of a (tightly reined-in) lesbian desire for an Andrews character, that of the young Italian maid in whose bed Stephanie takes refuge from her night fears in *Duet for One*, which might be seen as an invitation to lesbian identification, as well as recalling the sexualised elements of the female infant's bond with the mother.

Andrews's audiences pose two particular enigmas. The first is that of male under-response, since, despite her profound Oedipal meanings, Andrews is not notably popular with male audiences, apart from her cult camp homosexual status. Perhaps this is explained by a heterosexual male retreat from a too unmediated confrontation with the mother figure and a preference for more displaced encounters. The second is the apparent conservatism of the superstar's vast female audience, which has never revoked its fidelity, but nevertheless, in its absence in overwhelming numbers from her later films, announces a preference for the earlier surrogate mother over the imago tested in more complex circumstances of the later works. Perhaps for this largest audience the displacement from surrogate to metaphorical mother figure, whatever its logic, omits a vital component of the image.

Sexuality

Julie Andrews's 'sexual awkwardness', noted by Dyer in discussing *The Sound of Music*,[11] is a complicated thing, often seemingly contradicted, never justified by pathology (that is, Andrews nowhere plays women designated as frigid), and inconstant, though provoking unease in certain highly sexualised situations. Even before *The Sound of Music*, *The Americanization of Emily* began the sexualisation necessary for romantic stardom, which initially looks unproblematic as Emily, fetching in a military uniform that plays on Andrews's disciplinary associations, becomes the lover of Charley (James Garner, with his macho–virile connotations). But three oddities play across this. First, Joyce Grenfell, that paragon of somatic embarrassment in 1950s British comedies, is Emily's mother. Second, Emily's relationship with Charley is enveloped by serious ethical debates. Third, Emily's sexuality is extraordinarily inflected by the war deaths of her husband, brother and father which have led her to become an eroticised all-pitying mother figure, sleeping with young soldiers about to die. All three elements rehearse features attached to Andrews's sexuality in later films, the presence of the teacherly ethical and the solic-itously maternal often intertwined, as in *Hawaii*, where Jerusha tries to persuade her husband that God does not condemn his sexual desire for her. If the assertion that Grenfell is the mother of Andrews rings true, despite the fact that Andrews's characters do not exhibit similar repres-sions, it may do so as shorthand for more complex auras of inhibition sur-rounding her maternality. Perhaps the two most obviously unsettling instances where such inhibitions are invoked are Stephanie's hugely embarrassing outburst of variations around the word 'fuck' in *Duet for One*, and Lili's Madonna metamorphosing to whore imitation of 'Crepe Suzette''s striptease in *Darling Lili* which, as her body nears exposure, causes something like a nervous breakdown in the film, which becomes increasingly agitated, fragmenting the performance into a hysterical montage of rapid cuts, coloured lights, odd angles etc.

Her maternal primacy means that with Andrews's romantic heroines the erotic is potentially problematic because the maternal allusion, no longer distanced as with most heroines, is so strongly foregrounded. A way of reconciling the two is to surround the sexual with the teacherly and solicitous, but the incestuous desires and prohibitions underlying the child–mother relationship are hard to quiet, as witness the recurring scene which enacts a displaced version of the child's spying on the mother's body – when David (Burt Reynolds) looks up Mariana's skirt in *The Man who Loved Women* during his mother-oriented psychoanalysis, when King spies on Victoria as she bathes, literally to ascertain whether she has a penis, and in related voyeuristic moments in *10*, *Darling Lili* and *S.O.B.* Only a narrow reading would see these disturbances solely as the male viewer's, rather than including the female viewer's equally ambiva-lent relations to the mother figure.

Parody and deconstruction

S.O.B and *Star!* differ from other Andrews's films in their deconstruc-tiveness. In *S.O.B.* Andrews plays Sally Miles who projects Andrews-like fantasies of infantile appeal, suggested in the playroom setting of her 'Polly Wolly Doodle' number. But whereas the Julie Andrews 'myth' asserts the unity of self and screen role, *S.O.B.* violently ruptures it. This takes two forms – one simpler, where, as Sally rages or plots, the mask of the good mother simply drops; the second more unsettling in that the familiar semiotic surface remains undisturbed even while she behaves contrastingly, as when, solely for image, she sings a schmaltzily religiose number at her unlamented husband's funeral, not in burlesque mode but with all the precious signs of an Andrews performance intact, thus casting a more radical doubt on her signs as essences. Where *S.O.B.*'s deconstructions belong to a clear satiric project, *Star!*'s are harder to categorise. Many are generated by the predispositions of the post-studio musical, with its schizophrenic drives towards both deconstruction and celebration, to split its protagonists between performance and life, transparency on stage and confusion off. Andrews herself was reportedly drawn to the role by biographical parallels between herself and Gertrude Lawrence, and the film's makers must have envisioned Lawrence sharpening Andrews and Andrews sweetening Lawrence. But *Star!* was Andrews's greatest failure, rejected by her mass audience, for whom the problem seems to have been that she was no longer the teacher but the insufficient pupil (Noël Coward, Daniel Massey having the wisdom role), no longer the mother but the narcissistic child, appropriating, in the number 'Someone to Watch Over Me', her daughter's doll as a prop to transform herself from the one to the other. What is gracefully acted out there was no doubt less pleasing in the narrative where the heroine fails to bond with her own daughter, not so much a modulation of Andrews's image as its unravelling into a nefarious ambush by the bad mother.

Homosexuality

Julie Andrews's association with (male homosexual) camp derives from Mary Poppins's and Maria's cleanliness, affiliation with the idealised family and incorrigible optimism (not to mention her faint aura of discipline and Maria's connection with nuns). But when Hugh, George's gay colleague in *10*, insists how wonderful Samantha is, mockery is absent, signalling that the camp appropriation of Andrews (recently revived in the 'Singalong' *The Sound of Music*) masks deeper meanings.

A homosexual thematic (distinct from camp celebration or denigration) becomes central in *Victor Victoria* and *Our Sons*. In the latter, the persona's teacherly aspects are deployed in Audrey's attempt, on behalf of her gay son (Hugh Grant), to reconcile the son's lover, dying of AIDS, with his homophobic mother (Ann Margret). This teacherliness in the cause of sexual tolerance echoes *Victor Victoria*, where the heroine's romance with King includes chastising his machismo. In the commentary surrounding the film, the consistent oddity is that Andrews, the film's centre, should be treated as a neutral function, when her undeviating straightness definitively affects meaning, precisely because she (Andrews/Victoria) is never remotely destabilised in sexual orientation (in this paralleled by Toddy, as immune to heterosexual desire as she is to homosexual). Her stage impersonations, despite the convoluted sex reversals, amount, ultimately, to Andrews personifying herself. Only in the 'Shady Dame' number does her performance follow the lessons given her by female impersonators to overemphasise female movements parodically, and thus make her appear in any sense like a female impersonator. In the others, whether in female dress, or male, she is unmediated Andrews. But even in 'Shady Dame' a double layering of semiotics – Andrews's performance gestures overlaid by, but still visible through, the exaggerations – means that a reverse doubleness (or tripleness) accompanies the moment of the drag queen's removal of her/his wig to reveal his identity. Victoria in surface narrative terms is revealed as Victor. In deeper narrative terms we know that Victor is Victoria. And in deep performative terms the removal of the disguise, while at one level disclosing the man she is not, asserts Julie Andrews within her disguise, a disguise never adopted by her voice, which finishes the number in inimitably hyperbolical female coloratura mode by shattering glasses.

Out of this obstruction to the queering of the text at its centre, a double discourse of the mother and the homosexual child emerges. Explicitly, Victoria fulfils her social role of the good mother by teaching King tolerance. Implicitly, the social text shifts to the psychic territory of 'Matelot', and enacts the restoration of the mother to the homosexual child. That the camp appropriation of Andrews contains this meaning is clarified by the 1992 film *Beautiful Thing*, where the two boys first make love as the hero's mother and her boyfriend watch *The Sound of Music* on television.[12] This sequence goes to extraordinary lengths simultaneously to invoke and deny Julie Andrews as presiding good mother over the boys' homosexual initiation, displacing her singing to Liesl of 'Sixteen, Going on Seventeen' with Rolf's, and building in a reference to the bad mother, the Countess (Eleanor Parker) rather than Maria (Andrews), as if, in the only way to avoid the superficialities of the camp image, her invocation has to be in absentia (too deeply meaningful to be openly spoken). Andrews's straightness in *Victor Victoria* is thus essential to her deepest function, since to make her merely the double of the homosexual child would make impossible the restorative meanings acted out.

The dying mother

In two late films, *Duet for One* and *That's Life* (both 1986) Andrews's persona undergoes late variations as she ages and faces death. Both films begin by announcing sentences of terminal illness, *That's Life* as Gillian has throat tissue removed, with the ensuing narrative balefully punctuated by laboratory test shots. Ultimately, comic form prevails, with sentences suspended or lifted. Nevertheless both present Andrews in extremis, whether in the stoic other-oriented mode of *That's Life* or in the disintegrative vein of *Duet for One*, shocking in its fracturing of the star's image when she loses physical co-ordination when performing, and, most of all, in the life affirmer's attempted suicide. Both are also highly self-referential in having her play musical performers whose careers are threatened with termination, even if they survive, reminding the viewer that the performer's life too is finite. This may be the logic of ceding to other singers (Helen Reddy in *The Man who Loved Women*, Tony Bennett in *That's Life*) the final credit overvoice songs we expect Andrews to sing.

Given my argument, Andrews's mortification stages the death of the mother, either within the biological family in *That's Life* or within a network of family and surrogate relationships in *Duet for One*. The latter allows entry to the stressed interiority of the symbolic figure; *That's Life*, where all the fragmentation is her husband's (Jack Lemmon) and children's, conservatively preserves her as the healing (but sparingly subjectivised) centre. The films threaten, but only threaten, the protagonist's death, activating the audience into a recapitulation, or prefiguring, of their own orphaning, but finally relenting in a display of the mother's benign powers: Stephanie allowing her husband/son (Alan Bates) and his secretary a new independent life, and Gillian curing Harvey's psychic disintegration by threatening to leave. The latter remind us that the good mother incorporates the disciplining, denying figure within the all-giving one. (Remember how Maria, though not betraying the children to their father, reduces them to dinner-table tears as punishment for their anarchy.)

Coda

Why was Julie Andrews so charismatic? What was the meaning of her popularity? There have been other stars in whom the suffusing maternal has dominated, like Ingrid Bergman and June Allyson, but none so emphatically as Andrews. (I am discounting actresses who play literal mothers simply because they signify homeliness and domesticity, the difference being that Andrews, like Bergman and Allyson, embodies a fantasy combining the maternal and the erotic.)

When Mary Poppins floated down in 1964 it was at the time of 'second-stage' feminism, amid widely perceived dislocations in sex and family roles, and disruptive discourses against the primarily nurturing female, the centrality of the family and the naturalness of heterosexuality. It is *within* these dislocations that Julie Andrews needs analysing, not simply *against*. *Mary Poppins* responds to the perceived crisis of the assertion of adults' (particularly women's) individual interests against those of child and family, by adopting the child's all-demanding viewpoint and returning Mrs Banks to a Rousseauistic mother role (though it should be noted that Mr Banks too is returned to the domestic). However, Mary's active mastery provides a significant counterbalance – if she acts for the family she is certainly not reductively contained by it – so that Janet Thumim's comment that the film is deeply chauvinist[13] neglects the likelihood of audiences concurring at some, but not all, levels with the film's child-centredness, and moving between the positions acted out by Mrs Banks (Glynis Johns) and Mary Poppins and the children, as between past and present, and fantasy and reality. (Unless one thinks of Andrews's female audience as simply victimised by the film, one needs a more sophisticated approach.) The later films, though crucially mother-centred, not only expel the literal child from the narrative but also place the maternal imago in circumstances precluding easy solutions (for example simple good versus bad mother polarities). This means that Andrews's extraordinary abilities both to be the object of maternal fantasies and to project nurturing, empathic values in manifold narrative situations, even though we may feel that the first, with its backward pull towards infantile demands for the all-giving, can easily be employed regressively, are in the later films implicated with, rather than simply seen as the antidote to, feminism, the working woman, homosexuality etc. We should hardly expect these meanings to be worked out point by point, but the texts struggle percipiently, seldom in a simply regressive way, to match those archaic meanings to the contemporary world.

This chapter has centred more on the filmic persona than the Andrews of biography and publicity. Nevertheless, the Andrews of offscreen discourse parallels the onscreen Andrews in various ways. Constructed as the epitome of niceness, she embodies the superstar unspoiled by fame, a paradox much wondered at.[14] Concurrently, though, while her films place her maternality in increasingly complex circumstances, so her publicity has foregrounded a darker narrative – divorce, long-term psychoanalysis, her adopted Vietnamese daughter's drug addiction. But just as the serial film character finds a post-sceptical affirmation of the original image, so does the archetypal Andrews article or interview, reading her psychoanalysis as a symptom less of narcissism than of sensibleness against the 'wobbly' feeling fame brought, and viewing her children's problems in terms of a deconstructed or reconstructed Maria, coping with the family's difficulties in a fragmented age.

> 'She's as clean as a whistle now, and just graduated from college', says Julie proudly. 'She did an enormous amount of work and had a lot of help from a great many people, a lot of therapy. And a lot of vigilance on all our parts. I think the teens are a tremendously hard time for children. It's a narcissistic period where children turn inwards, so they are difficult anyway; but imagine being adopted, not sure of your roots and parentage and foundations. They both had problems but they are on the other side of the mountain now. We were wondering what the hell we did wrong. It's not easy being two kids brought from a strange country into a very high powered environment. We asked ourselves if we'd done the right thing'[15]

The script is moving as a difficult (post-Bettelheim) version of the fairy-tale of families and good mothers, combining echoes of Maria in 'clean as a whistle' and 'the other side of the mountain now' with the self-interrogating vocabulary of psychoanalysis. That it is a quintessentially English middle-class voice (give or take a few accretions from long-term American residence) is an important part of her meaning, though it may be hard to say exactly why. For some English viewers it is perhaps not so difficult, since many inherited texts, mixing the mythological and the actual, pass on the image of the caring middle-class mother, closer to her children and more concerned for their progress than the upper-class parent, and with more time and education than the lower-class mother. Even Andrews's precise enunciation carries messages of the importance of order and neatness, yet at the same time there is space for individual imagination and fantasy. Combined with an ethical, though not revolutionary, view of the less privileged in society (Mary's friendship with Bert, the Blakean sweeps, and the old bird woman, the last two, like the nuns in *The Sound of Music*, pointing to a post-Christian preservation of Christian values centred on a secular inflection of the Madonna), what emerges is a characteristic high bourgeois mixture of altruism and self-advancement, which, though in an English inflection, has its meanings in American culture, where for the American audience (remembering that Andrews's films are American) her Englishness also revives historical parent–child relations, and combines with Hollywood's tendencies to associate British female stars with cultivation and education. And, like the middle England stereotypes of Agatha Christie, Julie Andrews's Englishness is meaningful to many other cultures in some form. Thus the trans-historical, trans-cultural fantasy of the good mother restored that Julie

Andrews incarnates in highly defined but broadly appealing national and social forms appeared at a particular time of crisis in the intimate order of the western social world. Although part of this appeal is undoubtedly nostalgic (since the middle-class values with which Andrews is associated seem to be in decline), the persona and films struggle to adapt as well as conserve in their inflection of that which 'reduces social [and even metaphysical] anguish'.

Notes

1 Julia Kristeva, 'Stabat Mater', in *The Kristeva Reader*, ed. Toril Moi (Basil Blackwell, Oxford, 1986), p. 163.
2 Bruno Bettelheim, *The Uses of Enchantment: The Meaning and Importance of Fairy Tales* (Penguin, Harmondsworth, 1978), *passim*, but especially pp. 66–76. Bettelheim does not cite Klein, but his arguments seem to me Kleinian. See Juliet Mitchell, ed., *The Selected Melanie Klein* (Penguin, Harmondsworth, 1986), and Hanna Siegel, *Klein* (Fontana, London, 1979).
3 B. H. Travers, *Mary Poppins* (Collins Modern Classics, London, [1934] 1998).
4 Richard Dyer, *Stars* (BFI, London, 1979), p. 3.
5 Julia Kristeva, 'Stabat Mater', p. 169.
6 Sigmund Freud, 'Family Romances', Pelican Freud Library, vol. 7, *On Sexuality* (Penguin Books, Harmondsworth, 1977), pp. 221–5.
7 *The Lass with the Delicate Air* (RCA Records, Decca Recording Co., RD-27061 LPM-1403).
8 On *The Best of Julie Andrews*, R 2 77281 A 26680 Rhino Records, originally on *Julie Andrews Sings*, RCA Victor SP 1681 (June 1958).
9 *Noël Coward: Legends of the 20th Century*. 0724 3 499923 2 0 (version recorded 14 September 1945).
10 See the discussion by Claudia Gorbman in *Unheard Melodies: Narrative Film Music* (BFI, London, and Indiana University Press, Bloomington and Indianapolis, pp. 60–3). The phrase 'sonorous envelope' comes from Didier Anzieu, 'Enveloppe sonore du soi', *Nouvelle Revue de Psychoanalyse* (Spring 1976), 161–79.
11 Richard Dyer, 'The Sound of Music', *Movie*, 23 (1976–7), 39–49.
12 *Beautiful Thing*, dir. Hattie MacDonald, Channel 4 Corporation, 1996. Thanks to James Knowles for suggesting this film to me.
13 Janet Thumim, *Celluloid Sisters: Women and Popular Culture* (Macmillan, London and Basingstoke, 1994), p. 124.
14 For the tip of the iceberg, see *Time* cover story, 9 October 1964; *Sun*, 25 October 1964; *Daily Sketch*, 15 July 1968; and Jan Moir, *Daily Mail*, 5 October 1992.
15 Vicky Ward, *Daily Mail Weekend*, 11 July 1993.

'There's something about Mary ...'

16

From 1975 to 1982 there was always at least one of her films playing in London's West End. The first feature in which she played a sizeable role, *Come Play with Me*, ran in London for nearly four years, the longest uninterrupted run of any movie in the capital, taking £550,000. It also played on a thousand separate screens in the UK and broke box-office records in Manchester, Birmingham, Blackpool and elsewhere. It cost a mere £120,000 and has to date taken well over £4 million. Just before she committed suicide in August 1979, four of her films – *Queen of the Blues*, *The Playbirds*, *Come Play with Me*, and *Erotic Inferno* – were all playing concurrently in the West End.

Mary Millington. Topless and even totally naked in Leeds, Oldham, Hull, Wolverhampton and Stockton on Tees.

She was Mary Millington, described by David Sullivan, the executive producer of her best known British features, as 'the only really uninhibited, natural sex symbol that Britain ever produced and who really believed in what she did'.[1]

However, she was in a real sense a star without a cinema, a porn star in one of the few western countries in which hard-core pornography was then illegal. She also had the misfortune to embark on her feature film career when the British cinema was entering one of its more than usually moribund phases, as well as to work within genres such as the sex comedy which make even the best disposed to British cinema cringe with embarrassment. It is perhaps for these reasons, along with the British reticence about sex that, despite her immense popularity and high-profile media image, both in her short lifetime and after her death, it wasn't until twenty years after her suicide that a serious, book-length study of her life and work appeared. This was *Come Play with Me: The Life and Films of Mary Millington*, whose author, Simon Sheridan, neatly sums up her unique career and the appeal of her star persona:

> Few, if any, actresses can lay claim to a celluloid career encompassing everything from hardcore pornography to European arthouse, clever satire, 'B' grade thrillers, hoary old British comedy, and even a punk rock documentary. Come to think of it, most would not actually want to. It is a dubious distinction perhaps, but nonetheless one unique to Mary Millington. Her roles were, admittedly, terribly cliched (sexpot nurses, night-club strippers and so on), but however small the part, however seemingly insignificant her role, Mary brought an irresistible charm to each of the films in which she appeared. It was this charm that was responsible for her remarkable cinema track record.[2]

The fact that, as Christine Gledhill has noted, 'stars reach their audiences primarily through their bodies',[3] and, as Colin McArthur has argued, the meanings of stars are offered through 'qualities that are largely physical',[4] makes it all the stranger that there are so few serious studies of those most physical of stars, porn stars. Furthermore, the persona of a porn star such as Millington, for whom appearances in porn magazines as well as in the tabloid press were equally as important as, if indeed not more important than, her appearances in movies, very clearly backs up Richard Dyer's point that:

> The star phenomenon consists of everything that is publicly available about stars. A film star's image is not just his or her films, but the promotion of those films and of the star through pin-ups, public appearances, studio hand-outs and so on, as well as interviews, biographies and coverage in the press of the star's doings and 'private' life. Further, a star's image is also what people write or say about him or her, as critics or com-

mentators, the way the image is used in other contexts such as advertisements, novels, pop songs, and finally the way the star can become part of
the coinage of everyday speech ... A star image consists both of what we
normally refer to as his or her 'image', made up of screen roles and obviously stage-managed public appearances, and also of images of the manu-
facture of that 'image' and of the real person who is the site or occasion of
it. Each element is complex and contradictory, and the star is all of it taken
together.[5]

Indeed, Mary Millington's tragic end meant that her private life came
under the spotlight after her death even more intensely than it had done
in her life time, and inevitably there were strong suggestions that her
porn star persona had contributed to her suicidal state. In some cases this
was simply rather unpleasant moralism; however, if we want to understand the popular appeal of her star persona then we need to know something of her life, with the obvious caveat that what we 'know' is the
product of representations of one kind or another, including this one.

Mary Millington was born Mary Quilter in 1945 and grew up with her
unmarried mother Joan in Willesden, and then in Mid Holmwood, near
Dorking in Surrey, when single parenthood was not as common as it is
now, and certainly not amongst the middle classes to which Joan
belonged, having worked as a civil servant in the Foreign Office until she
became pregnant by a music critic. Mary was extremely close to her
mother. She was a high-spirited child who hated school and whose
great love, apart from her mother, was animals. She was also sexually precocious. Leaving school at 15, she drifted through secretarial college and
Reigate School of Art before training as a veterinary nurse, a job which
she loved. By now, however, her mother's health was deteriorating, giving
her daughter considerable concern. In 1964 she married, becoming Mary
Maxted, and the couple lived with Joan. Later she became deputy man-
ageress in a boutique in Dorking. However, during a visit to London she
was 'discovered' in a Kensington coffee bar by glamour photographer and
blue-movie-maker John Lindsay.

By this point Mary, although lacking in confidence about her looks,
something that would plague her career, had decided that she wanted to
be a fashion model and was happy to pose for him; however, at 4 feet 11
inches she simply wasn't tall enough for fashion shoots, so he offered to
photograph her for softcore magazines. She soon became Lindsay's most
popular model. She then began working in hard-core shorts such as *Miss
Bohrloch* and *Oral Connection* for his Taboo company, starring in eighteen
hard-core films between 1970 and 1974, although not all for Lindsay. It
needs to be reiterated that hard-core porn was completely illegal in
Britain, and much of what was distributed on the flourishing black

market was made, processed and duplicated abroad. It was then sold on 8 mm (although made in 16 mm) through mail order or under the counter in Soho and East End sex shops. However, in the 1970s, in London and other big cities, it was also shown in cinema clubs, such as Lindsay's own Taboo Club, which survived by exploiting police corruption and a loophole in the 1952 Cinematograph Act, until the latter was closed in 1982 by the Cinematograph Amendment Act. Lindsay himself was prosecuted unsuccessfully during the 1970s under the Obscene Publications Act; however, in 1983 a charge was finally made to stick (Lindsay claims that the evidence was planted) and he was sent to prison for twelve months.

By now Mary was becoming over-familiar to hard-core audiences, and Lindsay reluctantly let her go. She then began to work for soft-core magazines such as *Knave*, *Rustler* and *Club International*, under different names. It was at this point that she encountered David Sullivan, who had already established a highly successful mail order business selling soft-core magazines and sex aids. Sullivan decided to produce a mass-circulation soft-core porn magazine, *Private*, as a down-market challenge to *Penthouse* and *Playboy*. As Mark Killick points out, Sullivan 'did not feature models who were so beautiful that they were obviously beyond the reach of the readership. The girls were attractive but they looked as though they could be found in any British town. The models in his competitors' magazines looked as though they could only be found in Hollywood.'[6] Unsurprisingly, it was Sullivan who introduced the 'Readers' Wives' innovation into British soft-core porn magazines. *Private*'s first editor was Doreen Millington. Within eighteen months, it made Sullivan's company the second biggest publisher in the soft-core magazine field. He then went on to found *Whitehouse*, which cheekily was named after the anti-porn campaigner Mary Whitehouse and which set out deliberately to test the bounds of the acceptable. Mary rapidly became the most prominent model in both magazines, her surname changed to 'Millington' in order to make her appear to be Doreen's sexier sister. She also began a close personal relationship with Sullivan. (Although they were separated by the end of her life, she remained married to Maxted, who seems to have tolerated her sex star career.)

Mary was soon receiving over two thousand letters a week, and she became Sullivan's biggest star, even though she was pushing 30 (relatively old for a glamour model) and neither 21 nor 5 feet 10 inches as the magazines claimed. She also featured heavily in his new venture *Playbirds*, which included her version of Fiona Richmond's 'sex tours' around Britain, a popular feature of Paul Raymond's *Men Only*. These accounts of 'her' sexual exploits around the country were ghost-written, but Mary insisted on being photographed, often topless or even totally naked, in the articles' locations, such as Oldham, Wolverhampton and Hull. She also worked in Sullivan's Whitehouse sex shop in Norbury, south London, which she thoroughly enjoyed, even admitting that she found cashing up at the end of the day better than sex, and which she did so well that Sullivan gave her a stake in the business. By issue 15 of *Whitehouse* in 1976 Mary was named both editor and proprietor. As Sheridan puts it, thanks to Sullivan's promotional skills and her own qualities, 'the words Mary Millington had become the most famous brand name in the British sex business'.[7] Now her fame began to spread beyond the confines of softcore magazines and into the tabloids, thanks to Sullivan's publicity stunts – for example, having her pose naked with half-dressed members of the crew of the submarine HMS Otter in Nassau, and topless outside the Palace of Westminster and even No. 10. It was not long before Sullivan was planning a feature film career for his top model.

Two points need to be stressed here. First, Mary had already appeared briefly, in a number of features. As Mary Maxted she'd been in *Eskimo Nell* (Campbell, 1974), an unusual sex comedy in that it's actually amusing and well made, where, as a traffic warden, she does a high-speed strip auditioning for a sex film; spicing up the pre-credits sequence of *I'm Not Feeling Myself Tonight* (McGrath, 1975); the rather 'arty' Swedish hardcore film *I Nod Och Lust* / *Private Pleasures* (Gerber, 1975), in the UK print of which most of her role is missing thanks to the British Board of Film Censors; and *Erotic Inferno* (Wrenn, 1975), an unusual British sex film in that it isn't a comedy and contains a good deal of sex, albeit simulated, and in which a dubbed Mary plays a lesbian stable-hand. As Mary Millington she'd appeared in the unlikely role of a choirgirl in a flashback in *Intimate Games* (Gates, 1976), and, in her biggest role to date, as a scullery maid in the truly appalling *Keep It Up Downstairs* (Young, 1976), written and produced by *Crossroads'* Hazel Adair and scored by Michael Nyman. She also appears briefly (and dubbed) as a near-naked temptress in *What's Up Superdoc?* (Ford, 1978). None of these films was produced by Sullivan, who, as the commentary to Mary Millington's *True Blue Confessions* (Galtress and East, 1980) clearly demonstrates, later tried to write them out of her mythology. Nor were they particularly successful.

Second, Mary had entered the most godforsaken area of the British film industry. As Laurence O'Toole stresses: 'Britain has never had a home-based hard-core porn industry. Not magazines, nor movies. There have been a few brief periods of reckless enterprise, short-lived acts of solo derring-do, but never an industry, nothing like it.'[8] The only chance UK audiences had of seeing anything remotely arousing was in imported sex films, although these were usually stripped of most of their erotic content by the

BBFC, or else in insipid home-grown ones made with the Board's strict standards firmly in mind. One way of making displays of naked flesh and mild sexual activity palatable to the censors was to concoct what were essentially animated seaside postcards or slightly spiced-up *Carry On*'s. Thus were born those ghastly British cinematic abominations, sex comedies, the majority of which were neither sexy nor comic.

However, as Sullivan stated, 'I just knew that if I put Mary in a film, with the power of my magazines backing it up, it just couldn't fail'.[9] He discovered that Harrison Marks, Britain's most famous photographer of nudes, renowned for his work with the beautiful Pamela Green, had written a script called *Come Play with Me*, but hadn't been able to raise the finance. Sullivan put up the money and hired Marks as director. Mary was cast as a stripper working in a health-farm-cum-brothel. Long before the film was released he was ruthlessly promoting it across his publications, promising, among other entirely unlikely ingredients, unsimulated sex. Mary was described as the new Linda Lovelace and the movie as 'the British *Deep Throat*'. Soon the tabloids were inveigled into action, and Irene Handl and Alfie Bass were quoted in the *News of the World* as complaining that they hadn't realised it was that kind of film. (In fact, three hard-core scenes, one of which features Mary Millington and Penny Chisholm, were filmed, but only for the continental market.)

Once the film was released, its promotion in Sullivan's magazines went into overdrive, with Mary, for all the brevity of her appearances, featured as the principal star. Sullivan's forecast of its success was soon to prove an underestimate. He followed it up with a film in which Mary had a bigger part, which delighted her as the success of *Come Play with Me* had to some extent overcome her fear of speaking roles. This was *The Playbirds* (Roe, 1978), in which she plays an undercover policewoman investigating the murders of a number of models from Sullivan's own *Playbirds* magazine. For this her most substantial part she was heavily coached by her friend and soon-to-be publicist John M. East. This ran in London for thirty-four continuous weeks and took £177,000. In December 1978 *Come* became the longest-running British film of all time, with an unbroken eighteen-month residency at the Moulin. As Sheridan puts it, Mary Millington had

> broken free from the limited shackles of girlie magazines to quickly become a name on everybody's lips. Newspapers wanted to interview her; mainstream film journals wrote about her; and thanks to her image on the posters for *Come Play With Me* and *The Playbirds* her face and name were plastered throughout the whole of the UK. She had surpassed the dreams of any glamour actress in the film industry, and her own personal ambition had been fulfilled. She had attained 'real' fame.[10]

Mary promoted her films personally in provincial cinemas, and also presided over regional openings of sex shops in Sullivan's growing empire. She was invited to meet the contestants of the 1978 Miss World contest, opened boutiques, restaurants and pet parlours, and raised considerable funds for her favourite charity, the People's Dispensary for Sick Animals.

For Mary's next film, *Confessions from the David Galaxy Affair* (Roe, 1979) Sullivan shamelessly attempted to cash in on the popularity of Columbia's execrable *Confessions* series. Here Mary is limited to two scenes as Millicent Cumming, a woman unable to achieve orgasm until she goes to bed with the eponymous hero; in spite of one of these scenes being relatively explicit by British standards, and Sullivan's promotion notwithstanding, the film flopped. She was equally under-used in the woeful *Queen of the Blues* (Roe, 1979), in which she played a stripper, albeit highly professionally. By now Mary was tiring of this kind of film, but she also blamed herself for *Galaxy*'s failure, even though she had barely appeared in it and her sex scene is its highlight. It was not that she minded appearing naked or in sex scenes, but having acquired a taste for acting she now wanted something more substantial. But no such roles were forthcoming.

In order to understand why, one has to appreciate that, by the end of the 1970s, not only was the era of the British sex film dragging to an end but the entire British cinema industry had virtually collapsed. The BBFC was now passing rather stronger material from Hollywood and the continent, and the nascent video industry was taking full advantage of the brief interlude before stringent video censorship was imposed. These factors, taken in conjunction with others such as the inflation which rendered virtually all low-budget production financially unviable, sounded the sex film's death knell. And David Sullivan, with a keen eye for what the punters wanted and sights firmly fixed on the bottom line, was well aware of this. Thus even after the huge success of the extremely low-budget *Come*, Sullivan insisted that *Playbirds* be made for even less, whilst *Queen of the Blues* was not even feature length and was intended to be double- or even triple-billed with cheap, cut-down, continental or American sex films.

There were other factors which blighted her success. First, her mother had died in 1976, and Mary never really recovered from her loss. She lacked confidence in her looks and acting abilities. And then there were the police.

Mary had always had disliked the pornography laws, and the police who enforced them. This may have been at least partly because they interfered with the profits from her business, but she also clearly possessed a strong libertarian impulse and was an outspoken advocate of sexual liberation and freedom of expression. She openly encouraged her readers to demand the abolishing of the OPA, publicly criticised police raids on sex shops, and published the addresses and phone numbers of Scotland Yard, the DPP and MPs in her magazines. However, her determination to express her libertarian views publicly earned her powerful enemies, not least in the Metropolitan Police, by whom she was increasingly targeted. At the same time as being subjected to this campaign of harassment, she was also shelling out the 'protection' money to the Met that was more or less *de rigueur* for anyone involved in the porn business in London in the 1970s. She was repeatedly personally abused by police officers, the lives of her beloved dogs were threatened, and drugs and weaponry were planted on her.[11]

Her willingness to sell hardcore material from the Norbury shop had become an increasing source of tension with Sullivan, whose business empire had been no stranger to police raids since 1973. It was partly because of this that they had parted company in 1977. However, this didn't stop Sullivan being harassed, and later that year he was charged under the OPA. Because Mary was a director, albeit purely on paper, of the publishing company concerned, she herself had to appear in court in November 1977, facing the possibility of going to prison, a prospect which she dreaded and whose horrors the police emphasised at every opportunity. In the event, six of the seven charges were dropped owing to lack of evidence, and Mary (although not her two co-defendants) was found not guilty on the seventh.

In March 1978 Mary had severed her links with the Whitehouse shop in Norbury, and opened one of her own in Tooting, called Mary Millington's International Sex Centre, with a cinema club on the first floor. However, this resulted in demands for increased protection money and in yet more raids. But by this time she was beginning to face other problems; as a result of her cavalier attitude to paying tax she was facing huge demands from the Inland Revenue, with whom she refused to negotiate, and the kleptomaniac tendencies apparent in childhood were becoming more pronounced and causing yet more hassles with the police. Finally, she was taking cocaine and becoming increasingly confused, paranoid and depressed. She took a lethal cocktail of gin and paracetamol on the night of 18 August 1979, after having been arrested for shoplifting in Banstead, Surrey, and died in the early hours of 19 August. In her suicide note to David Sullivan she wrote: 'please print in your magazines how much I wanted porn legalised, but the police have beaten me.'[12]

Considering her star status, Mary Millington's cinematic legacy is by no means extensive. Of her hardcore shorts, only *Miss Bohrloch*, *Oral Connection* and *Betrayed* appear to have survived, although, thanks to a combination of the OPA and Video Recordings Act, these could still be open to prosecution if commercially distributed outside the confines of a licensed sex shop and are thus not easily available. However, many of her commercial features are now on video, enabling contemporary audiences to understand the appeal of her star persona. Some of these films do her no favours, but others are much more revealing and rewarding. Thus, in *Erotic Inferno* her two sex scenes with Heather Deeley are the only genuinely erotic moments in a film which otherwise consists of mechanical heterosexual coupling. Similarly the sub-*Carry-On* plot of *Keep It Up Downstairs*, with its endless innuendoes, is relieved only by the liveliness of Mary's two heterosexual scenes and the sheer strangeness of her lesbian threesome in a bathroom; the BBC clearly thought that two of these still packed such an erotic charge that they excised them entirely when the film was shown on late-night television in 1998! Also characteristic is her massaging of a male client in *Come Play with Me*, where, in Russ Meyer style, her breezy, carefree eroticism contrasts so sharply with the ludicrously uptight behaviour of her customer and indeed of most of the other men around her. Equally typical is her matter-of-fact but nonetheless erotically charged strip in *The Playbirds* in which she demonstrates to her superiors why she is so well suited to undercover work in the porn business, and an immaculately professional photo session which shows why she was such a popular model with photographers.

Mary's star persona, as it evolved during her lifetime, but even more so after her death, is nothing if not contradictory. As Leon Hunt has pointed out in a highly perceptive study of the star, she has been 'posthumously constructed as both liberated and doomed, ordinary and polymorphously insatiable, a male fantasy figure whose persona genuinely belittled male sexuality, a suburban libertine and a child, a girl-next-door and a freak'.[13] The qualities which Mary displays in her most typical roles are those of what David McGillivray aptly describes as the 'sexpot-next-door'.[14] This was a quality of her persona which she carried over directly from her magazine work; as Simon Sheridan puts it:

> Mary's fans perceived her as being easily the sort of attractive young woman they could meet down the pub, go on a date with to the Odeon, introduce to their parents and then have wild sex with in the back of a car. Her innocent hazel eyes belied her huge sexual appetite. She was, in her fans' eyes, the perfect fantasy girlfriend who would never say no.[15]

A journalistic contact, Colin Wills of the *Sunday Mirror*, explaining her peculiarly potent mix of the ordinary and the extraordinary, remarked that 'she brought porn out of Soho and into Esher', and it's hard to avoid the impression that, on occasion, her undubbed voice has distinct similarities with that of one-time suburban sitcom queen June Whitfield![16] However, there's also a certain parallel with Marilyn Briggs/Chambers, the one time down-home icon of the Ivory Snow soap powder advertisements in the USA, who turned overnight into a highly visible hardcore porn star.

Along with 'ordinary' (in its non-pejorative sense), the word invariably applied to Millington's star persona is 'natural'. Of course, we have to note the paradox that the 'natural' is a highly cultural concept, but one does not have to be a particular aficionado of sex films to notice that what defines Mary's star persona is not simply her spontaneity but also her obvious pleasure in what she is doing. This is most apparent in her hard-core films (a genre in which performers all too often appear to be simply going through the motions), and especially in *Miss Bohrloch*, in which she plays a prostitute energetically and imaginatively servicing two clients simultaneously. The film scored a huge success on the continent (where hard-core was by then commonplace), even winning the coveted Golden Phallus Award at the Wet Dream festival in Amsterdam; this was undoubtedly down to the remarkable performance of its fresh-faced but seemingly insatiable young star.

Unsurprisingly perhaps, Mary's on-screen portrayals of sexual activity mirrored her straightforward attitude towards sex in real life. This was nothing if not down-to-earth; as John M. East put it: 'to her sex was no big deal. She would always want to pay back people's kindness to her. She did this in the only way she knew how, usually with a quick bonk or at least a wank.' Or as David Sullivan put it, for her sex 'was just something nice to do with people'.[17] She sold kisses to fans for small sums and, on occasion, considerably more for much larger ones. There were rumours that her clients had even included Harold Wilson and the Shah of Iran. In a sense, then, Mary really was what most people would consider an impossible adolescent wish-fulfilment fantasy – the sex star who is, to some extent at least, actually 'available'.

There are certain parallels with Marilyn Monroe (quite apart from the fact that both committed suicide). Both were blonde, both adopted names with the same initials, both worked for soft-core magazines before entering feature films, and Richard Dyer's observation that 'Monroe was understood above all through her sexuality – it was her embodiment of current ideas of sexuality that made her seem real, alive, vital'[18] could equally well apply to Mary Millington, as could Diana Trilling's remark that 'none but Marilyn Monroe could suggest such a purity of sexual delight'.[19] Furthermore, Monroe's response ('I'm not ashamed of it. I've done nothing wrong') to the outcry that greeted her famous 'Golden Dreams' centrefold in the first *Playboy* in December 1953 was precisely the same as Mary's. But the most significant similarity between the two stars is the key role which they both played, in their very different cultures, in bringing at least soft-core pornography out from under the counter and making it seem less sleazy and disreputable. As Dyer points out: 'What *Playboy* succeeded in doing was making sex objects everyday',[20] which it did by turning the pin-up into the girl next door.

The other important feature of Mary's star persona, as will by now have become apparent, is bisexuality. Indeed, Simon Sheridan succinctly defines her somewhat contradictory appeal as being that of 'the predatory, insatiable, bi-sexual English rose'.[21] Of course, for obvious reasons, 'lesbian' scenes are a frequent feature of porn aimed at heterosexual men, but in fact Mary was openly bisexual, and at a time when there was even more prejudice than now against deviations from the heterosexual norm. No wonder, then, that her performances in sex scenes, both simulated and unsimulated, with other actresses have a certain intensity – witness in particular *Betrayed*, *Erotic Inferno* and the soft-core but extremely highly charged short *Response* (1974), which she made for Russell Gay, the glamour photographer, publisher of *Knave* and owner of Mistral films.

Even before her suicide there was a potent Mary Millington mythology which, like all star mythologies, was an inextricable mix of fact and fiction. In particular, her porn magazine persona as randy 'sex tourist' both was a fabrication and contained elements of truth. Meanwhile *The Amazing Mary Millington*, co-written with David Weldon and published in 1978, is more fiction than the 'autobiography' which it claims to be. Inevitably, the mythologising process was enormously boosted by her suicide, and swelled by the rushed-out *True Blue Confessions*, which purports to answer the question 'What was Mary really like?', a sure sign that mythmaking is in the offing. And thus we're told, in true tabloid tones, that 'she became hooked on glamour, something that people who are not sure of themselves cling to'; 'she yearned for affection and was full of self doubts. It's not surprising that Mary became a tormented woman'; 'even her friends didn't realise that Mary Millington was on a crash course and there was only one way out', all of which contain elements of truth but whose melodramatic language propels us towards myth. Elsewhere the real tabloids were revealing the more prosaic truth behind the myths cultivated in Sullivan's magazines: Doreen and Mary weren't sisters, the fancy-free Mary had been married for fifteen years, and the happy-go-lucky girl was a suicidally depressed woman in her thirties. At the same time, however, other sources (some owned by Sullivan) were stressing Mary's positive qualities (friend to humans and animals alike, charity worker, enemy of censorship, living marital aid, and so on) to such an extent that, as Sheridan perceptively points out: 'looking back at the events twenty years on it can seem that Mary had been elevated almost to the position of a pornographic Princess Diana'.[22] And then, finally, there's her appearance, filmed in the spring of the year she died, in *The Great Rock 'n' Roll Swindle* (Temple, 1979), which establishes a clear link not only with the Sex Pistols' anarchy but also with another 1970s icon who met an untimely end, Sid Vicious. This is a classic instance of a case in which, as Dyer puts it, 'the sheer multiplicity of the images, the amount of hype, the different stories told become overwhelmingly contradictory' so that what remains is not a sense of the 'real' person but, rather, of 'the extraordinary fragility of their inner selves, endlessly fragmented into what everyone else, including us, wanted them to be'.[23] A fitting epitaph, indeed, for Mary Millington.

Notes

1 Quoted in J. Adamson, *Sex and Fame: The Mary Millington Story*, a Speakeasy production in association with Fulcrum for Channel 4, broadcast 12 October 1996.

2 Simon Sheridan, *Come Play with Me: the Life and Films of Mary Millington* (FAB Press, Guildford, 1999), p. 147. Sheridan's book is a veritable Millington cornucopia, to which this chapter is indebted for a great deal of factual information.

3 Christine Gledhill, ed., *Stardom: Industry of Desire* (Routledge, London, 1991), p. 210.

4 Colin McArthur, 'The Real Presence', in Richard Dyer, ed., *Teacher's Study Guide 1: The Stars* (BFI Education, London, 1979), p. 99.

5 Richard Dyer, *Heavenly Bodies: Film Stars and Society* (Macmillan/BFI, London, 1986), pp. 2–3, 7–8.

6 Mark Killick, *The Sultan of Sleaze: The Story of David Sullivan's Sex and Media Empire* (Penguin, London, 1994), p. 23.

7 Sheridan, *Come Play with Me*, p. 69.

8 Laurence O'Toole, *Porntopia: Porn, Sex, Technology and Desire* (Serpent's Tail, London, 1999), p. 99.

9 Quoted in Sheridan, *Come Play with Me*, p. 77.

10 Sheridan, *Come Play with Me*, p. 89.

11 The corrupt nature of the Obscene Publications Squad at this time was extreme, and the extraordinarily seedy quality of Soho's streets, which today seems such a notable feature of *Eskimo Nell*, *The Playbirds* and *Mary Millington's True Blue Confessions*, was largely attributable to the fact that the officers policing the pornography trade were playing a key role in running it. In 1970 a major investigation by the *Sunday People* into the Soho porn business was sabotaged by the police, but by the end of the decade, after the biggest investigation into police corruption undertaken by the Met, culminating in three Old Bailey trials, thirteen officers up to and including the rank of Commander were sent to prison for a total of 96 years. More than forty others were investigated, of whom a significant number were allowed to leave the force rather than risk facing prosecution. As Mr Justice Mars-Jones stated at the Old Bailey, the corruption 'was done on a scale which beggars description' and he accused Commander Wallace Virgo and OPS head Bill Moody of controlling 'an evil conspiracy which turned the Obscene Publications Squad into a vast protection racket'. (See Barry Cox, John Shirley and Martin Short, *The Fall of Scotland Yard* (Penguin, Harmondsworth, 1977).) Needless to say, the police and

pornographers were happy with the pornography laws as they stood, since it was these which had created the situation which both sides were very profitably exploiting, and thus neither took kindly to demands for the de-criminalisation of pornography

12 Quoted in Sheridan, *Come Play with Me*, p. 133.

13 Leon Hunt, *British Low Culture: From Safari Suits to Sexploitation* (Routledge, London, 1998), p. 137.

14 David McGillivray, *Doing Rude Things: The History of the British Sex Film 1957–1981* (sun tavern fields (*sic*), London, 1992), p. 78.

15 Sheridan, *Come Play with Me*, p. 68.

16 For a useful discussion of the mundane and suburban in the British sex film see Ian Conrich, 'Forgotten Cinema: The British Style of Sexploitation', *Journal of Popular British Cinema*, I (1998), 87–100.

17 Both quoted in Sheridan, *Come Play with Me*, p .95.

18 Dyer, *Heavenly Bodies*, p. 13.

19 Quoted in Dyer, *Heavenly Bodies*, p. 32.

20 Ibid, p. 39.

21 Sheridan, *Come Play with Me*, p. 63.

22 Ibid., p. 136.

23 Dyer, *Heavenly Bodies*, p. 16.

ANDREW SPICER

Sean Connery: loosening his Bonds

In the popular imagination, Sean Connery is forever identified with James Bond, and jokes about his being 'in Bondage' were a journalistic cliché for twenty years. But Connery's distinction has been to embody not one mythic figure but two. Beginning with *The Name of the Rose* (Annand, 1986), he reinvented himself as an ancient archetype, the tribal elder, the wise mentor of a younger hero. In between he played a number of roles that explicitly dealt with the contradictions of mythical heroism. Connery's success has been as an *international* star, one whose brawn, looks and distinctive accent always set him apart from conventional English leading men. This chapter will explore the construction of these myths through a contextualised analysis of a representative selection of his films grouped into four phases. In doing so it also sheds light on the nature of stardom – that complex interaction between stars' attempts to control their image, the commercial imperatives of the film industry and the development of cultural myths.

Pre-Bond: problems of the British tough guy

Born and raised in Edinburgh's deprived Fountainbridge tenements, Connery's basic assets were his height, good looks and magnificent physique. His pre-cinematic career was based upon bodily display, as artist's or fashion model, as a body-builder who represented Scotland in a Mr Universe contest or as a chorus boy in the 1953 British tour of *South Pacific*. He enrolled in Swedish choreographer Yat Malmgeren's movement school to help control his body so that he became 'a much better tuned instrument'. His physicality was emphasised in the part which brought him recognition, the fading boxer Mountain McClintock in *Requiem for a Heavyweight* (BBC, March 1957), where he replaced Jack Palance. One commentator dubbed him 'Britain's Brando', 'the contemporary hero ... designed on American lines. Tall, broad, with features more rugged than regular, he looks earthy, unschooled and basic.'[2]

However, there were few opportunities for the rugged, American-style hero in British films at this point. Connery played only a tiny role in Rank's *Hell Drivers* (Endfield, 1957), where Stanley Baker was the tough lead.[3] It was Twentieth Century-Fox that offered him a contract. However, Fox used him merely as a hired hand, loaned out to other studios for dull supporting roles, including his bearded, brawling Irishmen in *Action of the Tiger* (Young, 1957) and *Tarzan's Greatest Adventure* (Guillermin, 1959). He was a romantic singing Irishman in Disney's *Darby O'Gill and the Little People* (Stevenson, 1959), but played second fiddle to the special effects. He looked uncomfortable as a BBC war correspondent in Paramount's *Another Time, Another Place* (Allen, 1958), a Lana Turner vehicle that did little for his reputation: 'Connery, in his first big part, gives the impression that he is reading his lines from a none-too-helpful prompt board.'[4] In *The Frightened City* (Lemont, 1961) some of the Bond characteristics were first visible in his Irish villain: the muscular grace of movement, the mordant wit and sardonic smile; but this was only a routine crime thriller. Over a five-year period, Fox had created nothing specifically

Sean Connery as Bond in *Dr No*, the first of the star's two mythic incarnations.

for him except a role as the 'seasoned veteran', Private Flanagan, in *The Longest Day* (Annakin et al., 1962), where again he was overshadowed by the main American stars. By this point, the impact of *Requiem* had been lost and his career was moribund.

Bond and 'Bondmania'

This changed decisively when he was cast as James Bond, becoming an integral part of the transformations made to translate that figure for a new medium and a different audience. Before this point the mid-Atlantic thriller always had an American lead, but Albert Broccoli, who formed Eon Productions in partnership with Harry Saltzman, the owner of the rights to Ian Fleming's novels, was convinced that Bond must be played by a British actor. Established stars such as Rex Harrison and David Niven (Fleming's choice), or newcomer Roger Moore ('the "Arrow collar" look: too buttoned-down smart'), were rejected:

> while very talented, [they] lacked the degree of masculinity Bond demanded. To put it in the vernacular of our profession: Sean had the balls for the part ... The whole point about having Sean in the role, with his strong physical magnetism and the overtones of a truck driver, was that it thrilled the women, but, more important, young men in the audience could feel there was a guy up there like them.[5]

Connery's lack of status also worked to his advantage. Eon wanted a virtual unknown who could, if the first film was successful, become identified with the role in an extended series.

Connery's rugged masculinity made his Bond a more demotic figure than in the novels; as Fleming observed, 'a somewhat rougher diamond than I had envisaged'.[6] His Edinburgh burr made him sound classless rather than patrician and gave a truculent and insubordinate edge to his relationship with 'M' not present in the novels. But Connery retained the ease and confidence of the elegantly stylish and sophisticated Man About Town, having been coached in those intricacies by his first director, Terence Young.[7] Connery's Bond was therefore a potent blend of the virile, athletic American action man and the insouciant Clubland hero whose *sang froid* is equal to any crisis. He incarnated both the unwavering patriotism of the traditional British gentleman hero and the guiltless sexual philandering of the international playboy who embodied the Swinging Sixties.[8] Bond became, on both sides of the Atlantic, a hero of consumption, refined, hedonistic and liberated. His Aston Martin was the symbol of traditional excellence and the latest in technological wizardry. He was both a 'guy like them' and the projection of audiences' aspirational fantasy of stylish and successful living, the classless hero of a modern, expansive international meritocracy. One of the reviewers for *Dr No* (Young, 1962) praised Connery as 'a flawless choice for the snob hero, Bond; virile, tough, perfectly tailored and faultlessly knowing.'[9]

Connery's dark good looks, thin, cruel mouth and calculating self-possession offered, as Kingsley Amis noted, a modern version of that potent male fantasy figure, the Byronic hero. This Byronic male is a refined sensualist, dark, handsome, sadistic, cynical but above all enigmatic, creating the impression of hidden depths which heightened the eroticism.[10] But Bond's sadism is lightened by the laconic, deadpan humour, those one-liners which Connery delivers with relish and immaculate timing. By the third film, *Goldfinger* (Hamilton, 1964), some commentators began to understand how shrewdly the films played on the knowingness of the audience, who could share the jokes, and thereby distance themselves from the palpable absurdities of the fantasy and participate in the comfortable pleasures of a familiar game: 'we all know the clichés and can have a little fun with them'.[11]

By the time of *Goldfinger* these knowing, playful and spectacular fantasies had made Bond *the* modern folk hero with an instantly recognisable style and image. 'Bondmania' reached such heights that Connery was mobbed wherever he went on a scale that rivalled the Beatles.[12] 'Connery is Bond and Bond Connery' proclaimed the publicity, and indeed, as a self-made working-class Scot, Connery empathised with Bond's self-reliant, competitive individualism as an extension of his own efforts to succeed: 'There's so much social welfare today that people have forgotten what it is to make their own decisions rather than leave them to others. So Bond is a welcome change.'[13] However, this near complete identification with the role became an oppressive strait-jacket, exacerbated by what Connery perceived as an increasing tendency to subordinate characterisation to special effects. He withdrew, temporarily, from the series after *You Only Live Twice* (Gilbert, 1967).

Beyond Bond?

Connery's contract with Eon always allowed him to make other films, but the scale of his success as Bond made it difficult for audiences to accept Connery in other roles. His engaging performance as a frustrated, boorish, womanising Greenwich Village poet in the comedy *A Fine Madness* (Kershner, 1966) flopped, as did the British Western *Shalako* (Dymtryk, 1968), which offered Connery as an ersatz Eastwood, the mysterious loner. The case of *Marnie* (1964) was more complex. Hitchcock cast Connery in order to subject the Bond persona to ruthless analysis.[14] Mark Rutland (Connery) has the invincible confidence of the attractive, wealthy playboy, but his jaded sensibilities can be goaded into life only by the piquancy of marrying a thief. As an erudite zoologist, he can justify his actions anthropologically as the close examination of an enigmatic and beautiful predator, whose primness offers a challenge to his own powers of seduction and analysis. For all his chivalrous concern, Rutland is prepared to 'rape' Marnie (Tippi Hedren), the camera drilling into his cold, ruthless eyes. Although he congratulates himself, as a self-styled psychoanalyst, on engineering her 'cure', it is far from clear that this is what she wants; or that the ending, which apparently tidies everything up, performs any kind of lasting resolution for the characters. Rutland is Bond stripped of the seductive fantasy, becoming the typically compulsive, obsessive, fetishistic, postwar Hitchcock male protagonist. In retrospect, Hitchcock judged Connery to have been unconvincing as a Philadelphia gentleman.[15] But the film's poor box office was more likely to have been an audience's inability to identify with or admire such a flawed and disturbing hero.

Bond may have typecast Connery, but the role also gave him the commercial clout to cultivate his twin aims to promote Scotland and to extend himself as an actor. The first was accomplished by the huge pay cheque for his return as Bond in *Diamonds Are Forever* (Hamilton, 1971), which helped launch the Scottish International Education Trust for his underprivileged countrymen.[16] The second was achieved by *The Hill* (1965) and *The Offence* (1972), both directed by Sidney Lumet, noted for his left-liberal social melodramas and his ability to work closely with actors.[17] *The Hill* was a modestly budgeted black-and-white film about a North African prison camp during the Second World War, 'the sort of film that might have been considered a non-commercial art-house property if my name were not on it'.[18] Its attraction for Connery was a radically different role as a working-class rebel, 'busted' Sergeant-Major Joe Roberts, crop-haired and with a moustache, goaded into revolt by the weakness, corruption and stupidity of his superiors. Roberts's intelligence, strength and self-conviction allow him to survive the physical barbarity of pounding up and down the 'hill', a man-made mountain of sand, in the blistering heat, but, at the very point where he traps the psychotic Sergeant Williams (Ian Hendry) into another assault that will condemn him, his fellow prisoners undermine his case by beating Williams. Sobbing 'I won, I won', Roberts is left in frustrated rage and pain.

The Offence, financed as part of the deal over *Diamonds Are Forever* that allowed Connery to make two films of his own choice, was set in the deracinated environment of a Home Counties New Town (Bracknell) with its bleak, decentred landscapes, Styrofoam pubs, cavernous underground car parks and impersonal, soulless flats. It is a world which produces victims not heroes, and Connery's Detective-Sergeant Johnson, with his cheap sheepskin coat, battered deerstalker rammed on his head, the mouth curling under a heavy moustache, is a man approaching disillusioned middle age and marital breakdown. Johnson's menopausal crisis is intensified by his interrogation of a suspected child molester, Baxter (Ian Bannen), during which he comes gradually to recognise these hideous potentialities within himself. The harsh, jarring music, unbalanced compositions and inchoate colour tones convey Johnson's confusion and terror at what is being revealed and he beats Baxter to death.

These deglamorised, stark and violent films contain two of Connery's most compelling performances that greatly enhanced his reputation as an actor. But, like *Marnie*, they asked too much of audiences wedded to his Bond persona. Connery's box-office value was sustained by routine action thrillers in which he was the tough lead – *Ransom* (Wrede, 1974), *The Next Man* (Sarafan, 1976), *Meteor* (Neame, 1979), *The Man with the Deadly Lens* (Brooks, 1982) or cameos: *Murder on the Orient Express* (Lumet, 1974), *A Bridge Too Far* (Attenborough, 1977) and *Time Bandits* (Gilliam, 1981). However, his accomplishments as an actor and his association with Bond made him attractive to *auteur*-directors keen to explore the myth of the hero.[19] Connery did not initiate these films, but his epic presence is an integral part of their meaning.

Two of these – *Robin and Marian* (1976) and *Cuba* (1979) – were directed by Richard Lester, who had an abiding concern with the contradictions of heroism.[20] In *Robin and Marian* Connery, with thinning hair, heavy beard and creaking joints, plays a jaded and disillusioned Robin Hood, the veteran of twenty years' soldiering in the Crusades: 'I've hardly lost a battle and yet I don't know what I've won.' His return to England shows a man trapped by his own legend. It is far from clear whether he has any desire to be the people's champion, and no good comes of the revolt he unwittingly leads. His defeat of his old adversary the Sheriff of Nottingham (Robert Shaw) in single combat has been emptied of any significance, and simply perpetuates a confused belief in his 'destiny'. Only Marian (Audrey Hepburn) truly understands the situation and poisons them both, an act of loving compassion as it will save Robin from further disenchantment by offering him a romantic death. It is their love which softens the film's coruscating scepticism and offers Connery in a new light: vulnerable, anxiously trusting, uncertain of his own gestures and unselfconsciously appreciative of Marian's loyalty and loveliness.

Cuba refuses this consolation. Connery's Major Robert Dapes is a modern soldier of fortune who has gone the rounds of British colonial conflicts secure in the knowledge that his legendary skills have been deployed in a just cause. Although Connery looks extremely handsome in his immaculate suits and sports jackets, the Ronald Colman moustache complemented by a full head of hair greying at the temples, Dapes is a Blimp operating by an anachronistic chivalric code: 'You know soldiering has changed. It's not as clean as it was. An honourable profession, or was.' In his new role as military adviser to the ailing Batista regime, he is forced to undergo an ideological and sexual education, opposed by an army that represents the aspirations of the people and by a former mistress, Alexandra (Brooke Adams), who is much too wary and independent to regard their affair as anything more than a brief encounter. The anticlimactic denouement, in which he flees and she remains, was a deliberate reversal of *Casablanca*.[21] This proved unacceptable to audiences, and the film was even less successful than *Robin and Marian*.

Both *The Wind and the Lion* (Milius, 1975) and *The Man who Would Be King* (Huston, 1975) were more romantic and more popular, but equally concerned with the contradictions of heroism and the construction of myths. John Milius's *The Wind and the Lion*, based loosely on an actual incident in 1904, gives epic scope to the conflict between Raisuli, a renegade Moroccan sheik (Connery) and President Theodore Roosevelt (Brian Keith) over Raisuli's abduction of Eden Pedecaris (Candice Bergen). In a series of deft parallels, the actions of each are shown to be dictated by a self-conscious cultivation of their own mythical status as leaders of their people obeying an unalterable destiny. Roosevelt assiduously promotes his image as the American frontiersman, imbued with the rugged energy of the Wild West. Raisuli resplendently incarnates the ancestral virtues of the Berber chieftain, the nomadic horseman, driving the hated foreigners from his lands with his sword. Both are charismatic anachronisms in a changing world, but preferable to the deceitful machinations of European power politics.

John Huston's brilliant adaptation of Kipling's allegorical short story *The Man Who Would Be King*, exploded the myth of the imperial hero. This lush and expansive picaresque epic concerns Peachy Carnehan (Michael Caine) and Daniel Dravot (Connery), two ex-Army 'Loafers', an Anglo-Indian underclass of devious rogues. Their grand scheme is nothing less than gaining a kingdom, remote Kafiristan, where men of enterprise and daring might prosper by exploiting the warring tribes as hired mercenaries. With devastating irony, their dreams of conquest and riches are shown to be no different from the dreams of every imperialist, every Englishman in India. Through accidental good fortune, Dravot becomes the 'second Sekunder', son of Alexander, the God-king. Intoxicated with the vanities of power, Dravot mystifies chance as fate: 'You may call it luck, I call it destiny.' Connery beautifully captures Dravot's slow-building wide-eyed wonder at his new eminence; his unselfconscious pomposity as he tries to rule his kingdom with dignity, tempering justice with mercy: 'a nation I shall make of it, with an anthem and a flag'. He dreams of an audience with Queen Victoria, 'as an equal'. His disarming credulity is perfectly complemented by Caine's droll wariness as the quick-thinking Cockney pragmatist, intent on departing with as much gold as possible. After the deception is blown and Dravot led away to his execution, the reaffirmation of their comradeship adds weight to the pathos. As the crippled Carnehan recounts his tale to the appalled Kipling (Christopher Plummer), he, like the audience, is unsure whether it is authentic or self-dramatising myth.

There was a strong element of conscious myth-making in Connery's return, aged 53, as the 'true' Bond, in *Never Say Never Again* (Kershner, 1983). The popular press was much exercised by the 'Battle of the Bonds', weighing up the merits of Connery against Roger Moore in *Octopussy* (Glen, 1983).[22] Warners offered Connery greater artistic control; he engaged Dick Clement and Ian La Frenais to ensure that the humour was both droll and British, emphasising character, not gadgetry.[23] Douglas Slocombe's subtle, subdued cinematography creates a mellow mood complementing Connery's intelligent performance as an agent who harbours his energies carefully. Of course, being Bond, he can still outperform his younger rival and save the world, but there are some neat ironies in the final image of an exhausted agent soothing his aching limbs in a Jacuzzi as the 'Bond girl', Kim Basinger, swims energetically around the pool.

The tribal elder

Connery's last bow as Bond reclaimed his status as a 'bankable' star and the first to sign with Michael Ovitz's Creative Artists Agency, which became the leading force in the 'package system' of commercial film production. However, in the more eclectic and decentred international film industry of the 1980s, Connery's new career path emerged through two off-beat films financed by Twentieth Century-Fox, *Highlander* (Mulcahy) and the European art-house picture *The Name of the Rose*, both released in 1986. Connery's Ramirez, an Egyptian immortal in a peacock courtier's attire, was all part of *Highlander's* flip postmodernism. But Jean-Jacques Arnaud's adaptation of Umberto Eco's cult novel *The Name of the Rose*

offered him a much more substantial role as a fourteenth-century Fran-
ciscan friar, William of Baskerville, the 'man of reason in an age of faith'.
A medieval Sherlock Holmes, Baskerville battles the credulity, blind obedience and fear induced by a tyrannical church. His quest to unravel the
murders uncovers the cause as heretical, forbidden, subversive pagan
knowledge, the 'lost' book of Aristotle's *Poetics* on comedy. Like Ramirez,
Baskerville is a mentor, his wisdom directed to the moral and emotional
education of his young novice Adso (Christian Slater). Connery's subtle
performance, mixing philosophising with irascibility, vanity and hubris,
was much admired in a film which became a major success in Europe.[24]

Connery's successful reincarnation as a father figure led to further
similar roles in three Paramount films, *The Untouchables* (De Palma,
1987), *Indiana Jones and the Last Crusade* (Spielberg, 1989) and *The Hunt
for Red October* (McTiernan, 1990), gave currency to this new persona for
American audiences. In *The Untouchables*, Brian De Palma's knowing
retro-stylishness is anchored by David Mamet's taut script that offers two
complementary images of the man of integrity. Connery's Jim Malone,
the lone bachelor, wily and unorthodox – knowing all about 'the Chicago
way' – becomes the mentor and surrogate father to Kevin Costner's Eliot
Ness, the stiff-necked, conventional family man. Connery's charismatic
performance, a complex, volatile mixture of wit, vulnerability, and stubborn, flinty roughness, was completely credible and made Johnson's
death, riddled with bullets, a moment of great pathos. The film was
extremely successful and Connery, gaining his only Oscar, now had a
popularity 'unmatched since the Bondian heydays of the 1960s'.[25]

This was enhanced by his role in *The Last Crusade*, the third part of the
Lucas/Spielberg Indiana Jones trilogy. This exuberant pastiche, hurtling
along the well-worn paths of 'Boys' Own' adventure, was executed suit-
ably tongue-in-cheek for contemporary audiences. Part of its joky allu-
siveness was to have the old Bond, Connery's Dr Henry Jones, play the
father of the new, Harrison Ford's bull-whipping, sardonic Indiana. Connery's performance beneath the battered deerstalker is keyed to the style
of the film without straining for profundity, but with a pawky humour
that has a distinct edge to it.

Connery's Henry Jones contrasted with his handsome and dignified
Captain Ramius in *The Hunt for Red October*, based on Tom Clancy's best-
selling novel. Ramius, an incipient nonconformist from a marginalised,
unorthodox background (son of a Lithuanian fisherman), is another man
of integrity, who has the courage to disown his own country when he discovers that his nuclear submarine was built for only one purpose: to get
in the first, decisive strike. His adversary turned surrogate son Dr Ryan
(Alec Baldwin), is another family man who recognises in Ramius an

idealised father, wise, austere, loving, incorruptible. Their mythical relationship, which bonds East and West in a shared humanity beyond political machinations, was, to judge from the scale of the film's popularity, a highly acceptable message to cinemagoers at the beginning of the 1990s.

For all their differences of style and mode, these films offered a coherent persona for audiences: the tribal elder, a man of exceptional wisdom and integrity, reflective, philosophical, pondering the fruits and the lessons of his own experiences which he imparts to the younger man. It has affinities to Robert Bly's influential philosophy popularised in *Iron John* (1990) where the mentor instructs the neophyte in how to recover the 'inner warrior'.[26] The archetype was King Arthur, the role Connery played in *First Knight* (Zucker, 1995). Connery's performances were highly accomplished: the wry humour, the patience and stillness which command a scene more than histrionics; the careful timing of the apparently long pondered remark so that even the baldest platitude carries weight and authority; the moments of tenderness and vulnerability contrasted with the irascible anger which prevent his character becoming pious or inert. They are roles which allow Connery to blossom with age, rather more successfully than Clint Eastwood, his exact contemporary. But despite his age, the famous *People* survey revealed that Connery was, at 60, 'The Sexiest Man Alive'. He had the artistic dexterity to play either widowers or even a bachelor lover as in *The Russia House* (United Artists, 1990) with equal assurance.[27]

This persona, which gains cumulative force from each new embodiment, has often dignified otherwise rather undistinguished films, providing moments of repose in often frenetic thrillers. In *The Presidio* (Hyams, 1988) Connery was an honourable Scottish-American soldier, still nursing the belief in freedom that had welled up inside him at his first glimpse of the Statue of Liberty and mourning those who fought in Vietnam, heroes of the 'war that nobody liked'. In *Medicine Man* (McTiernan, 1992), he played an eco-warrior, a maverick Scottish-American biochemist who has discovered a cure for cancer amongst an unspoilt tribe of the Amazon rainforest, but cannot reproduce it. In *Rising Sun* (Kaufman, 1993) he was a special investigator whose unrivalled knowledge of Japanese culture, precisely the understanding that the young policeman (Wesley Snipes) lacks, prevents catastrophe. He played an incorruptible Scottish doctor in *A Good Man in Africa* (Beresford, 1994) and a Harvard Professor of Criminology from a deprived Scottish upbringing, in *Just Cause* (Glincher, 1995), where he proves to be the only man capable of defending justice, even if he has to grow in understanding himself. Connery's latest film at time of writing, *Finding Forrester*

(Van Sant, 2000), is also his most palpable embodiment of this figure, as a misanthropic author who recovers his belief in humanity through developing the writing of a black Bronx teenager Jamal (Rob Brown). Having secured Jamal's social and cultural aspirations, Forrester disappears to die in his Scottish homeland.

His most successful recent film, *The Rock* (Bay, 1996), the last in the line of ultra-'high concept' thrillers produced by Don Simpson and Jerry Bruckheimer, was also the most ingenious celebration of the tribal elder. Connery plays Glaswegian John Mason, ex-SAS operative, incarcerated for thirty years as a 'non-person' after being caught with FBI tapes which expose the truth about political cover-ups. The highly educated Mason places himself in a line of celebrated dissidents whose voice went unheeded: Nelson Mandela, Alexander Solzhenitsyn, Sir Walter Raleigh and Archimedes. He is an exacting mentor to the young biochemist Dr Goodspeed (Nicholas Cage), whom he cajoles, bullies and instructs in order to release that 'inner warrior', forestall the threat of the Vietnam veterans and collect the tapes that Mason secreted. As in *Never Say Never Again*, Connery employed Clement and La Frenais to supply the witty dialogue that helps gives substance to his role and stop the film being sucked into an all-action vortex.[28] And, although his primary relationship is with a younger man, the masculine self-assurance of the tribal elder is shown to be incomplete without a sense of female companionship and love, in this case the brief reunion with his estranged daughter.

In his recent films, Connery has acted as executive producer, operating through his company Fountainbridge Films, so the heavy underscoring of his characters' flinty Scottish independence is surely deliberate. In *A Good Man in Africa*, his phlegmatic doctor turns on the 'old enemy', bellowing at the venal First Secretary Morgan Leafy (Colin Friels): 'Never talk to me like that you little English shit or I'll rip your fucking tongue out.' Such moments of rage are exciting because they are fissures through which the old persona can be glimpsed and Connery's menacing physicality reasserted. But they can be successfully accommodated into his new persona as the righteous anger of the tribal elder who has become a disowned man, neglected by his country, exiled or marginalised, but who seeks justice rather than revenge. As such, the tribal elder and the dissident are one and the same, offering an untainted integrity in a deracinated modern world in danger of losing its way and abandoning democratic values. His characters are always men of talent, embodying the values of individualistic self-help which unite them with Bond and with the widely circulated accounts of his own upbringing and his often abrasive independence as an actor, to create a classless hero who can appeal across the age range.[29]

The prewar generation of gifted British male actors, Ronald Colman, Robert Donat, Leslie Howard or David Niven, could sustain an international career playing variations of the debonair English gentleman. Kenneth More preserved that tradition right up to 1960. Connery was poured into that mould as James Bond, but with a muscular physicality that incorporated its apparent opposite, the rugged American tough guy, to produce a new cultural myth, the screen Bond, an image still in circulation. After a middle period in which his attempts to rebel against the Bond image sometimes produced, in the hands of talented directors, a searching exploration of the nature of heroic myths, Connery was gradually able to reinvent himself in the 1980s and 1990s as a new myth figure. His nonconformist tribal elder, at once Celtic and international, gives Connery, now over 70, a very distinctive presence in the roster of modern male stars and maintains his position as the only British star considered a major box-office draw around the world.

Notes

1 Michael Callan, *Sean Connery* (W. H. Allen, London, 1973), p. 90.

2 Patricia Lewis, *News Chronicle* (24 October 1957).

3 For the importance of Baker see my 'The Emergence of the British Tough Guy: Stanley Baker, Masculinity and the Crime Thriller', in Steve Chibnall and Robert Murphy, eds., *British Crime Cinema* (Routledge, London, 1999), pp. 81–93; for Connery's place within postwar British cinema see my *Typical Men: Representations of Masculinity in Popular British Cinema* (I. B. Tauris, London, 2001).

4 Anthony Carthew, *Daily Herald* (9 May 1958).

5 Cubby Broccoli (with Donald Zec), *When the Snow Melts* (Boxtree, London, 1998), pp. 165–6, 171.

6 Felix Barker, *Evening News* (4 October 1962).

7 Michael Freedland, *Sean Connery* (Weidenfeld & Nicolson, London, 1994), pp. 90–2.

8 Space precludes detailed discussion of the Bond films, for which see Tony Bennett and Janet Woollacott, *Bond and Beyond: The Political Career of a Popular Hero* (Macmillan, London, 1987); James Chapman, *Licence to Thrill: A Cultural History of the James Bond Films* (I. B. Tauris, London, 1999).

9 Margaret Hinxman, *Daily Herald* (6 October 1962).

10 Kingsley Amis, *The James Bond Dossier* (Jonathan Cape, London, 1965), pp. 36, 42.

11 Penelope Houston, '007', *Sight and Sound*, 34.1 (Winter 1964–5), 14-16.

12 See, inter alia, John Parker, *Sean Connery* (London, Gollancz, 1993), pp. 171–88.

13 Interview in *Playboy* (November 1965), p. 81. However, Connery made a documentary, *The Bowler and the Bunnet*, in 1967 to help promote the cause of the Clydeside shipworkers, who needed to be allowed to use their skills and energies. See also note 16 below.

14 *Marnie* is a much more intelligent and incisive film than the Relph–Dearden *The Woman of Straw* (United Artists, 1964) where Connery is simply a villainous playboy.

15 See François Truffaut, *Hitchcock*, rev. edn (Grafton Books, London, 1986), p. 469.

16 John Hunter, *Great Scot: The Life of Sean Connery* (Bloomsbury, London, 1993), pp. 118–22. Connery's sense of national identity has always been strong and his support of the Scottish National Party is well known. He is currently part of a group of businessmen planning a film studio in Scotland: *Sunday Times* (1 November 1998), 1–2.

17 Frank R. Cunningham, *Sidney Lumet: Film and Literary Vision* (University Press of Kentucky, Lexington, 1991).

18 Connery, quoted in Lee Pfeiffer and Philip Lisa, *The Films of Sean Connery* (Citadel Press, New York, 1993), p. 81.

19 Space precludes a consideration of John Boorman's *Zardoz* (1974), which explores this theme.

20 Neil Sinyard, *The Films of Richard Lester* (Croom Helm, London, 1985).

21 Ibid., pp. 150–1.

22 See, for example, 'Sean is your premium Bond', a selection of readers' responses, *Daily Express* (8 December 1983), 7.

23 Pfeiffer and Lisa, *The Films of Sean Connery*, p. 208.

24 Ibid., p. 219. Connery received a BAFTA Award as Best Actor for *Baskerville* and a similar accolade in the Federal Republic of Germany.

25 Ibid., p. 220.

26 J. Richards, 'From Christianity to Paganism: The New Middle Ages and the Values of "Medieval" Masculinity', *Cultural Values*, 3.3 (April 1999), 226.

27 In an Ann Summer's recent survey, Connery was Britain's second 'most kissable man', well behind Robbie Williams but above David Beckham: *Daily Mirror*, 5 July 1999, p. 8. *Entrapment* (Amiel, 1999), released in Britain in July 1999, offers him as the sexy master criminal.

28 M. Cousins, 'King of the Hill', *Sight and Sound* (May 1997), 24.

29 For Connery's appeal to 'more mature filmgoers' see *The Times* (4 May 1999), 18.

18

'Bright, particular stars': Kenneth Branagh, Emma Thompson and William Shakespeare

In a fabricated satiric interview which appeared in the *Independent on Sunday* in the late spring of 1999, a literary editor condenses Kenneth Branagh and Emma Thompson's six-year marriage into three short sentences punctuated by a wistful sigh: '[Ken] and Em just seemed so perfect for a while. It was nice. But then it faded away.'[1] As the couple themselves had announced four years earlier – not personally, of course, but in a written statement circulated to the international media – they merely 'drifted apart'.[2] In the only too telling words of the *Independent on Sunday*'s fictional editor, the story of Branagh and Thompson is not of epic proportions but of far more modest scale: something fit 'for a sad, comic script by Miss Emma Thompson'.[3]

The scripted version of their story would indeed be sadly comic. Some would say deservedly pathetic. The best that we can say of this couple is that they were comfortably pleasant, but never grandly passionate. Thompson likened Branagh to a 'plumber' while labelling herself a 'bluestocking'.[4] No volcanic temperaments here. No colossal egos. No Shakespeare, one might say. Despite the frantic pace of their earlier careers, Branagh and Thompson were never able – as a couple – to electrify the filmgoing public. But they did succeed in annoying a considerable segment of the public. The worst we might say of this couple is that they were *faux* stars, an obvious and pretentious degradation of legendary screen couples of the past: Olivier and Leigh, Hepburn and Tracy, Taylor and Burton. Indeed, their very existence repudiated the authenticity of glamorous stardom personified above all by Laurence Olivier and Vivien Leigh. Yet repudiation alone hardly constitutes an identity. And it bears remembering that Branagh and Thompson strove mightily to project the 'newness' of their star status: he was almost robotically professional, refusing to discuss in interviews anything that might suggest he had a personality, let alone a personal life. 'The more personal the enquiry,' *The Times* noted in an interview with Branagh, the 'more general his

response.'⁵ Thompson was predictably unpredictable. Naturally she kept
her Best Actress Oscar in the loo; naturally she defended Hugh Grant's
liaison with a Hollywood hooker. She was, moreover, calculatedly spontaneous: 'less real', as Ian Parker shrewdly observed, 'for her efforts to be
more real'.⁶

Certainly there was something outright irritating – even nauseating –
about this couple's facile iconoclasm. Yet after Branagh and Thompson
scorned the old gods of stardom, did they set up new idols of which they
themselves were the incarnation? What, in the end, was their bequest?
The answer must be, to quote the Constable of France in *Henry V*
(Branagh, 1989), 'a very little little'.⁷ One indication of the relative languor
surrounding them was the surprising absence of really juicy gossip. Even
in the weeks immediately before and after their 1995 separation, the
tabloids carried little salacious material. Their marriage was more stag-
nant than stormy. Here was a couple whose offscreen lives contained
nothing more scandalous than that most predictable of film star infideli-
ties, the affair with a co-star: Branagh with Helena Bonham Carter (*Mary
Shelley's 'Frankenstein'*, Branagh, 1989) and Thompson with Greg Wise
(*Sense and Sensibility*, Ang Lee, 1995). Nor was this a couple who together
accomplished wonders. Thompson's two Oscars – Best Actress for
Howards End (Ivory, 1992) and Best Screenplay for *Sense and Sensibility*
confirm that her best work has been on her own. Conversely, one cannot
imagine that Branagh's *Hamlet* (1997) could have successfully accommodated Thompson, for she would have been too old for Ophelia and too
young for Gertrude. Indeed, when Thompson did appear in Branagh's
films, critics frequently complained that hers was the weakest performance and that she had been cast only because she was married to the
director. While almost all reviews of *Henry V* (1989) lauded the 'best of
British' ensemble cast of Judi Dench, Ian Holm, Derek Jacobi, Geraldine
McEwan, Paul Scofield and Robert Stephens, they also singled out
Thompson as the only clunker in the cast. '[T]he new Mrs Branagh, a
stilted, ill-at-ease Emma Thompson,' *Today* baldly asserted, was the film's
only piece of 'distinctly ropey casting.'⁸

For the filmgoing public it has been difficult to care about these film
stars, at least in the way we care about more 'traditional' stars such as
Brad Pitt and Julia Roberts. In late 1992 *The Times* complained that the
couple had become 'tedious'.⁹ The actor, in a rare moment of self-revela-
tion, confessed that his wife called him a 'walnut because that's how
unemotional [he] could be'. Only too true. Branagh gave nothing of himself emotionally, in print or on film, except the impression that he had
nothing to give. Yet perhaps the lack of interest surrounding Branagh and
Thompson, perhaps the painfully contrived nature of their ordinariness

(plumbers do not act with the Royal Shakespeare Company; bluestockings do not pose nude for *Vanity Fair*) is precisely the point. We do not care about them because there is nothing to care about. And yet they behaved as if we cared; as if they were indeed Olivier and Leigh: they produced, directed, wrote, and played leading roles in their own films; they courted the attention of the international media; they received and accepted awards; they presented themselves to the world as a celebrity couple. If Branagh and Thompson were together not quite hypocritical stars, they were certainly self-avowedly 'ironic' stars. By this I mean neither petulance nor reclusiveness, for such attributes are merely classic stardom in its most acute state. Johnny Depp is a star because he destroys hotel suites; Greta Garbo was a megastar in her splendid isolation. Rather, I mean that ironic stars repudiate star 'quality' – a sensational singularity – while none the less fulfilling the public duties of a star. Yet just what does the ironic star give to the public? Neither sincerity nor *gravitas* (though these are clearly what Thompson and Branagh imagined their gifts to be) but only the vulgar degradation of glamour itself: Emma Thompson publicly announcing a moment of impending flatulence.

In a Cambridge Footlights sketch, Thompson once played an actress who began an awards acceptance speech by saying, 'I'd like to thank my husband, the director.' Over the intervening years, the words have acquired a richly ironic resonance. The Footlights alumna did indeed make her name as a film star through being cast by her director-husband (although her two Academy Awards were for films on which her husband was not involved). Within ten years after leaving Cambridge, Thompson found herself in precisely the situation she had earlier lampooned. As the actress herself noted after receiving a 1993 Evening Standard Film Award – for which she duly thanked her husband, the director – 'It's awful to discover you've become the subject of your own early satire.'[10] What, then, is a star to do, having become what she once mockingly beheld? The only possible response was irony. The game was up, Thompson quickly surmised, just as soon as it began.

A central feature of the couple's ironised stardom was always the repudiation of glamour. The media's impulse to glamorise Branagh and Thompson (how bizarre it now seems in retrospect) never went away, however, despite the stars' belaboured efforts to assert their own ordinariness. It bears recalling, as a testament to their distinct lack of allure, that Branagh and Thompson were never linked to Britain's ultimate icon of glamour – Diana, Princess of Wales. Indeed, it was Prince Charles, through his patronage of the Renaissance Theatre Company, who was the couple's royal connection. At a time when Diana was the world's most photographed woman, Branagh and Thompson could invoke only the tiresome mannerisms of in-bred English luvvies. The couple was far too 'knowing' about their own celebrity ever to acquire Diana's phenomenal mass appeal. Of course the screen couple's attempts to revise the norms of stardom seemed gauche in comparison not just to Diana but also in a comparison to the standard set for an earlier generation by Laurence Olivier and Vivien Leigh. They were dubbed the 'new Oliviers' in the late 1980s, a pedigree which seemed only too well deserved when their own marriage later failed. The *Daily Mail*, true to its hyperbolic form, declared in a headline that 'They were the Oliviers, and just like the Oliviers, their love was doomed'.[11] Surely that is overstating the case. The actors themselves knew that such comparisons were far-fetched, as they never tired of reminding star-struck journalists. In fact, Branagh and Thompson spent a good deal of time distancing themselves from unwanted (because unflattering, if we stopped for a second to think about it) comparisons to their predecessors. Yet the comparisons were as inevitable as they were misguided.

While Branagh first encouraged predictable comparisons with Olivier by filming *Henry V* (1989), such comparisons were more about the young actor's claim to an actorial legacy than about an offscreen celebrity status. Thompson in particular rebuffed every attempt to recast the couple as 'the greatest double act since Olivier and Leigh'.[12] Such comparisons were not odious but 'excruciating', Thompson explained to the critic Mark Sanderson: 'Olivier was a matinée idol and Leigh was an exquisite creature. Ken is a plumber figure. My godfather said that when you meet him you think he'd come to do the pipes and I'm a sort of blue-stocking.'[13] A year earlier Thompson had flatly declared to the *Daily Telegraph* that she and Vivien Leigh 'haven't got that much in common'. Leigh 'was a porcelain beauty,' the actress continued, 'and I am a great hulking ex-Footlights turn'.[14] Self-derogatory comments were not, however, uttered in isolation. Unlike the inveterate star-gazers at such tabloids as the *Daily Mail*, other journalists found themselves agreeing with Thompson's distinctly pedestrian self-image. 'I am sure [Thompson] will be the first to admit she will never be voted Sexiest Woman in the World', Anne Billson candidly noted in the *Sunday Times*.[15] Branagh, for his part, was simply too odd-looking, too short, too thin-lipped to be a leading man. Adam Mars-Jones wrote that Branagh's 'charm always had an edge of smugness'.[16] Indeed, one has only to compare Branagh with the other actors in *Much Ado About Nothing* (1993) to realise that he is simply overpowered by such prettier, sexier and butcher actors as Robert Sean Leonard, Keanu Reeves, and Denzel Washington. Branagh seemed always to be suffering from sexual anemia, a condition laughingly alluded to by Thompson herself when she dismissed questions about why they had not started a family with the quip that 'Ken's sperm are on crutches'.[17]

What seems beyond dispute is that, whatever Branagh and Thompson were, they were *not* latter-day versions of Olivier and Leigh. Nor were they even a canny, postmodern repackaging of film stardom itself. I would argue that the deepest irony about Branagh and Thompson is not that they failed to attain the super-sized stature of Hollywood stars but rather that in rejecting this classic model of stardom they failed to become a new kind of film star. To misquote Matthew Arnold, they were caught helplessly between two archetypes of stardom, 'one dead / The other powerless to be born'.[18] As I hope to detail in the remainder of this chapter, the couple themselves were unable either to reject fully their traditional celebrity status or to construct for themselves a new ironic, postmodern identity. In disclosing the couple's ultimate inability to appropriate the norms and conventions of stardom, we might profitably begin by looking at the kinds of roles they played on the screen. Not that I believe their film roles are grounded in any sort of biographical reality; but rather that such roles can be interpreted as vehicles for the public articulation of what ironic stardom may yet become. Precisely because the couples they played in *Henry V* (1989) and *Much Ado About Nothing* (1993) do not conform to romantic norms, these films present themselves as meditations upon the cultural phenomenon of stardom itself. That is, the roles which Branagh and Thompson played in these films offer the possibility of exploiting not romance but satire. In a 1992 interview with *OK* magazine, Thompson acknowledged that 'the couples we've played have, generally speaking, had fairly disastrous relationships ... Let's just say that in professional terms, Romeo and Juliet we ain't.'[19] The witticism is more suggestive than the actress herself might have realised since the couple both did and did not play 'Romeo and Juliet' in their screen versions of Shakespeare. To put the matter another way, the films *Henry V* and *Much Ado About Nothing* both wish to become *Romeo and Juliet* even as they seemingly repudiate traditional narratives of romance, courtship and marriage. The repudiation is ultimately overthrown in each instance by a final return to romanticised plot, theme and character.

Henry V, for example, ends not with the rapture of forbidden passion but with a politically arranged marriage masquerading as a comically inept profession of love. Emma Thompson's Katherine knows only too well that she is indeed the bartered bride, a commodity to be exchanged in the realm of international politics. And the exchange comes with Henry's awkward pretence of amorous devotion. He speaks to Princess Katherine as a 'plain soldier' and seeks to close the matrimonial deal quickly: 'so clap hands, and a bargain'[20] he urges his hesitant would-be betrothed. The actors themselves seemed to recognise the underlying cynicism of the wooing scene, and what the *Daily Telegraph* dismissed as Thompson's 'self-indulgence'[21] could be more insightfully read as the actress's own ironic commentary on the chauvinistic imperialism of Henry's geo-political romance. And yet somehow this recognition, achieved through satire, that Henry and Katherine are not ideally matched is quickly lost as the entrance of the French and English courts – 'Here comes your father' – interrupts the scene. In Branagh's adaptation, Isabel, Queen of France, has been written out of the scene and her lines given over to her husband, Charles VI.

It is precisely the absence of the Queen, I suggest, which allows us to accept so easily the blessed union of France and England in the persons of Katherine and Henry. For Isabel's presence in the scene would have reminded us of the strategic – and purely strategic – function of royal women: to ensure the protection of property and the purity of the sovereign's lineage. The absent Isabel symbolises the depressing future which awaits Katherine, the future which the film will not allow itself to acknowledge precisely because it dashes all our hopes for the happiness of the young royal couple. The audience has seen Katherine in only one other scene, the richly comic lesson in English with her lady-in-waiting. Branagh stages the scene humorously, but also romantically: sunlight streaming through the windows, the cooing of doves, and above all a cherished sanctuary from the world of war. After this scene of almost virginal purity, we do not wish to see Katherine become the tool of courtly Machiavels. We want the romance to continue, and Branagh fulfils our desire.

To be sure, the dark political future of the Anglo-French alliance is foreshadowed by Derek Jacobi's Chorus, who reminds us of the wars fought under Henry V (1989) which 'lost France' and made 'England bleed'.[22] But these are problems of statecraft, not of wedlock. Branagh thus attempts to decouple politics and romance in a way that is not true to Shakespeare's history play, but is true to our expectation that heroic princes and fairy-tale princesses (no less than theatrical newlyweds) live happily ever after. And thus the film, in its closing moments, becomes two films: one about a happy couple; the other about a warring nation. This divided consciousness in the film itself, this inability of Branagh and Thompson to sustain their ironised reading of Shakespeare's royal couple, is but another means of acknowledging that the stars themselves are unable either to embrace or to repudiate their own status as film stars. Branagh and Thompson are certainly *not* Henry and Katherine. But the ambivalent way in which the actors characterise this screen couple – an irony which dissolves into romance – testifies to their own bedevilled effort to define themselves as ironic stars who have emancipated themselves from the romance of Olivier and Leigh, from the romance which is the authenticating ground of film stardom.

The tensions between old and new definitions of stardom are even more striking in the couple's portrayal of Benedick and Beatrice in *Much Ado About Nothing*, a film which explicitly enacts the difficulty of finding 'a ground between stardom and the absolute subversion of stardom', as Ian Parker astutely observed after interviewing Emma Thompson.[23] In exploring how this film simultaneously articulates and disavows an ironic identity for screen celebrities, we might begin by acknowledging that Shakespeare's story, even as radically adapted by Branagh, is fundamentally unpleasant. The innocent Hero is publicly called a whore. Don John organises the plot of deception. Beatrice and Benedick, for all their sarcastic banter, are fugitives from their own emotions. Love comes to them, when it finally does, not as joyous release, but as suffering; as a force which confronts them against their will. We should acknowledge, moreover, the long history of stage productions which downplay the public calumny of the innocent Hero and prefer instead to emphasise the wit of Beatrice and Benedick and the courtly spectacle of soldiers, masques and dances.[24] Branagh's film version, though trumpeted by the director himself as a populist alternative to 'some cultural church',[25] none the less shares the seductive pictorial aesthetic which has marked productions of this Shakespearian comedy for over a century. The images which remain with us are not those of surveillance, vilification and the corrupting effect of leisure. Rather, we remember Emma Thompson's bronzed skin, the wide-angle shots of the Tuscan countryside and the splash of fountains on a summer's day. What Bernard Shaw wrote of Herbert Beerbohm Tree's spectacular 1905 production of *Much Ado About Nothing* at His Majesty's Theatre seems equally appropriate when considering Branagh's 1993 film version:

> All the lovely things Shakespeare dispensed with are there in bounteous plenty. Fair ladies, Sicilian seascapes, Italian gardens, summer nights and dawns ... dancing, singing, masquerading, architecture, orchestration culled from Wagner [and] Bizet ... [are] carried out with much innocent enjoyment, which is fairly infectious on the other side of the footlights.[26]

Yet no amount of directorially dictated jollity – what Adam Mars-Jones tartly termed 'shrieks of artificial Renaissance excitement'[27] – can successfully obscure the story's pronounced ambivalence toward love. Nor, moreover, does the 'innocent enjoyment,' to redirect Shaw's description, of the all-singing, all-dancing, all-confetti-throwing ending make us forget the betrayals we have just witnessed. The play, admittedly, has ended with music and dancing since at least the eighteenth century. But for Branagh to have the players (accompanied on the soundtrack by full orchestra and chorus) sing a jubilant rendition of 'Sigh no more, ladies' at a *wedding* seems more inattentive than ironic. Similarly, Branagh opens the film with an insistently pastoral lyricism, an 'idyllic picnic' on a 'grassy knoll'.[28] He does not, however, acknowledge that Thompson's beguiling recitation of 'Sigh no more, ladies' – a song which insists that, since men are 'deceivers ever', women can be 'blithe and bonny' only when they 'let them go'[29] – might function in suggestive counterpoint to the charm of his mise-en-scène. The recitation is staged not as a declaration but as a entertaining *divertissement*. Indeed, the possibility of women's emancipatory action, already diminished by the scene's bucolic tranquillity, utterly disintegrates when Beatrice, Hero, Margaret and even the elderly Ursula succumb to a disturbingly comic sexual frenzy at the imminent arrival of Don Pedro and his leather-clad entourage.

And yet the only too predictable festivity of Branagh's mise-en-scène is really only the blatant sign of his and Thompson's surprisingly romanticised view of the play and, more particularly, their own performances. For many reviewers, the film's charm, if that is the right word, derived principally from Branagh and Thompson themselves. The star couple's presumed offscreen intimacy cast a steady romantic glow over the entire proceedings. For how could a film starring the happily married actors (we insist that marriages always be happy) *not* be about a similarly well-matched couple? Partly owing to its audience's horizon of expectations and partly, as we shall see, to the couple's own equivocal reading of their work together, *Much Ado About Nothing* remains a film complicit with the widespread expectation that glamorous lovers should play glamorous lovers – much as Richard Burton and Elizabeth Taylor playing Antony and Cleopatra was in the natural order of things. Such a conviction echoed in much of the publicity which the film generated. The snappy photo caption 'Ken and Em as Ben and Bea' from Iain Johnstone's review must strike us as an utterly graceless attempt to force the connection between the onscreen and offscreen couples.[30] With Shakespeare's characters reduced to their Anglicised diminutives, one is reminded of Quentin Crisp's dictum that it's cheaper to drag the Joneses down to one's own level than to keep up with them.

Most journalists, gainsaying Crisp's downward directive, strove to raise Branagh and Thompson to the level, however much presumed, of their Shakespearian characters. Indeed, the general critical tendency was to uphold Beatrice and Benedick as idealised incarnations of the romantic perfection which Thompson and Branagh couldn't quite carry off in their own lives. The *Morning Star* praised the 'joyous enthusiasm' of the sparring couple's 'witty badinage'.[31] Even *Time Out* felt obliged to acknowledge the 'very obvious loving relationship' between the director and his leading lady.[32] The *Sunday Times* dubbed the actors the 'Beatrice and Benedick of our time'.[33] The *Mail on Sunday* offers an excruciatingly extended comparison between the screen couple and the Shakespearian couple:

> Love's Labours Won at last for Kenneth Branagh and Emma Thompson. Britain's high-profile luvvies have become a golden box-office double act. Love-struck in poetry and sun-stunned in Tuscany ... Their's is the togetherness which suits the play so wonderfully and our need for romance so splendidly. All the world loves a lover. And the pair, so ardently entwined, should ensure a box-office love affair to last a very long time.[34]

Of course it is painful to read such drivel, and not simply because the romance soon soured. To regret the couple's breakup would be only to reaffirm a naive, indeed selfish insistence that blazing stars never grow cold. Rather, we should actively challenge such a blatantly sentimental reading of Branagh's and Thompson's performances in *Much Ado About Nothing*. That challenge might begin by noting that Branagh and Thompson could not decide just who their characters were. In the Introduction to his screenplay, Branagh acknowledges that Shakespeare's play 'goes much further than the celebration of one gloriously witty couple' and thus declares his desire for the film to offer something more than 'star turns' for him and his wife.[35] Throughout this rambling preface, he touches upon a number of issues central to his directorial vision: international casting, realistic acting and scenic interpolations. Yet he devotes surprisingly little attention (two paragraphs only) to discussion of his and Thompson's characters. He states that Benedick and Beatrice are 'staunchly anti-marriage' because wedlock 'mutes the personalities' of husbands and wives. Yet he almost immediately disavows that view by asserting that the *real* Benedick and Beatrice, beneath their merely superficial wit and irony, are 'romantic, generous, and emotional'.[36]

Thompson, for her part, came to the role of Beatrice with a public record of scepticism towards love and marriage. In 1988, when she was romantically involved with Branagh, she told the *Sunday Express* that she had thus far avoided marrying because 'Lots of people's minds solidify quietly at my age, and younger, when they have children and marriage [sic]'.[37] In 1993, before the release of *Much Ado About Nothing*, the *Daily Mail* printed extracts from her interview with the American magazine *US* in which she declared that 'Marriage is an extremely dangerous step. I mean, how stupid can you get? You put all your eggs in one basket and say you're going to stay with the person for the rest of your life. Talk about taking a risk.'[38] The question thus arises as to exactly why Thompson would want to play Beatrice and, more pointedly, why she would want to play the role opposite her husband. One response, in light of her earlier pronouncements, would be that she was attracted to the cynical view of romance to which *Much Ado About Nothing* subscribes. Yet after the film's release Thompson told the *Guardian Weekend* that Beatrice and Benedick were 'Total equals' and an 'archetypically perfect blueprint for a relationship'.[39] As Thompson speculates, Beatrice is angry because she was never allowed 'to be a boy'. For the actress, then, Beatrice's anger at her own lack of power is precisely the source of her equality with men. Beatrice is a man's equal, at least in spirit, because her anger makes her capable of the heroic action which society prevents her from undertaking in the first place.

This sounds quite promising; and Thompson seems to be on the verge of a shrewd, if somewhat idiosyncratic perspective on the story. Beatrice's anger saves the play from being performed as yet another courtly romance which reinstates patriarchal authority under the guise of 'innocent enjoyment'. Such a view would temper Thompson's romantic scepticism without abandoning her explicitly feminist agenda. That is, the actress can accept the possibility of equality in marriage – something she had earlier doubted – but she can also rail against the social conventions which prevent such equality from ever being achieved. We seem to be witnessing what the *Village Voice* called, less approvingly, the actress's 'self-satisfied deconstruction of her character'.[40] But Thompson suddenly abandons her own evolving position. Having once spoken approvingly of Beatrice's 'fucking' rage, she now reveals that 'in its own sweet way' *Much Ado About Nothing* 'pointed towards true happiness between men and women'.[41] Surely such trite sentimentality must negate her vigorously 'feminist' reading of the relationship between Beatrice and Benedick.[42] Astonishingly, Thompson then takes one further step, confiding that in essence Ken and Em really are Ben and Bea because she and her husband have found for themselves the same 'true happiness' found by their characters. Thompson ultimately suggests, then, that Beatrice and Benedick really are role models for her and her husband: not because the characters are dubious or ironic about marriage (although they are); not because the characters combat gender inequalities (although they do, at least in Thompson's reading of the story); but rather because they have found 'true happiness' in a 'sweet way'.[43]

Branagh and Thompson, with their fundamentally benign readings of Benedick and Beatrice, foreclose the possibility of truly innovative characterisation which then might lead on to a redefinition of stars and stardom. In fact, their insistence on 'true happiness' and romance places their acting – or at the least the rhetoric surrounding their acting – squarely within the Victorian sentimental tradition. Branagh's view that Benedick and Beatrice were once in love, had broken each other's hearts and were now masking their love with caustic behaviour is not so terribly distant from Henry Irving's romanticised belief, a century earlier, that the pair unconsciously loved each other all along. Not all contemporary observers were seduced by the enduring charms of romance, for we can also find less naive, less congratulatory appraisals of the film. Anne Billson noted in the *Sunday Times* the distinct 'lack of crackle' in the 'verbal sparring' between Branagh's Benedick and Thompson's Beatrice. As for 'sexual excitement', Billson observed that the couple 'might well be tucked up in separate beds drinking a cup of cocoa' since they generated all the lust and passion of 'John and Norma Major'.[44] The *New Statesman*, in a more curious notice, praised the couple as the only actors in the film who 'really chime off each other'.[45] There was a convincing dash of 'vitriol' in their 'amorous warring'; but their performances recalled not so much Katherine Hepburn and Spencer Tracy as 'Kenneth Williams and Hattie Jacques in *Carry On Matron*'.

It is deliciously perverse that Branagh and Thompson, when recognised as failing to measure up to Olympian standards of film stardom, should be likened both to John and Norma Major for their lack of eroticism *and* to Kenneth Williams and Hattie Jacques for their high camp. These touchstones are not quite fallen stars, but rather dimmed or twinkling stars. And this, in the end, seems to be the depleted legacy of Kenneth Branagh and Emma Thompson. The irony they so desperately acted out was ultimately an empty irony, for they could not cast themselves successfully as the peers of Laurence Olivier and Vivien Leigh, Elizabeth Taylor and Richard Burton or even Hepburn and Tracy. Every word that issued from their mouths strikes us as disingenuously premeditated to display a lack of premeditation. Every disarming and self-derogatory statement – Thompson's absurd declaration 'Oh crumbs! We are not used to this sort of thing in England'[46] upon receiving a Golden Globe Award – only reveals the sanctimony behind their public personae.[47] Branagh and Thompson, for all their – and our – efforts, were never satisfying as stars. Neither glamorous nor ironic, neither iconic nor iconoclastic, they could finally offer us nothing more than boredom or camp. As *The Times* asserted as early as 1992, 'the Ken and Em show' had become a tiresome 'one-note samba'.[48] For the sake of film audiences, let us choose the more appealing alternative and imagine how successful the couple would have been had they filmed *Carry On, Much Ado*.

Notes

1 *Independent on Sunday* (9 May 1999).
2 *Sunday Times* (1 October 1995).
3 *Independent on Sunday* (9 May 1999).
4 *Time Out* (9 April 1992).
5 *The Times* (21 November 1992).
6 Ian Parker, *Independent* (3 September 1995).
7 *Henry V*, 4.2.33.
8 *Today* (6 October 1989).
9 *The Times* (21 November 1992).
10 *New York Times* (4 April 1993).
11 *Daily Mail* (2 October 1995).
12 *Time Out* (29 April 1992).
13 Ibid.
14 *Daily Telegraph* (24 September 1991).
15 *Sunday Times* (29 August 1993).
16 Anne Billson, *Sunday Times* (29 August 1993).
17 *Sunday Times* (12 November 1995).
18 'Stanzas from the Grande Chartreuse', C. B. Tinker and H. F. Lowry, ed., *The Poetical Works of Matthew Arnold* (Oxford University Press, London, 1950), p. 299.
19 Taken from, *Guardian* (9 January 1996).
20 *Henry V*, 5.2.153, 5.2.132.
21 *Daily Telegraph* (5 October 1989).
22 *Henry V*, 5.2.12.
23 Ian Parker, *Independent on Sunday* (3 September 1995).
24 See John F. Cox, ed., *Much Ado About Nothing* (Cambridge University Press, Cambridge, 1997), pp. 18–57.
25 Kenneth Branagh, Introduction, *Much Ado About Nothing* (W. W. Norton & Co., New York and London, 1993), p. ix.
26 Bernard Shaw, 'The Dying Tongue of Great Elizabeth', *Saturday Review* (11 February 1905).
27 Adam Mars-Jones, *Independent* (27 August 1993).
28 Branagh, *Much Ado About Nothing*, pp. 5–6.
29 *Much Ado About Nothing*, 2.3.58–72.
30 Iain Johnstone, *Sunday Times* (29 August 1993).
31 *Morning Star* (28 August 1993).
32 *Time Out* (18–25 August 1993).
33 *Sunday Times* (15 May 1994).
34 *Mail on Sunday* (29 August 1993).
35 Branagh, *Much Ado*, p. vii.
36 Ibid., p. xi.
37 *Sunday Express* (30 October 1988).
38 *Daily Mail* (16 February 1993).
39 *Guardian Weekend* (7 August 1993). The play, of course, does not unequivocally sustain this reading. After all, Beatrice twice laments 'O that I were a man!' as she must rely on Benedick to salvage publicly the reputation of her wrongly slandered cousin (4.1.299, 302).
40 *Village Voice* (11 May 1993).
41 *Daily Mail* (13 August 1993).
42 *Guardian Weekend* (7 August 1993).
43 As Branagh similarly told the *Mail on Sunday*, 'Emma and I were not a thousand miles away from the characters of Beatrice and Benedick' (15 August 1993).

44 *Sunday Times* (29 August 1993).
45 *New Statesman* (27 August 1993).
46 *Independent* (23 February 1996).
47 On a similar occasion, Helen Mirren told an American audience that she was 'dead chuffed', the sort of bluff, straightforward, even common remark that Thompson and Branagh could never pull off.
48 *The Times* (21 November 1992).

Select bibliography

Works on British cinema

Adair, Gilbert, and Roddick, Nick, *A Night at the Pictures* (Columbus Books, Bromley, 1985).

Aldgate, Anthony, and Richards, Jeffrey, *Best of British: Cinema and Society 1930–1970* (Basil Blackwell, Oxford, 1983).

Aldgate, Anthony, and Richards, Jeffrey, *Britain Can Take It: The British Cinema in the Second World War* (Blackwell, Oxford, 1986).

Armes, Roy, *A Critical History of the British Cinema* (Secker & Warburg, London, 1978).

Aspinall, Sue, and Murphy, Robert, eds, *BFI Dossier No. 16: Gainsborough Melodrama* (BFI, London, 1983).

Balcon, Michael, *Michael Balcon Presents ... A Lifetime in British Films* (Hutchinson, London, 1969).

Barr, Charles, ed., *All Our Yesterdays: 90 Years of British Cinema* (BFI, London, 1986).

Barr, Charles, *Ealing Studios* (Cameron & Tayleur, David & Charles, London, 1977).

Barr, Charles, *English Hitchcock* (Cameron & Hollis, Moffat, 1999).

Berry, David, *Wales and Cinema: The First Hundred Years* (University of Wales Press, Cardiff, 1994).

Betts, Ernest, *The Film Business: A History of British Cinema, 1896–1972* (Allen & Unwin, London, 1973).

Brown, Geoff, *Launder and Gilliat* (BFI, London, 1977).

Brownlow, Kevin, *David Lean* (Richard Cohen Books, London, 1996).

Caughie, John, and Rockett, Kevin, *The Companion to British and Irish Cinema* (BFI, London, 1996).

Cook, Pam, *Fashioning the Nation: Costume and Identity in the British Cinema* (BFI, 1996).

Cook, Pam, ed., *Gainsborough Pictures* (Cassell, London, 1997).

Curran, J. and Porter, V., eds, *British Cinema History* (Weidenfeld & Nicolson, London, 1983).

Dixon, Wheeler Winston, ed., *Re-viewing British Cinema, 1900–1992: Essays and Interviews* (State University of Albany Press, Albany, New York, 1994).

Durgnat, Raymond, *A Mirror for England: British Movies from Austerity to Affluence* (Faber & Faber, London, 1970).

Elsaesser, Thomas, 'Images for England (and Scotland, Ireland, Wales ...)', *Monthly Film Bulletin*, September 1984, 267–8.

Geraghty, Christine, 'Post-war Choices and Feminine Possibilities', in Ulrike Sieglohr, ed., *Heroines Without Heroes: Reconstructing Female and National Identities in European Cinema, 1945–51* (Cassell, London, 2000), pp. 15–31.

Gledhill, Christine, and Swanson, Gillian, 'Gender and Sexuality in Second World War Films: A Feminist Aproach', in Hurd (1984), pp. 52–62.

Harper, Sue, *Picturing the Past: The Rise and Fall of the British Costume Film* (BFI, London, 1994).

Harper, Sue, 'The Representation of Women in British Feature Films, 1939–1945', in Taylor (1988).

Harper, Sue, and Porter, Vincent, 'Cinema Audience Tastes in 1950s Britain', *Journal of Popular British Cinema*, 2 (1999), 66–82.

Higson, Andrew, *Waving the Flag: Constructing a National Cinema in Britain* (Clarendon Press, Oxford, 1995).

Hill, John, *British Cinema in the 1980s: Issues and Themes* (Clarendon Press, Oxford, 1999).

Hill, John, 'British Cinema as National Cinema: Production, Audience and Representation', in Murphy (1997), pp. 244–54.

Hurd, Geoff, ed., *National Fictions: World War Two in British Film and Television* (BFI, London, 1984).

Korda, Michael, *Charmed Lives* (Allen Lane, London, 1980).

Low, Rachael, and Manvell, Roger, *The History of the British Film, 1896–1906*, vol. I (Routledge, London, 1997; reprint of Allen & Unwin edition, 1948).

Low, Rachael, *The History of the British Film 1906–14*, vol. II (Allen and Unwin, London, 1950).

Low, Rachael, *The History of the British Film 1914–18*, vol. III (Allen and Unwin, London, 1950).

Low, Rachael, *The History of the British Film 1918–29*, vol. IV (Allen and Unwin, London, 1971).

Low, Rachael, *The History of the British Film 1929–39*, vol. VII (Allen and Unwin, London, 1985).

McArthur, Colin, *Scotch Reels: Scotland in Cinema and Television* (BFI, London, 1982).

McFarlane, Brian, *An Autobiography of British Cinema* (Methuen, London, 1997).

McFarlane, Brian, *60 Voices: Celebrities Recall the Golden Age of British Cinema* (BFI, London, 1992).

Macnab, Geoffrey, *J. Arthur Rank and the British Film Industry* (Routledge, London, 1994).

Mayer, J. P., *British Cinemas and their Audiences: Sociological Studies* (Dobson, London, 1948).

Mayer, J. P., *Sociology of Film* (Faber & Faber, London, 1946).

Murphy, R., ed., *The British Cinema Book* (BFI, London, 1997).

Murphy Robert, *Realism and Tinsel: Cinema and Society in Britain 1934–49* (Routledge, London, 1989).

Murphy, Robert, *Sixties British Cinema* (BFI, London, 1992).

Noble, Peter, ed., *The British Film Yearbook 1949–50* (Skelton Robinson, London, 1949).

Oakley, Charles, *Where We Came In: Seventy Years of the British Film Industry* (Allen & Unwin, London, 1964).

Perry, George, *The Great British Picture Show: From the Nineties to the Seventies* (Hart-Davis MacGibbon, London, 1974).

Powell, Michael, *A Life in Movies* (Methuen, London, 1987).

Powell, Michael, *Million-Dollar Movie* (Heinemann, London, 1992).

Richards, Jeffrey, *The Age of the Dream Palace: Cinema and Society in Britain 1930–1939* (Routledge and Kegan Paul, London, 1984).

Richards, Jeffrey, *Films and British National Identity: From Dickens to Dad's Army* (Manchester University Press, Manchester, 1997).

Richards, Jeffrey, ed., *The Unknown Thirties: An Alternative History of the British Cinema 1929–1939* (I. B. Tauris, London, 1998).

Richards, Jeffrey, and Sheridan, Dorothy, eds, *Mass Observation at the Movies* (Routledge and Kegan Paul, London, 1987).

Sedgwick, John, 'Cinema-going Preferences in Britain in the 1930s', in Richards (1998), pp. 1–35.

Street, Sarah, *British National Cinema* (Routledge, London, 1997).

Swann, Paul, *The Hollywood Feature Film in Post War Britain* (Croom Helm, London, 1982).

Taylor, Philip, ed., *Britain and the Cinema in the Second World War* (Macmillan, Basingstoke and London,1988).

Trilby, Jeffrey, ed., *British Film Annual 1949* (Winchester Publications, London, 1949).

Trilby, Jeffrey, ed., *British Films of 1947* (Winchester Publications, London, 1948).

Trilby, Jeffrey, ed., *Daily Mail Film Award Album 1948* (Winchester Publications, London, 1948).

Vargas, A. L., 'British Films and their Audiences', in *Penguin Film Review* (Penguin, Harmondsworth, January 1949), pp. 71–6.

Walker, Alexander, *Hollywood England: The British Film Industry in the Sixties* (Michael Joseph, London, 1974).

Walker, Alexander, *National Heroes: British Cinema in the Seventies and Eighties* (Harrap, London, 1985).

Wilcox, Herbert, *Twenty Five Thousand Sunsets* (Bodley Head, London, 1967).

Wood, Alan, *Mr Rank* (Hodder & Stoughton, London, 1952).

General and theoretical works on stars or bearing on stars

Affron, Charles, *Star Acting: Gish, Garbo, Davis* (Dutton, New York, 1977).

Birdwhistle, Ray L., *Kinesics and Context* (Allen Lane, London, 1971).

Bowser, Eileen, *The Transformation of Cinema 1907–15* (University of California Press, Berkeley, 1990).

Burrows, Jon, *The Whole English Stage to Be Seen for Sixpence: Theatrical Actors and Acting Styles in British Cinema, 1908–18* (PhD thesis, University of East Anglia, 2000).

Cook, Pam, 'Star Signs', *Screen*, 20.3/4, Winter 1979–80.

deCordova, Richard, *Picture Personalities: The Emergence of the Star System in America* (University of Illinois Press, Urbana and Chicago, 1990).

Donald, James, 'Stars', in Cook, Pam, ed., *The Cinema Book* (BFI, London, 1985), pp. 50–6.

Dyer, Richard, *Heavenly Bodies: Film Stars and Society* (BFI and Macmillan, London, 1986).

Dyer, Richard, *Stars* (BFI, London, 1979).

Eckert, Charles, 'The Carole Lombard in Macey's Window', in Gledhill (1991), pp. 30–9.

Eckert, Charles, 'Shirley Temple and the House of Rockefeller', in Gledhill (1991), pp. 60–73.

Ellis, John, *Visible Fictions* (Routledge, London, 1991).

Findler, Joel W., *The Hollywood Story* (Octopus, London, 1988).

Gandhy, Behrose, and Thomas, Rosie, 'Three Indian Film Stars', in Gledhill (1991), pp. 107–31.

Gledhill, Christine, 'Re examining Stardom: Questions of Texts, Bodies and Performance', in Christine Gledhill and Linda Williams, eds, *Reinventing Film Studies* (Arnold, London, 2000).

Gledhill, Christine, ed., *Stardom: Industry of Desire* (Routledge, London, 1991).

Hansen, Miriam, 'Pleasure, Ambivalence, Identification: Valentino and Female Spectatorship', in Gledhill (1991), pp. 259–82.

Harris, Thomas, 'The Building of Popular Images', in Gledhill (1991), pp. 40–4.

Herzog, Charlotte Cornelia, and Gaines, Jane Marie, 'Puffed Sleeves before Teatime: Joan Crawford, Adrian and Women Audiences', in Gledhill (1991), pp. 74–91.

King, Barry, 'Articulating Stardom', in Gledhill (1991), pp. 167–82.

King, Barry, 'The Star and the Commodity: Towards a Performance Theory of Stardom', *Cultural Studies*, 1, 2 (1987), 145–61.

King, Barry, 'Stardom as an Occupation', in Paul Kerr, ed., *The Hollywood Film Industry* (Routledge & Kegan Paul, London, 1986), pp. 154–84.

Koszarski, Richard, *An Evening's Entertainment: The Age of the Silent Feature Picture, 1915–1928* (UCLA Press, Berkeley, 1994).

Lusted, David, 'The Glut of the Personality', in Gledhill (1991), pp. 251–6.

MacDonald, Paul, supplementary chapter and bibliography to new edition of Richard Dyer, *Stars* (BFI, London, 1998).

MacDonald, Paul, 'Star Studies', in J. Hollows and M. Jancovich, eds, *Approaches to Popular Film* (Manchester University Press, Manchester, 1995).

May, Larry L., *Screening Out the Past: The Birth of Mass Culture and the Motion Picture Industry* (University of Chicago Press, Chicago, 1980).

Morin, Edgar, *The Stars* (Grove Press, New York, 1960) (first published in French 1957).

Naremore, James, *Acting in the Cinema* (University of California Press, Berkeley and Los Angeles, 1988).

Pirie, David, *Anatomy of the Movies* (WHS Distributors, London, 1981).

Shaffer, Lawrence, 'Reflections on the Face in Film', *Film Quarterly*, 31.2, Winter, 1977–8.

Shaffer, Lawrence, 'Some Notes on Film Acting', *Sight and Sound*, 42.2, Spring, 1973.

Shipman, David, *The Great Movie Stars: The Golden Years* (2nd ed., MacDonald, London, 1989).

Shipman, David, *The Great Movie Stars: The Independent Years* (MacDonald, London, 1992).

Shipman, David, *The Great Movie Stars: The International Years* (Angus & Robertson, London, 1972).

Stacey, J., *Star Gazing: Hollywood Cinema and Female Spectatorship* (Routledge, London, 1994).

Stallings, Penny, with Mandelbaum, Howard, *Flesh and Fantasy* (MacDonald and Jane's, London, 1978).

Taylor, Helen, *Scarlett's Women: Gone with the Wind and its Female Fans* (Rutgers University Press, New Brunswick, New Jersey, 1989).

Thompson, John O., 'Screen Acting and the Commutation Test', in Gledhill (1991), pp. 183–206.

Thompson, Kristin, *Exporting Entertainment: America in the World Film Market 1907–34* (British Film Institute, London, 1985).

Thumim, Janet, *Celluloid Sisters: Women and Popular Culture* (Macmillan, Basingstoke and London, 1992).

Tudor, Andrew, *Image and Influence: Studies in the Sociology of Film* (George Allen & Unwin, London, 1974).

Wolfe, Charles, 'The Return of Jimmy Stewart', in Gledhill (1991), pp. 92–106.

Wolfenstein, Martha, and Leites, Nathan, *Movies: A Psychological Study* (Free Press of Glencoe, Glencoe, 1950).

British stars: biographies, autobiographies, analytical studies

Alexander, Norah, 'Frustrated, Lonely and Peculiar', in John Sutro, ed., *Diversion: 22 Authors on the Popular Arts* (Max Parrish, London, 1950). [on Richard Attenborough's fan club]

Allen, David Rayvern, *Sir Aubrey: A Biography of C. Aubrey Smith, England Cricketer, West End Actor, Hollywood Film Star* (Elm Tree, London, 1982).

Andrews, Emma, *The Films of Michael Caine* (BCW Publishing, Bembridge, Isle of White, 1977).

Baker, B., 'Picturegoer', *Sight and Sound*, 53.3, 1985, 206–11.

Barker, Felix, *The Oliviers: A Biography* (Hamilton, London, 1953).

Barrow, Kenneth, *Mr Chips: The Life of Robert Donat* (Methuen, London, 1985).

Billson, Anne, *My Name is Michael Caine* (Muller, London, 1991).

Bloom, Claire, *Limelight and After: The Education of an Actress* (Weidenfeld & Nicolson, 1982).

Bogarde, Dirk, *Snakes and Ladders* (Triad–Granada, London, 1978).

Bouchier, Chili, *Shooting Star: The Last of the Silent Film Stars* (Atlantis, London, 1995).

Bragg, Melvyn, *Rich: The Life of Richard Burton* (Hodder & Stoughton, London, 1989).

Branagh, Kenneth, *Beginning* (Chatto & Windus, London, 1991).

Braun, Eric, *Deborah Kerr* (W. H. Allen, London, 1974).

Bret, D., *Gracie Fields: The Authorized Biography* (London Books, London, 1995).

Brooks, Xan, *Choose Life: Ewan McGregor and the British Film Revival* (Chameleon Books, London, 1998).

Caine, Michael, *Acting in Film: An Actor's Take on Moviemaking* (Applause Theatre Book Publishers, London, 1997).

Callan, Michael Feeney, *Anthony Hopkins: In Darkness and Light* (Pan, London, 1994).

Callan, Michael Feeney, *Julie Christie* (W. H. Allen, London, 1984).

Carmichael, Ian, *Will the Real Ian Carmichael ... An Autobiography* (Macmillan, London, 1979).

Colman, Juliet Benita, *Ronald Colman: A Very Private Person* (W. H. Allen, 1975).

Cottrell, John, *Julie Andrews: The Unauthorized Life Story of a Super-star* (Dell, New York, 1968).

Cottrell, John, *Laurence Olivier* (Weidenfeld & Nicolson, London, 1975).

Cushing, Peter, *Peter Cushing: An Autobiography* (Weidenfeld & Nicolson, London, 1986).

Dacre, Richard, *Trouble in Store: Norman Wisdom, A Career in Comedy* (T. C. Farries, Dumfries, 1991).

Dors, Diana, *Behind Closed Dors* (W. H. Allen, London, 1979).

Dors, Diana, *Dors by Diana* (MacDonald Futura Press, London, 1981).

Dors, Diana, *Swingin' Dors* (World Distributors, London, 1961).

Emyr, John, *Anthony Hopkins* (Canolfan Astudiaethau Addysg, Aberystwyth, 1997).

Eyles, Allen, and Fitzgibbon, Lesley, eds, *James Mason: Actor* (BFI, London, 1970).

Falk, Quentin, *Albert Finney in Character* (Robson Books, London, 1992).

Falk, Quentin, *The Golden Gong: Fifty Years of the Rank Organisation, Its Films and Its Stars* (Columbus Books, London, 1987).

Farrar, David, *No Royal Road* (Mortimer Publications, Eastbourne, 1948).

Faulkner, Trader, *Peter Finch* (Angus & Robertson, London, 1979).

Fields, Gracie, *Sing As We Go* (Frederick Muller, London, 1960).

Film Index International CD Rom (Chadwyck–Healey, BFI, National Library) lists references (articles only) to many British stars in a very restricted number of cinema publications.

Fisher, J., *George Formby* (Woburn-Futura, London, 1973).

Fleming, Kate, *Celia Johnson: A Biography* (Weidenfeld & Nicolson, 1991).

Fowler, Karin J., *David Niven* (Greenwood Press, New York, 1995).

Freedland, Michael, *Sean Connery* (Weidenfeld & Nicolson, London, 1994).

Frewin, Leslie R., 'British Film Publicity, the Renascence', in P. Noble, ed., *The British Film Yearbook 1949–50* (Skelton Robinson, London, 1949).

Geraghty, Christine, 'Albert Finney – Working Class Hero', in Kitchen, P., and Thumim, J., eds, *Me Jane: Masculinity, Movies and Women* (Lawrence & Wishart, London, 1995).

Geraghty, Christine, 'Diana Dors' in Barr (1986), pp. 341–5.

Gielgud, John, *An Actor and His Times* (Penguin, London, 1981).

Granger, Stewart, *Sparks Fly Upward* (Granada, London, 1981).

Guinness, Alec, *Blessings in Disguise* (Hamish Hamilton, London, 1985).

Guinness, Alec, *My Name Escapes Me: The Diary of a Retiring Actor* (Hamish Hamilton, London, 1996).

Guinness, Alec, *A Positively Final Appearance* (Hamish Hamilton, London, 1999).

Haining, Peter, *The Last Gentleman: A Tribute to David Niven* (W. H. Allen, 1984).

Hall, William, *Raising Caine: The Authorized Biography* (Sidgwick & Jackson, London, 1981).

Hampshire, Susan, *Susan's Story: An Autobiographical Account of My Struggle with Words* (Sidgwick & Jackson, London, 1981).

Harper, Sue, 'Thinking Forward and Up: The British Films of Conrad Veidt', in Richards (1998), pp. 121–37.

Harrison, Rex, *Rex: An Autobiography* (William Morrow, New York, 1975).

Hawkins, Jack, *Anything for a Quiet Life* (Elm Tree Books, Hamish Hamilton, London, 1973).

Hepworth, Cecil, *Came the Dawn* (Phoenix House, London, 1951).

Hickey, Des, and Smith, Gus, *The Prince: Being the Public and Private Life of Larushka Mischa Skikne ... Otherwise Known as Laurence Harvey* (Frewin, London, 1975).

Higham, Charles, *Charles Laughton: An Intimate Biography* (W. H. Allen, London, 1976).

Higham, Charles, *Princess Merle: The Romantic Life of Merle Oberon* (Coward–McCann, London, 1983).

Howard, Leslie, ed. Ronald Howard, *Trivial Fond Records* (Kimber, London, 1982).

Howard, Ronald, *In Search of My Father: A Portrait of Leslie Howard* (Kimber, London, 1981).

Jenkins, Garry, *Daniel Day Lewis: The Fire Within* (Pan, London, 1995).

Keown, Eric, *Margaret Rutherford* (Rockliff, London, 1956).

Knight, Vivienne, *Trevor Howard: A Gentleman and a Player* (Muller, Blond &

White, London, 1986).

Lee, Christopher, *Tall, Dark and Gruesome: An Autobiography* (W. H. Allen, London, 1977).

Lewis, Roger, *The Life and Death of Peter Sellers* (Arrow Books, London, 1995).

Lewis, Roger, *The Real Life of Laurence Olivier* (Arrow Books, London, 1997).

Lockwood, Margaret, *Lucky Star: The Autobiography of Margaret Lockwood* (Odhams Press, London, 1955).

Loder, John, *Hollywood Hussar* (Baker, London, 1977).

Macnab, Geoffrey, *Searching for Stars: Stardom and Screen Acting in the British Cinema* (Cassell, London, 2000).

Martin, Roy, and Seaton, Ray, *Good Morning Boys: Will Hay, Master of Comedy* (Barrie & Jenkins, London, 1978).

Mason, James, *Before I Forget: An Autobiography* (Hamish Hamilton, London, 1983).

Matthews, Jessie, *Over My Shoulder* (W. H. Allen, London, 1976).

Medhurst, Andy, 'Dirk Bogarde', in Barr (1986), pp. 346–54.

Milland, Ray, *Wide Eyed in Babylon: An Autobiography* (Coronet, London, 1997).

Mills, John, *Up in the Clouds, Gentlemen Please* (Weidenfeld & Nicolson, London, 1980).

Moline, Karin, *Bob Hoskins, An Unlikely Hero* (Sphere, London, 1989).

More, Kenneth, *Happy Go Lucky: My Life* (Hale, London, 1959).

More, Kenneth, *More or Less* (Hodder & Stoughton, London, 1978).

Morley, Sheridan, *The Other Side of the Moon: The Life of David Niven* (Weidenfeld and Nicolson, 1985)

Munn, Michael, *Trevor Howard: The Man and His Films* (Robson, London, 1989).

Nathan, David, *Glenda Jackson* (Coronet, Sevenoaks, 1986).

Neagle, Anna, *'There's Always Tomorrow'* (W. H. Allen, London, 1974).

Niven, David, *Bring on the Empty Horses* (Hamish Hamilton, London, 1975).

O'Connor, Garry, *Ralph Richardson: An Actor's Life* (Athaneum, New York, 1982).

Olivier, Laurence, *Confessions of an Actor: An Autobiography* (Simon & Schuster, New York, 1982).

O'Toole, Peter, *Loitering with Intent: The Apprentice* (Macmillan, London, 1996).

Palmer, Lilli, *Change Lobsters and Dance* (W. H. Allen, London, 1976).

Pendreigh, Brian, *Ewan McGregor* (Orion, London, 1998).

Petley, Julian, 'Reaching for the Stars', in Martyn Auty, and Nick Roddick, eds, *British Cinema Now* (BFI, London, 1985), pp. 225–41.

Picturegoer (under various minor changes of title the longest-lasting and most popular of the British cinema magazines, concentrating on stars, both Hollywood and British).

Randall, Alan, and Seaton, Ray, *George Formby* (W. H. Allen, London, 1974).

Rathbone, Basil, *In and Out of Character* (Doubleday, New York, 1962).

Redgrave, Michael, *Mask or Face: Reflections in an Actor's Mirror* (Heinemann, London, 1958).

Richards, Jeffrey, 'Gracie Fields: Concensus Personified', in Richards (1989), pp. 169–90.

Richards, Jeffrey. 'George Formby: The Road from Wigan Pier', in Richards (1989), pp. 191–206.

Richards, Jeffrey, 'The Romantic Adventurer: Robert Donat and Leslie Howard', in Richards (1989), pp. 225–41.

Richards, Jeffrey, 'Jessie Matthews: The Dancing Divinity', in Richards (1989), pp. 207–24.

Richards, Jeffrey, 'Tod Slaughter and the Cinema of Excess', in Richards (1998), pp. 139–59.

Rutherford, Margaret, *Margaret Rutherford: An Autobiography* (W. H. Allen, London, 1972).

Sanders, George, *Memoirs of a Professional Cad* (Putnam, New York, 1960).

Sedgwick, John, 'The Comparative Popularity of Stars in mid-30s Britain', *Journal of Popular British Cinema*, 2, 1999, 121–7.

Sheridan, Simon, *Come Play with Me: The Life and Films of Mary Millington* (FAB, Guildford, 1999).

Shuttleworth, Ian, *Ken and Em* (Headline Books Publishing Ltd, London, 1995).

Sim, Naomi, *Dance and Skylark: Fifty Years with Alastair Sim* (Bloomsbury, London, 1987).

Simmons, Dawn Langley, *Margaret Rutherford: A Blithe Spirit* (Sphere, London, 1985).

Smith, R. Dixon, *Ronald Colman: Gentleman of the Cinema* (McFarland, London, 1991).

Spicer, Andrew, 'The Emergence of the British Tough Guy: Stanley Baker, Masculinity and the Crime Thriller', in Steve Chibnall, and Robert Murphy, eds, *British Crime Cinema* (Routledge, London, 1999), pp. 81–93.

Spicer, Andrew, 'Male Stars, Masculinity and British Cinema, 1944–1960', in Robert Murphy, ed., *The British Cinema Book* (BFI, London, 1997), pp. 144–53.

Spindle, Les, *Julie Andrews: A Bio-bibliography* (Greenwood Press, New York, 1989).

Storey, Anthony, *Stanley Baker: Portrait of an Actor* (W. H. Allen, London, 1977).

Street, Sarah, 'A Place of One's Own? Margaret Lockwood and British Film Stardom in the 1940s', in Ulrike Sieglohr, ed., *Heroines Without Heroes: Reconstructing Female and National Identities in European Cinema, 1945–51* (Cassell, London, 2000), pp. 33–43.

Terry-Thomas, *Filling the Gap* (Parrish, London, 1959).

Terry-Thomas, and Daum, Terry, *Terry-Thomas Tells Tales* (Robson, London, 1999).

Thornton, Michael, *Jessie Matthews* (Hart-Davis, London, 1974).

Tims, Hilton, *Once a Wicked Lady: A Biography of Margaret Lockwood* (Virgin, London, 1989).

Todd, Ann, *The Eighth Veil* (William Kimber, London, 1980).

Trewin, J. C., *Robert Donat: A Biography* (Heinemann, London, 1968).

Troyon, Michael, *A Rose for Mrs Miniver: The Life of Greer Garson* (University Press of Kentucky, Lexington, 1998).

Vanderbeets, Richard, *George Sanders: An Exhausted Life* (Robson, London, 1991).

Walker, Alexander, *Fatal Charm: The Life of Rex Harrison* (Weidenfeld & Nicolson, London, 1986).

Walker, Alexander, 'Random Thoughts on the Englishness (or Otherwise) of English Film Actors', in *'It's Only a Movie, Ingrid': Encounters On and Off Screen* (Headline Book Publishing, London, 1988).

Warner, Jack, *Jack of All Trades* (W. H. Allen, London, 1975).

Wild, Roland Gibson, *Ronald Colman* (Rich & Cowan, London, 1933).

Wilding, Michael, *Apple Sauce: The Story of My Life as Told to Pamela Wilding* (George Allen & Unwin, London, 1982).

Wilson, S., *Ivor* (Michael Joseph, London, 1975).

Windeler, Robert, *Julie Andrews: A Life on Stage and Screen*, revised and updated (Aurum, London, 1997).

Woodward, Ian, *Glenda Jackson: A Study in Fire and Ice* (Spellmount, Tunbridge Wells, 1984).

Index

Note: page references in italics indicate film stills.